AN EMDR PRIMER

From Practicum to Practice

ABOUT THE AUTHOR

Barbara J. Hensley, EdD, served on the EMDR International Association Board of Directors as president and treasurer and has represented EMDRIA in Stockholm, Sweden and Brussels, Belgium. She is an EMDRIA-Certified Therapist, and Approved Consultant, and Regional Coordinator for the Greater Cincinnati EMDRIA Regional Network. For the past 10 years, she has been a facilitator and logistician for EMDR trainings in Japan and throughout the United States.

Dr. Hensley is creator of the Francine Shapiro Library. It is an online source of EMDR research and writings and currently housed in the Steely Library of Northern Kentucky University. She is also the 2009 recipient of the Francine Shapiro Award. She also is the 2009 recipient of the distinguished Francine Shapiro Award for her extraordinary service and contributions to EMDR.

Dr. Hensley is co-founder of the Cincinnati Trauma Connection in Cincinnati, Ohio, an EMDR-based trauma center.

AN EMDR PRIMER

From Practicum to Practice

BARBARA J. HENSLEY, EdD

SPRINGER PUBLISHING COMPANY

NEW YORK

Springer Publishing Company, LLC
11 West 42nd Street
New York, NY 10036
www.springerpub.com

Acquisitions Editor: Sheri W. Sussman
Project Manager: Judy Worrell
Cover Design: TG Design
Composition: Six Red Marbles

Transcripts of the outlines were adapted from The EMDR Approach to Psychotherapy —EMDR Institute Basic Training Course, Weekend I, 2009, by Dr. Francine Shapiro for Calm (or Safe Place), Breathing Shift, Spiral Technique, Affect Scan, and Direct Questioning Approach. Tables were adapted for: Single Incident Targeting Sequence, EMDR Selection Criteria; Resuming Reprocessing in an Incomplete Session; Strategies to Open Processing; Activation Components of EMDR; Future Template-Anticipating Anxiety—Key Points; Future Template Flow Chart—Skill Building and Imaginal Re-hearsal; Assessment—Identify, Assess, Measure, and The Presenting Problem and the Three-Pronged Approach; Future Template Script; Strategies for Maintaining Process-ing: Deceleration/Acceleration, with permission from The EMDR Institute, Copyright (2009).

Ebook ISBN: 978-0-8261-1987-2
13 14 15 / 5 4

Library of Congress Cataloging-in-Publication Data
Hensley, Barbara J.
 An EMDR primer : from practicum to practice / Barbara J. Hensley.
  p. ; cm.
 Includes bibliographical references and index.
 ISBN 978-0-8261-1986-5
 1. Eye movement desensitization and reprocessing. I. Title.
 [DNLM: 1. Desensitization, Psychologic—methods. 2. Stress Disorders,
Post-Traumatic—therapy. WM 425.5.D4 H526e 2009]
 RC489.E98H46 2009
 617.7—dc22
                                                                    2009021561

Printed in the United States of America by SCI

To Francine Shapiro,
creator of EMDR, a ripple in still water.

And to Robbie Dunton, Scott Blech, and Robert Gelbach
and
Irene Giessl, Jennifer Lendl, Victoria Britt, Marilyn Schleyer, Kay Werk,
Zona Scheiner, and Deany Laliotis
in honor of your dedication and commitment to EMDR.

And to all the clinicians and clients who have been caught up in the
wave, creating ripples of their own.

*A single act does make a difference...it creates a ripple effect that can be
felt many miles and people away.*
—Lee J. Colan

Contents

Contributing Editors xiii
Foreword xv
Preface xix
Acknowledgments xxv

1   EMDR Overview   1

Reintroduction to EMDR   1
Trauma   2
    What is Trauma?   2
    Types of Trauma   3
Adaptive Information Processing   5
Three-Pronged Approach   11
    Past, Present, Future   11
    Three-Pronged Targets   12
    Why Is the Concept of Past, Present, Future so Important?   14
Targeting Possibilities   15
    Targets May Arise in Any Part of the EMDR Process   15
    Types of EMDR Targets   16
        Targets from the Past   16
        Targets from the Present   17
        Targets from the Future   17
        Other Potential Targets   18
Dual Attention Stimulation   25
    What Does It Do?   25
    Preferred Means of Dual Attention Stimulation   25
    Is Dual Attention Stimulation EMDR?   26
    Shorter or Longer? Slower or Faster?   26
Important Concepts to Consider   27
    What Once Was Adaptive Becomes Maladaptive   27
    State vs. Trait Change   27
    Dual Awareness   28

Ecological Validity (i.e., Soundness)   28
Side Benefits of EMDR   30
Holistic Nature of the Approach   31
Useful Train Metaphor   31
Practical Tips to Remember   33
  Practice, Practice, Practice   33
  Follow the Script Verbatim   33
  Know Your Client   34
  Stay off the Tracks   35
  Tracking the Client   35
  Keep It Simple   36
  Then or Now?   36
  One More Time   37
  Solo Run   38
Summary Statements   39

2   Eight Phases of EMDR   41

PHASE 1: Client History and Treatment Planning   41
  Informed Consent and Suitability for Treatment   44
  Client Selection Criteria   45
  Client's Suitability and Readiness for EMDR   46
  Screening for Dissociative Disorders   47
  Client Willingness to Do EMDR   48
  Assessment   48
  Treatment Planning in EMDR   49
  Elements Pertinent to EMDR   51
  Candidates for EMDR   51
  Case Example 2A: Sally   52
  Case Example 2B: Marie   53
PHASE 2: Preparation   54
  Setting the Stage for Effective Reprocessing   54
  Calm (or Safe) Place   59
  *Resource Development and Installation, Dissociation, and
    Ego State Therapy*   60
  Addressing the Client's Fears and Expectations   62
PHASE 3: Assessment   63
  Identify, Assess, and Measure   63
PHASE 4: Desensitization   65
  When Does It Begin?   65
  What About Reprocessing?   66
  Purpose of Desensitization Phase   67

Associative Processing 67
Assessment of the Channels of Association 68
End of Channel? 68
When to Return to Target 74
How Long Does It Last? 74
When to Proceed to Installation Phase 75
Taking a Break 76
PHASE 5: Installation Phase 77
What Occurs? 77
Evaluate Appropriateness of Original Cognition 77
Validity of the Positive Cognition 77
Link to Original Target 78
When Is Installation Complete? 78
How to Discern the Presence of a Blocking Belief 78
PHASE 6: Body Scan 79
PHASE 7: Closure 80
Levels of Closure 80
Strategies for Closing Sessions 80
Assessment of Client's Safety 81
What Can Happen After a Session? 82
PHASE 8: Reevaluation 82
What Has Changed and What Is Left to Do? 82
Resuming Reprocessing in an Incomplete Session 83
Reevaluation of Treatment Effects 84
Reevaluation and Treatment Planning 84
Reevaluation of Targets 84
Final Stage Reevaluation 85
Pivotal Points in the Reevaluation Phase 86
Summary Statements 86

3 Stepping Stones to Adaptive Resolution 87

Assessment Phase 87
Back to Basics 87
How Much Do You Need To Know? 88
Target Assessment 88
Effective EMDR Equals Effective Targeting 88
Characteristics of Effective Targets 89
How Is the Memory Encoded? 89
Case Example 3A: Jennifer 89
Appropriateness of the Target 90
Assessment of Cognitions 91

Elements of Negative and Positive Cognitions   91
What Is a Cognition?   92
Teasing Out Negative and Positive Cognitions   93
Assessment of the Validity of Cognition (VOC)   99
VoC Scale   99
Assessment of Emotions   100
Emotional Sensations   100
Assessment of Current Level of Disturbance   101
Subjective Units of Disturbance (SUD) Scale   101
Assessment of Physical Sensations   103
Body Sensations   103
Case Examples   105
Case Example 3B: Terry   105
Case Example 3C: Julia   109
Case Example 3D: Jerry   113
Case Example 3E: Henry   115
Recent Traumatic Events and Single-Incident Traumas   118
Recent Traumatic Events   119
Case Example 3F: Patrick   119
Single-Incident Traumas   124
Targeting Sequence Plans   124
Summary Statements   125

4   Building Blocks of EMDR   127

EMDR is a Three-Pronged Approach   127
Building Blocks of EMDR: Past, Present, and Future   128
Clinical Presentation Possibilities   129
Single-Incident Presentations   131
Multiple Issues/Symptoms Presentations   132
Vague or Diffuse Presentations   133
First Prong: Earlier Memories/Touchstone Events   134
Touchstone Event   134
Strategies for Accessing the Touchstone Memory   135
Case Example 4A: Betty   138
Touchstone Revisited   141
Second Prong: Present Events and Triggers   142
What to Look Out For   142
*How Can Triggers Remain Active After So Much
    Processing?*   143
Case Example 4B: Peter   144
*Present Triggers Subsumed by the Reprocessing of the
    Touchstone Event*   149

Third Prong: Future Events and Future Templates   150
    Goals of the Future Template   150
    Skills Building and Imaginal Rehearsal   150
    Steps Needed Prior to Creating a Positive Template   153
    Third Prong: Misunderstood, Disregarded,
        Forgotten   154
    Case Example 4C: Michael   156
Summary Statements   160

5   **Abreactions, Blocked Processing, and Cognitive Interweaves   161**

When the Engine has Stalled   161
    Stalled Processing   161
Abreaction   162
    What Is It?   162
    Preparing the Client for Abreactions   163
    What Happens When a Client Abreacts?   163
    Abreaction Guidelines   165
Strategies for Maintaining Processing   168
    Overresponders and Underresponders: Guidelines
        for Clients Who Display Too Little or
        Too Much Emotion   168
    Cautionary Note   170
    Returning to Target Too Soon?   170
Strategies for Blocked Processing   171
    Blocked Processing   171
    Identifying Blocked Processing   171
    Primary Targets for Blocked Processing   172
    Ancillary Targets for Blocked Processing   172
The Art of the Cognitive Interweave   174
    What Is a Cognitive Interweave?   175
    Using a Cognitive Interweave Effectively   176
    When to Use a Cognitive Interweave   177
    Case Example 5A: Renee   178
    Choices of Cognitive Interweaves   179
    Comparison Between Strategies for Blocked Processing
        and Cognitive Interweaves   184
    Responsibility, Safety, and Choice   184
    Case Example 5B: Susie   186
    Use the Cognitive Interweave With Caution   192
Summary Statements   198

6   Past, Present, and Future   199

    EMDR Case Examples   199
        Questions   *200*
    Past   202
        Case Example 6A: Jessica   *202*
        Case Example 6B: Karen   *213*
    Present   220
        Case Example 6C: Delores   *220*
        Case Example 6D: Brenda   *235*
    Future   240
        Case Example 6E: Jimmy   *240*
    Summary   247
    Conclusion   248

Appendices   249

    Appendix A: Definition of EMDR   251

    Appendix B: Exercises
    Grounding   257
    Diaphragmatic Breathing   258
    Anchoring in the Present   259
    Calm (or Safe) Place   260
    Sacred Space   264

    Appendix C: EMDR Scripts
    Breathing Shift   267
    Spiral Technique   268
    Future Template Script   268
    Tices Log   270

    Appendix D: Informed Consent and EMDR   273

    Appendix E: EMDR and Trauma-Related Resources   277

    Appendix F: Efficacy of EMDR   283

References   289

Index   **297**

Contributing Editors

Dana C. Braun, MEd
Educator
Cincinnati State College, OH

Victoria Britt, MSW
Private Practice
Clinical Social Worker and Marriage and Family Therapist
Montclair, NJ

Irene B. Giessl, EdD
Psychologist, Private Practice
Co-Founder
Cincinnati Trauma Connection
Cincinnati, OH

Deany Laliotis, LCSW
Private Practice
Bethesda, MD

Jennifer Lendl, PhD
Psychologist
San Jose, CA

Marilyn Schleyer, PhD, ARNP
Professor and First Chair
Department of Advanced Nursing Studies
College of Health Professions
Northern Kentucky University, KY

Zona Scheiner, PhD
Psychologist, Partner, and Co-Founder
Family Therapy Associates
Ann Arbor, MI

Deborah Smith-Blackmer, LISW
Private Practice
Cincinnati, OH

Kay Werk, LISW
Manager
Community Crisis Response and Critical Incident Stress Management for NetCare
Columbus, OH

Foreword

Although Dr. Francine Shapiro's now-famous walk in the park took place in 1987, the first EMDR study was published 2 years later in 1989. The EMDR community is celebrating its 20th anniversary at this year's EMDRIA Conference in Atlanta, Georgia. Twenty years later, there are EMDR therapists trained around the world. The efficacy of EMDR has been proven repeatedly, and it is included as the treatment of choice by mental health groups in the United States (American Psychiatric Association, 2004; Department of Veteran Affairs and the Department of Defense, 2004) and abroad (Australian Centre for Posttraumatic Mental Health, 2007; Bleich, Kotler, Kutz, & Shaley, 2002; Clinical Resource Efficiency Support Team [CREST], 2003; and United Kingdom Department of Health, 2007). We have come a long way!

Back History

In the summer of 1989 in San Jose, California, there was a brownbag luncheon for therapists sponsored by the Giaretto Institute. The guest speaker was an unknown psych intern who presented a case with video clips showing work with a client who was a Vietnam War veteran. As Dr. Shapiro explained her method of treatment from her recently published dissertation (Shapiro, 1989a, 1989b), there was a lot of eye-rolling and uncomfortable shifting in chairs. Then she showed the video. The audience quieted. She had our attention. The client was changing before our eyes. We were witnessing the rapid processing of trauma but not understanding why it was happening.

In the winter of 1989, the Santa Clara County Psychological Association held a special trauma response meeting for earthquake debriefing. After my presentation (Lendl & Aguilera, 1989), Dr. Shapiro approached me and invited me to her upcoming training. She was looking for trauma trained community therapists to join her "EMD" team.

EMD was considered at the experimental stage, but she wanted to start judiciously training as research proceeded. She did not think it was ethical to withhold treatment when it seemed to alleviate suffering so quickly and thoroughly. In the spring–summer of 1990, the first U.S. EMD training began.

At the 2002 EMDRIA Conference in Coronado, California, I met Dr. Barbara Hensley, who was in her first year on the EMDRIA Board and serving as treasurer. I was immediately impressed by her dedication to EMDR and her no-nonsense work ethic. She was the epitome of an EMDR therapist Dr. Shapiro encouraged us all to become . . . utilizing all her talents to benefit EMDR and her community.

Dr. Hensley had spent 30 years mostly in management for the State of Ohio and honed the ability to pinpoint needs, harvest resources, and bring solutions to fruition. With her colleague, Dr. Irene Giessl, she founded the multidisciplinary Cincinnati Trauma Connection practice with its roots in EMDR. They are Regional Coordinators for their fellow EMDR therapists and for many years have sponsored top specialty trainings in their community. Dr. Hensley served a term-and-a-half as EMDRIA Board president during a very difficult reorganization period. She did it quietly, gracefully, and masterfully. Despite her shyness, one of her personal goals as president was to meet as many of the EMDRIA members as possible. She wanted everyone to feel welcome and part of the EMDR community.

When I asked her why she wanted to write this Primer, Dr. Hensley confessed that it was not her intention to write a book. She was becoming aware that many people who were trained in EMDR were hesitant to continue training or use EMDR in their practices. When questioned, they often stated that they were afraid to try such a different, "a possibly dangerous" method. She thought that a few examples might be useful. Voila! A book was born. She also said, "I wanted to make a contribution. I don't think you can do enough for EMDR . . . It has changed so many lives."

It has been my pleasure and honor to be on the editing team for this book. I believe that Dr. Hensley has written a book that is simple, basic, and can mentor therapists who are EMDR trained and yet intimidated. It is the perfect complement to Dr. Shapiro's text (Shapiro, 2001). Learning EMDR can be likened to learning a language. Having a strong foundation in grammar helps many years down the line.

Ever since my Catholic grammar school education stressed diagramming sentences and studying Latin, I have appreciated the necessity for laying a strong foundation in the understanding, maintenance, and facile utilization of learned information. The importance of going back to basics cannot be overemphasized. Beyond the therapeutic relationship, a thorough understanding and meticulous use of the EMDR methodology will nurture the best EMDR treatment and therefore the greatest therapeutic effects when applied appropriately. This book brings us back to the basics.

I can see EMDR therapists rereading Dr. Shapiro's book chapter by chapter as they move through Dr. Hensley's Primer. And I can hear what Dr. Shapiro would say to us after every training, "Did you learn something? Are you having fun?" Please keep this in mind as you are reading the Primer.

—Jennifer Lendl, PhD

REFERENCES

American Psychiatric Association. (2004). *Practice guidelines for the treatment of patients with acute stress disorder and posttraumatic stress disorder.* Arlington, VA: Author.

Australian Centre for Posttraumatic Mental Health. (2007). *Australian guidelines for PTSD.* Melbourne, Australia: University of Melbourne.

Bleich, A., Kotler, M., Kutz, E., & Shaley, A. (2002). Guidelines for the assessment and professional intervention with terror victims in the hospital and in the community. Jerusalem, Israel: Israeli National Council for Mental Health.

Clinical Resource Efficiency Support Team. (2003). *The management of post traumatic stress disorder in adults.* Belfast: Northern Ireland Department of Health, Social Services and Public Safety.

Department of Veterans Affairs and the Department of Defense. (2004). *VA/DoD Clinical Practice Guideline for the Management of Post-Traumatic Stress.* Washington, DC: Veterans Health Administration, Department of Veterans Affairs and Health Affairs, Department of Defense, Office of Quality and Performance publication 10Q-CPG/PTSD-04.

Lendl, J., & Aguilera, D. (1989). Multidisciplined survey of therapist-reported patient response to the October 17, 1989 earthquake. Research assessment tool used by the UCSF Center for the study of trauma.

Shapiro, F. (1989a). Efficacy of the eye movement desensitization procedure in the treatment of traumatic memories. *Journal of Traumatic Stress, 2*(2), 199–223.

Shapiro, F. (1989b). Eye movement desensitization: A new treatment for post-traumatic stress disorder. *Journal of Behavior Therapy and Experimental Psychiatry, 20*(3), 211–217.

Shapiro, F. (2001). *Eye movement desensitization and reprocessing: Basic principles, protocols and procedures* (2nd ed.). New York: Guilford Press.

United Kingdom Department of Health. (2001). Treatment choice in psychological therapies and counselling evidence based clinical practice guideline. London, England: Author.

Preface

Tuning Into the Creative Force

Sit back and visualize the small but exciting moment in 1987 when Francine Shapiro became aware of her eyes shifting involuntarily and simultaneously back and forth as she focused on some disturbing events in her life. If she had not stopped to notice the relief she felt as a result of this back-and-forth movement of her eyes, the EMDR journey could have ended that fateful day. Dr. Shapiro's visionary and creative spark began a quiet revolution in the field of psychotherapy . . . a ripple in still water.

In his book *Creativity: Flow and the Psychology of Discovery and Invention*, Mihaly Csikszentmihalyi distinguishes between what he defines as "small-c" and "big-C" creativity as he describes how creative individuals influence their respective fields and domains of knowledge. While small-c creativity is somewhat subjective, Csikszentmihalyi states that big-C is the kind of creativity that drives culture forward and redefines the state of the art (1997).

Francine Shapiro belongs to a select group of big-C creators in our world. Small-c creativity involves personal creativity while big-C requires the type of ingenuity that "leaves a trace in the cultural matrix" (Csikszentmihalyi, 1997), something that changes some aspect of how we view or treat something in a big way. Anyone who has conducted a successful EMDR session or has experienced its results firsthand can attest to the expanding ripples that Dr. Shapiro began and that continue to grow as we progress further into the future.

From the day of her fateful walk in Vasona Park in Los Gatos, California, Dr. Shapiro's destiny began to change. Excited by her chance revelation, she leapt into action, finding friends and subjects to test her new discovery. She quickly set out to develop well-structured principles, protocols, and procedures around the effects of eye movements based on the consistent treatment results she and others had observed. She trained interested and excited clinicians who in turn encouraged others to learn this new methodology. The big-C ripple mounted as the first controlled study of EMDR appeared in the *Journal of Traumatic Stress* in 1989. Other studies were soon to follow, and the rest is history. Dr. Shapiro's big-C creativity changed and continues to change the way trained clinicians conceptualize and treat trauma. EMDR has redefined the state of the art in terms of mental health.

The big-C ripple now encompasses the world many times over—from North to South America, Africa, Europe, India, China, Japan, and Australia. It continues to grow and multiply along with many new ripples that are created every day as clients and clinicians around the world experience for the first time the power of Dr. Shapiro's personal discovery.

Who Could Benefit From Reading This Primer?

EMDR is a powerful therapeutic approach. However, without the proper training and consultation, an untrained therapist (and this includes very experienced clinicians) could put their clients at risk. A goal of this Primer is to target those clinicians who have attended what is now called Weekends 1 and 2 EMDR Training and have read Dr. Shapiro's basic text (2001; i.e., *Eye Movement Desensitization and Reprocessing: Basic Principles, Protocols and Procedures, Second Edition*) but still want additional information on using it skillfully. They may have experienced fear or apprehension about trying something so new and different or they may simply want to maximize their preparation and skills as they begin using EMDR.

In consultation groups, clinicians often report being skeptical before EMDR training, yet amazed by their practicum experiences afterward. They concede that using EMDR has potential to help their clients. However, even after reading Dr. Shapiro's basic text and other books on the subject, many still feel a reluctance to utilize what at first appears to be a radically different treatment approach. Some live in remote areas where they are the only EMDR-trained clinician for miles or where their only access to other clinicians is by boat or airplane. I hope this Primer encourages and raises the confidence levels of those trained but wanting to increase their ability to use EMDR with consistent success.

I also want to provide assurance to those using EMDR that they are on the right track.

Learning to implement EMDR in session with a client is a process of its own; it is not an event. Thus it is important to understand the basic theory underlying EMDR before attempting to implement it. The manner in which you as the therapist set up the procedural steps with a client to do the actual EMDR will vary with each and every client assessed for treatment. Every client is unique, and EMDR is not a "cookbook" approach. Therefore, familiarity with Dr. Shapiro's Adaptive Information Processing model is crucial to enhance your understanding as to why some clients make shifts readily and others experience more difficulty. As you become more adept at EMDR with *practice, practice, practice*, your EMDR approach and delivery will likely change and evolve as you become more comfortable, more knowledgeable, and more expert in this approach. Each client can teach you something about the process as he or she resolves his or her own issues.

What Is Included

Much of the information contained in the following pages has already been described by Dr. Shapiro and others in the rapidly growing body of EMDR literature and research. The primary intention of this Primer is to supplement Dr. Shapiro's explanation of EMDR. It is not meant to be a substitute for her training or previous writings. The reader is urged to read and study them all. This Primer attempts to augment what she has presented in a different way, adding case histories and extensive examples of successful EMDR sessions. The cases represent composite or conglomerate portraits of the many clients with whom I have performed EMDR over the past 15 years.

This text is a primer and, as such, the writing, examples and illustrations are presented in a less formal and more personal manner, alternating the pronoun "he" and "she" throughout the book. The Primer has been written from a practical, learning-focused approach so that the clinicians who read it can become more familiar with the principles, protocols, and procedures of EMDR. It is my desire to facilitate the flow of information so that clinicians can easily and naturally begin to use their EMDR training as soon as possible. This book is also geared to help clinicians to reaccess information that was lost in the weeks, months, or years since they were trained.

Purpose of Primer

Throughout this Primer are transcripts embellished with relevant details to illustrate important learning points. Other sessions have been created to demonstrate how to identify the touchstone event (if any), set up the procedural steps, deal with blocked processing and blocking beliefs during the desensitization and installation phases, reassess the state of previously targeted material, and identify material for new processing. An attempt is made to take the clinician through complete and incomplete EMDR sessions, explaining treatment rationale at given points.

The Primer is laid out in the following manner:

- **EMDR Overview**—A straightforward explanation of the Adaptive Information Processing model, the three-pronged approach, the types of targets accessed during the EMDR process, and other relevant information to assist in distinguishing EMDR from other theoretical orientations are provided.
- **Eight Phases of EMDR**—The eight phases of EMDR are summarized.
- **Stepping Stones to Adaptive Resolution**—The components of the standard EMDR protocol used during the Assessment Phase are explained and actual cases are included to demonstrate how the procedural setup is possible with various clients.
- **Building Blocks of EMDR**—The foundation of EMDR—past, present, and future—is assessed in terms of appropriate targeting and successful outcomes.
- **Abreactions, Blocked Processing, and Cognitive Interweaves**—Strategies and techniques for dealing with challenging clients, high levels of abreaction, and blocked processing is the focus.
- **Past, Present, Future**—Actual cases demonstrate various strategies to assist the client in reaching adaptive resolution of trauma.

The definitions of EMDR provided by the EMDR Institute and EMDRIA are also included in the Appendices. These definitions, particularly the one developed by EMDRIA for clinicians, are the yardsticks used to assure that the explanation and rationale for EMDR remain consistent from session to session, client to client. In order for clinicians to experience more comfort and familiarity with EMDR, it is suggested that they keep these definitions close at hand and refer to them frequently until an adequate understanding of the methodology is attained.

A sacred space exercise has been added in the Appendices which can be used side by side with the traditional calm (or safe) place exercise. Simple exercises to give clients on grounding, diaphragmatic breathing, and anchoring in the present can also be found in the Appendices. In addition, scripted use of calm (or safe) place, spiral technique, future template, and breathing shift are also included.

The purpose in writing this book is to offer a Primer that can further facilitate mental health professionals in becoming more confident and experienced EMDR clinicians. The process has been simplified as much as possible with diagrams, tables, and other illustrations.

Dr. Shapiro's basic text, *Eye Movement Desensitization and Reprocessing: Basic Principles, Protocols and Procedures, Second Edition,* is a masterpiece in itself and contains a wealth of information on EMDR. One needs to read her text over and over again to savor all the kernels of significant information. These kernels have been separated out by providing explanations, as well as anecdotal and illustrative examples throughout. EMDR is a significant contribution to psychology in the 20th and 21st centuries, and this Primer is offered as a further learning tool.

What is covered in this Primer is but the tip of the iceberg when it comes to all the possibilities in terms of using EMDR with clients that present from different populations, such as children, combat veterans, and couples, and those who present with more complex issues, such as dissociation, phobias, obsessive–compulsive disorder, and substance abuse. Regardless of the client populations or the types of issues that the client brings, the basics in this Primer are essential to the overall outcome and success of EMDR.

Acknowledgments

My thanks to Dr. Francine Shapiro for providing me with an opportunity to be part of the ripple she created after taking her famous walk in the park. From that memorable walk, I was motivated to create my own small ripples in writing this Primer and in creating the Francine Shapiro Library. Dr. Shapiro has had an enormous impact on my life both personally and professionally as a result of her revolutionary work. My hope is that my efforts on behalf of EMDR will feed her spirit as hers have fed mine.

It never was my intent to write a book, let alone a primer on the basics of EMDR. While involved in working on an EMDR presentation to local colleagues, I began to think about the significance of understanding the intricacies of the EMDR model. Letting that slip from my lips, friends and colleagues started to offer ideas and give feedback. It became a personal challenge to boil down "EMDR talk" into small portions so more clinicians might be intrigued to follow the trail and not be daunted by the process. So I started writing to the novice, imagining the questions, creating tables of explanations and diagrams. Thus, the birth of this Primer. What an adventure!

There are nine exceptional individuals who put part of their life on hold to help me edit this Primer to ensure the fidelity of EMDR. It was an editing marathon in which they volunteered to engage. These wonderful women—Irene Giessl, Marilyn Schleyer, Victoria Britt, Kay Werk, Jennifer Lendl, Dana Braun, Deborah Smith-Blackmer, Zona Scheiner, and Deany Laliotis—helped to make this Primer a reality. Their names are listed in the order they became involved in the project, not by their importance or level of involvement. Thanks to all of you for reading my manuscript, sometimes more than once, for your invaluable comments, and for your encouragement.

Special thanks to Irene Giessl for her relentless pursuit of perfection and clarity. Her support, inspiration, faith in my ability to write this Primer, and sharp eye for the flaw, moved me when courage wavered.

Thanks to Marilyn Schleyer who urged me to "keep it simple" and to provide tables and diagrams to nurture the reader's learning process. Her mentoring and constant assurance that the Primer could be an important contribution to EMDR literature spurred me on.

Thanks to Jennifer Lendl. Jennifer truly is an EMDR pioneer, "a trainer before there were trainers." I am eternally indebted to her for all the time, hard work, guidance, encouragement, and support she has given throughout the entire process of writing this Primer. Jennifer read the entire manuscript over and over again to ensure its fidelity to the EMDR model.

Thanks to Victoria Britt for "holding my feet to the fire," as she promised, and for consistently and continually pointing out inadvertent deviations from EMDR standard procedure. Her commitment, ideas, and suggestions were deeply appreciated and valued.

Thanks to Kay Werk and Zona Scheiner for providing invaluable input from their experience as clinicians and teachers of EMDR. Kay allowed me to interrupt her complicated schedule to lend an ear at all times of day and night with no admonishments for my uncertainties. Her gracious demeanor and complete knowledge of the EMDR model calmed me when I started second guessing my efforts. Zona was called upon later in the writing stage. She worked with amazing speed and generosity to edit all the chapters. She added valuable comments from her deep understanding of the protocol and procedures and their optimal effectiveness.

Thanks to Deany Laliotis for her astute editing assistance on "Chapter 5, Abreactions, Blocked Processing, and Cognitive Interweaves." She graciously took time out of her busy teaching schedule to lend assistance when asked. Having EMDR Trainers and Facilitators oversee my writing is the only way I could dare to endorse these chapters.

Thanks to Dana Braun, a retired school teacher, friend, and non-clinician, and Deborah Smith-Blackmer, colleague, office mate, friend, and nontrained EMDR clinician, for offering their constructive eyes by reading the Primer for simplicity and ease of understanding. They both provided a view from the outside without the bias and complication of being EMDR trained.

As can be seen, all these women made special and unique contributions to the editing of this Primer. I know they made sacrifices and encountered personal challenges along the way. I owe all of these amazing women a deep debt of gratitude for their time, talents, and expertise.

These women are dear friends and colleagues. They are all ripple creators extraordinaire! From my grateful heart, I offer my sincere thanks.

Thanks also to Sheri Sussman, Senior Vice President of Springer Publishing, for her encouragement and assistance throughout. Sheri's interest in and support of this Primer was evident from the beginning when I first was introduced and approached her about the Primer at the EMDRIA Conference in Phoenix.

I have always believed in the spirit of generosity, giving freely without strings attached. This philosophy includes making financial contributions, offering pro bono therapy services, and sharing personal and professional resources to support those who might need a step up. I am so rewarded in life for taking this stance. For me, EMDR is a work of the heart, spurred on by my belief in the power of EMDR's healing properties. I chose to write to assist those beginning to study EMDR as a way of continuing to "pay forward." In offering this Primer to the EMDR community, it is my hope that many clinicians and their clients will reap the benefits of my efforts.

1

EMDR Overview

REINTRODUCTION TO EMDR

This chapter summarizes the information covered in the most recent Eye Movement Desensitization and Reprocessing (EMDR) trainings, as well as Dr. Shapiro's primary text, *Eye Movement Desensitization and Reprocessing: Basic Principles, Protocols, and Procedures, Second Edition* (2001), in the hope of providing additional clarity for the newly trained clinician. It takes a look at different ways trauma can be conceptualized and includes a reintroduction to the Adaptive Information Processing (AIP) model, the concept of the three-pronged approach, targets associated with EMDR, and clinical guidelines pertinent to EMDR. References to educational learning materials, research, other relevant supplementary information, and key points that are important to remember during the EMDR learning process are also covered.

Although the EMDR principles, protocols, and procedures have been simplified with tables and figures in this Primer, it is not a mechanistic or cookie-cutter approach. EMDR is a fluid process, and the results will vary from client to client. Formal EMDR training allows clinicians to initiate understanding the mechanism, model, and methodology of EMDR. This knowledge, combined with their own clinical intuition, allows them to begin practicing this therapeutic approach. No one should read this book thinking that it is a substitute for formal training. EMDR seems simple on its face; however, in reality, its competent execution is fairly complicated.

Extensive familiarity with Dr. Shapiro's primary text is a prerequisite for the reading of this Primer, which is intended to supplement, not replace, Dr. Shapiro's required pretraining readings. No clinician who intends to utilize EMDR with clients can afford to be without *Eye Movement Desensitization and Reprocessing: Basic Principles, Protocols, and Procedures, Second Edition* (Shapiro, 2001). In the early days of implementation, you may need to refer to Dr. Shapiro's book on a daily basis. Read it often and use it as your primary EMDR reference guide. Every time you read it, you will probably notice something that you did not quite understand or retain the first few times around. Read it thoroughly and refer to it often. It is not necessary that you memorize the book; just remember that it is there for you as an ongoing guide to your clinical work.

EMDR is a psychotherapeutic treatment approach that has eight distinct phases. It is not just dual attention stimulation. For it to be called EMDR, we must incorporate all eight of these phases. They include taking a thorough client history, preparing the client for the EMDR process, setting up the protocol, desensitizing and reprocessing the trauma, installing a positive cognition, doing a body scan to check for residual trauma, closing down the session, and reevaluating the status of the trauma. All of these eight phases must be in place in the order described above. Chapter 2 contains an in-depth discussion of these phases. There have been many offshoots of EMDR since its inception. These techniques have their supporters and many successes may have been reported, but these treatments to date have not been validated in the research literature. The efficacy of these models has not been tested within a scientific, empirical setting. EMDR's validity has been proven over and over again.

TRAUMA

What is Trauma?

The diagnostic criteria for posttraumatic stress disorder (PTSD; 309.81) cited in the *Diagnostic and Statistical Manual of Mental Disorders, text revision (DSM–IV–TR)* is the definition used most frequently to describe acute trauma in adults. In essence, this definition describes trauma as an event experienced, witnessed, or confronted by a person that: (a) "involved actual or threatened death or serious injury, or a threat to the physical integrity of self or others" and the person's response to that event; or (b) "involved intense fear, helplessness, or horror," or, in children, is displayed "by disorganized or agitated behavior" (American

Psychiatric Association [APA], 2000). Flannery describes trauma as "the state of severe fright that we experience when we are confronted with a sudden, unexpected, potentially life-threatening event, over which we have no control, and to which we are unable to respond effectively no matter how hard we try" (1995).

A child who was sexually abused by her older brother may grow up to believe, "I am bad" or "The world is unsafe." When an individual experiences a traumatic event, the event can become entrenched (or fixed) in the form of irrational beliefs, negative emotions, blocked energy, and/or physical symptoms, such as anxieties, phobias, flashbacks, nightmares, and/or fears. Regardless of the magnitude of the trauma, it may have the potential for negatively impacting an individual's self-confidence and self-efficacy. The event can become locked or "stuck" in the memory network in its original form, causing an array of traumatic or PTSD symptoms. Triggers activate images, physical sensations, tastes, smells, sounds, and beliefs that might echo the experience as though it were the day it originally happened or cause other distortions in perception of current events. Reminders of the event have the potential for triggering an emotional or physical response. With the use of EMDR, the client can unblock the traumatic information and can fully experience and integrate the trauma toward a healthy resolution.

Types of Trauma

Dr. Shapiro distinguishes between large "T" and small "t" traumas (2001; see Figure 1.1). When a person hears the word "trauma," he usually thinks of man-made events, such as fires, explosions, automobile accidents, or natural disasters, which include hurricanes, floods, and tornados. Sexual abuse, a massive heart attack, death of a loved one, Hurricane Katrina, and the 9/11 attacks on the World Trade Center by international terrorists are graphic examples of large "T" traumas. Among other descriptors, these types of traumas can be defined as dangerous and life-threatening and fit the criteria in the *DSM–IV–TR* (APA, 2000).

Then there are the traumas Dr. Shapiro (2001) has designated as small "t" traumas. Small "t" traumas may be more subtle. These types of traumas impact one's beliefs about self, others, and the world. Small "t" traumas are those that can affect our sense of self, self-esteem, self-definition, self-confidence, and optimal behavior. They influence how we see ourselves as a part of the bigger whole. They are often ubiquitous (i.e., constantly encountered) in nature and are stored in state-dependent mode in our memory network. Unless persistent throughout the client's childhood, small "t" traumas usually do not have much impact on overall development, yet

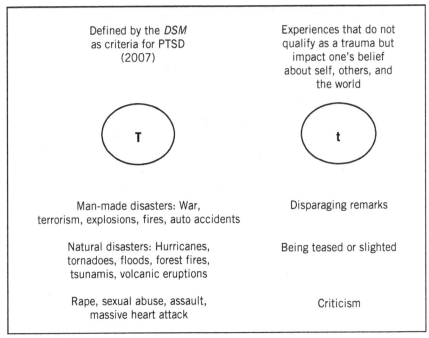

Figure 1.1 Types of traumatic events.

maintain the ability to elicit negative self-attributions and have potential for other long-term negative consequences.

To illustrate the difference between a small "t" and a large "T" trauma, let's consider the case of Rebecca who grew up as "the minister's daughter." As the offspring of a local pastor, Rebecca grew up, figuratively speaking, in a glass house. She believed that her father's job rested on her behavior inside and outside of her home. In her world, everyone was watching. She was always in the spotlight, and no one seemed to want to share their life with her. She went through childhood with few friends. "I remember before and after church, the groups of kids forming. I was the outsider. No one invited me in." All the kids were afraid that every move they made would be reported to her daddy. She never would. She never did.

Being at home was not much better. Her father was never home. He was always out "tending to his flock" and had little time left for his own family. Her mother was not much comfort either because she spent much of her time trying to be perfect as well. Living in a glass house was not easy for any of them, especially Rebecca, the oldest of three.

By the time Rebecca entered therapy, she was a wife and mother. She thought she had to be perfect in motherhood and in her marriage as well. She became frustrated, angry, and lonely. She felt misunderstood and neglected by her husband. He was never there. He never listened. She thought she could do nothing right, as hard as she tried.

Probing into Rebecca's earliest childhood memories, no tragic or traumatic memories (i.e., large "T" traumas) emerged. As she continued to explore her past, the hardships and rigors of living in a glass house as the preacher's daughter slowly became apparent. The original target that initiated a round of EMDR sessions focused on Rebecca "sitting on my hands in church and being a good little girl." Her negative belief about herself as she focused on this global touchstone event was "I have to be good." She felt isolated, overlooked, and abandoned by her parents and the parishioners of her father's church. This was undoubtedly a small "t" trauma. There was no one single event or series of traumatic events that set her current problem or issue in place. It was her way of life . . . how, where, and why she was forced to live as a child caused a specific set of symptoms and interfered with her living happily and successfully in the present.

The differentiation between small "t" and large "T" trauma often appears too simplistic. Another way of discussing the types of trauma is to look at it in terms of shock or developmental trauma.

Shock trauma involves a sudden threat that is perceived by the central nervous system as overwhelming and/or life-threatening. It is a single episode traumatic event. Examples include car accidents, violence, surgery, hurricanes and other natural disasters, rape, battlefield assaults, and war.

Developmental trauma refers to events that occur over time and gradually affect and alter a client's neurological system to the point that it remains in a traumatic state. This type of trauma may cause interruptions in a child's natural psychological growth. Examples of a developmental trauma are abandonment or long-term separation from a parent, an unstable or unsafe environment, neglect, serious illness, physical or sexual abuse, and betrayal at the hands of a caregiver. This type of trauma can have a negative impact on a child's sense of safety and security in the world and tends to set the stage for future trauma in adulthood as the sense of fear and helplessness that accompany it go unresolved.

ADAPTIVE INFORMATION PROCESSING

EMDR is an integrative psychotherapeutic approach and is guided by an information processing model. Francine Shapiro developed a hypothetical model called the Adaptive Information Processing (AIP) model (changed from Accelerated Information Processing model in 1995) to provide a theoretical framework and principles for EMDR treatment. Accelerated information processing clarifies how EMDR works, and AIP guides how it is used (see Figure 1.2). Dr. Shapiro recognized the need to more efficiently explain the consistent treatment effects being obtained and reported from EMDR.

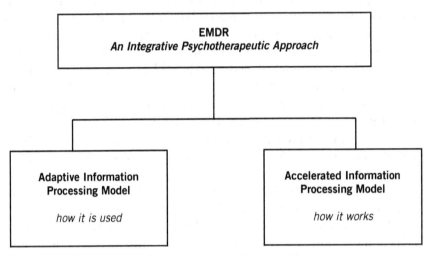

Figure 1.2 EMDR: An integrative psychotherapeutic approach.

AIP elaborates on the observed treatment effects of EMDR by describing an innate physiological system that helps to transform disturbing information into adaptive resolution by psychologically integrating the information. In this model, memory networks constitute the basis of our perceptions, attitudes, and behaviors. These memories consist of stored information, such as sensory input (i.e., captured by our five senses), thoughts, emotions, and beliefs. Dr. Shapiro believes that disturbing events, whether large "T" traumas or small "t" traumas, are the primary source of our current dysfunction. When trauma happens, it causes a disruption in our information processing system, leaving any associated sights, sounds, thoughts, or feelings unprocessed and, subsequently, dysfunctionally stored as they are perceived (Shapiro, 2001). See Figure 1.3 for an example of adaptive versus maladaptive resolution.

Dr. Shapiro posits that inherent in the AIP model is a psychological self-healing construct similar to the body's healing response to physical injury (2001). For example, if you get a splinter stuck in your

Erica's possible responses to recovering from an automobile accident:

Adaptive Resolution	**Maladaptive Resolution**
I survived.	Driving phobia
or	Intense anxiety while driving
I can learn from this.	

Figure 1.3 Adaptive vs. maladaptive resolution.

finger, your body's automatic response is to heal the area of injury. However, because the area is blocked by the splinter, healing cannot easily occur until the sliver is removed. In terms of mental processes, it is the inherent tendency of the information processing system to also move toward a state of health. So, when something mildly disturbing happens, you may think about it, talk about it, and process it. You usually find that, within a day or so, you are no longer thinking so intensely about the event and, when you do, you have come to a resolution. For instance, if you are angry at your spouse, you may start to remember that your spouse has some good qualities as well as these very annoying ones. It is a case of the mind adaptively processing the disturbing material and connecting that disturbance into the larger picture of the experience.

On the other hand, when a trauma occurs that is too large for your system to adequately process, it can become "stuck" (i.e., dysfunctionally stored) in the central nervous system. Maladaptive responses, such as flashbacks or dreams, can be triggered by present stimuli, and there may be attempts of the information processing system to resolve the trauma (Shapiro, 2001). When the system becomes overloaded as just described, EMDR is proving to be the treatment of choice for many to help restart this mental healing process and allow the traumas to be reprocessed. See Figure 1.4 for a graphical representation of the AIP model.

The AIP model also posits that earlier life experiences set the stage for later life problems. Information from earlier disturbing life events can be physiologically and dysfunctionally stored in our nervous system if not properly assimilated at the time of the event. Problematic behaviors and disorders can occur as a result.

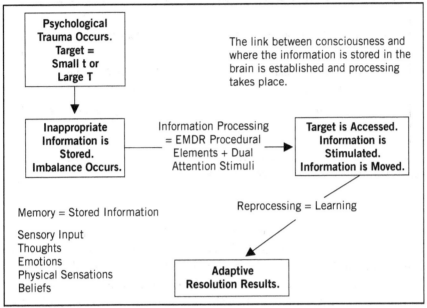

Figure 1.4 Adaptive Information Processing model: The information processing system at work.

At the time of disturbing or traumatic events, information can be stored in the central nervous system in state-specific form (i.e., the negative cognitive belief and emotional and physical sensations the client experienced at the time of the traumatic event remain stored in the central nervous system just as if the trauma is happening in the now). Over time, a client may develop repeated negative patterns of feeling, sensing, thinking, believing, and behaving as a result of the dysfunctionally stored material. These patterns are stimulated, activated, or triggered by stimuli in the present that cause a client to react in the same or similar ways as in the past. Dr. Shapiro (2001) states in many ways throughout her basic text that the "past is present." Negative beliefs and affect from past events spill into the present. By processing earlier traumatic memories, EMDR enables the client to generalize positive affect and cognitions to associated memories found throughout the "neuro" networks (i.e., memory networks), thus allowing more appropriate behaviors in the present. Figure 1.5 demonstrates a more simplified version of how EMDR works (Shapiro, 2008).

Cognitive behavioral techniques, such as systematic desensitization, imaginal exposure, or flooding, have the client focus on anxiety-

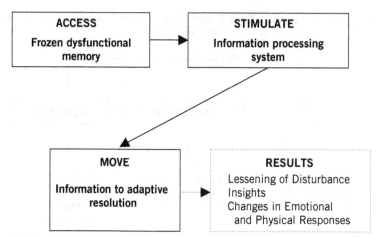

Figure 1.5 Activation components of EMDR.

provoking behaviors and irrational thoughts or relive the traumatic experiences with which he presents. More inclusively, EMDR targets the experiences that *caused* the negative cognition, affect, and physical sensations to become "stuck" in a client's nervous system. Once the memories have been processed utilizing EMDR, a physiological shift can occur that causes the disturbing picture to fade appropriately with the associated negative self-belief, feelings, and physical sensations. The "block" (i.e., dysfunctionally stored information) in the client's nervous system has been shifted, and the disturbance has been brought to an adaptive resolution as the natural healing process is activated. The primary byproduct of reprocessing is a decrease or elimination of the negative charge associated with the trauma.

Changes in perception and attitude, experiencing moments of insight, and subtle differences in the way a person thinks, feels, behaves, and believes are byproducts as well. The changes can be immediate. Take, for instance, a session with a young woman who had been brutally raped by her ex-boyfriend. During the assessment phase, Andrea's terror appeared raggedly etched in her face and slumped demeanor. After many successive sets of bilateral stimulation, her pale facial features began to redden, her posture to straighten, and her breath to gain strength and resolve as she spontaneously stated, "He took my power that night. No more! I am taking my power back. He no longer has the power to terrorize me." Figure 1.6 demonstrates in action the inherent

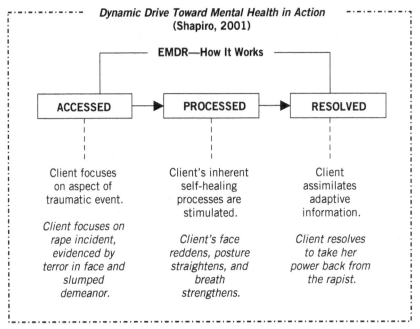

Figure 1.6 Adaptive Information Processing: Information processing mechanism.

information processing mechanism as it highlights the changes that occurred as a result of Andrea's dynamic drive toward mental health with the use of EMDR.

Because the heart of EMDR is the AIP model, it is critical that the clinician have a clear understanding of it before proceeding with EMDR. An adequate conceptual understanding helps the clinician determine a client's appropriateness for EMDR, as well as explain the process to the client during the preparation phase, so he has some understanding of the potential treatment effects. Table 1.1 highlights the before and after changes of EMDR in terms of the AIP model.

For a more comprehensive explanation of AIP, read "Chapter 2, Adaptive Information Processing, the Model as a Working Hypothesis," in *Eye Movement Desensitization and Reprocessing: Basic Principles, Protocols, and Procedures, Second Edition* (2001) by Francine Shapiro.

Table 1.1

ADAPTIVE INFORMATION PROCESSING BEFORE AND AFTER EMDR		
BEFORE		**AFTER**

Client experiences negative event, resulting in:
   Intrusive images
   Negative thoughts or beliefs
   Negative emotions
   and associated physical
   sensations
	NEGATIVE EXPERIENCE IS TRANSMUTED INTO AN ADAPTIVE LEARNING EXPERIENCE	Client experiences adaptive learning, resulting in:
		   No intrusive images
		   No negative thoughts or
		   beliefs
		   No negative emotional and/
		   or physical sensations
		   Client possesses
		   empowering new positive
		   self-belief

What happens?
   Information is insufficiently
   (dysfunctionally) stored
   Developmental windows
   may be closed
		What happens?
		   Information is sufficiently
		   (adaptively) processed
		   Adequate learning has
		   taken place

Resulting in:
   Depression
   Anxiety
   Low self-esteem
   Self-deprecation
   Powerlessness
   Inadequacy
   Lack of choice
   Lack of control
   Dissociation
		Resulting in:
		   Sense of well-being
		   Self-efficacy
		   Understanding
		   Catalyzed learning
		   Appropriate changes in
		   behavior
		   Emergence of adult
		   perspective
		   Self-acceptance
		   Ability to be present

THREE-PRONGED APPROACH

Past, Present, Future

EMDR is a three-pronged treatment approach that focuses on past events, current stimuli, and future situations (see Figure 1.7). This may seem to be a simple idea, but it is often a concept that escapes many newly trained EMDR clinicians because their first exposure to EMDR can be overwhelming, even to the most seasoned clinical professional.

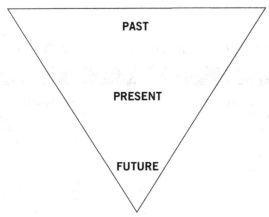

Figure 1.7 Self actualization: EMDR and the three-pronged hierarchy.

Regardless of what you as a participant were taught in the earlier didactic trainings, what you most likely will remember is what was on the instructional sheet that sat on your lap. The first question that you asked the client was, "What old issue or old memory would you like to focus on today?" It is important to note that this question was only used in the training exercises and not in daily clinical practice. Fortunately, this teaching method has changed as the training focus now is to establish a more formalized plan (*e.g., a targeting sequence plan; Shapiro, 2009*) that attempts to identify past events (and a touchstone event, if available), present triggers, a future template, and to encourage the participant to process in this order.

To completely resolve a client's issue and achieve adaptive resolution, EMDR is designed to: (a) address a client's past events; (b) clean out related current stimuli that might trigger distress in the client; and (c) prepare the client for future situations involving the same kind of circumstance (or reaction). The concept of the three-pronged approach is so important that an entire chapter in this Primer has been devoted to it (see chapter 4).

Three-Pronged Targets

The order of the processing is important. First, it is necessary to strive to adaptively resolve past traumas, then process current stimuli that trigger distress, and continue on to any future situations that have the potential or likelihood to do the same. See Figure 1.8 for a breakdown of what is identified and processed under each prong of the EMDR approach.

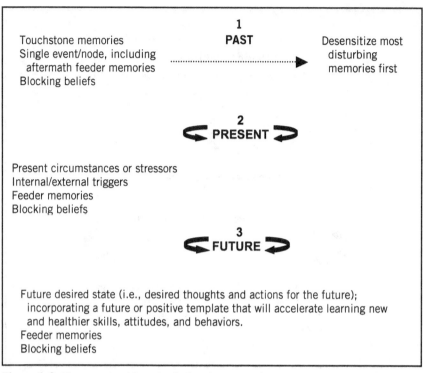

Figure 1.8 Three-pronged targets: Order of reprocessing.

What this means is that the clinician may want to consider targeting the memories that lay the groundwork for any present problems and/or issues first. It may be a single traumatic event or what is called a *touchstone event,* a primary and self-defining event in the client's life. In AIP language, Dr. Shapiro refers to the touchstone memory as a node to which similar events *will attach* in the continuous formation of a "neuro" or memory network that is critical to the client's sense of self (2001; see Figure 1.9).

Once all presently charged past events are processed (i.e., after the *touchstone event* is processed), other past events may or may not have a cognitive or affective charge remaining. The clinician may want to consider processing those that have a "charge" before continuing to recent events. Then any recent events, circumstances, situations, stressors, or other triggers that might elicit a disturbance are targeted. After the past events and present disturbances have been identified and reprocessed, focus on the future desired behavior and the client's ability to make better choices. This entails education, modeling, and targeting what Dr. Shapiro calls a future or positive template

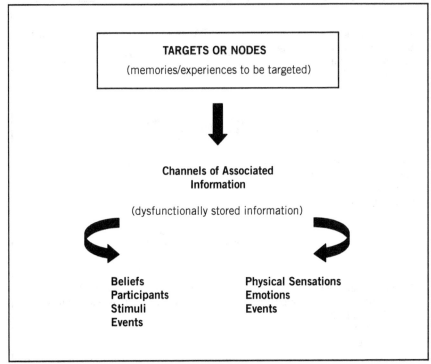

Figure 1.9 Targets or Nodes.

(2001). It is important for the client to appropriately and properly assimilate the new information gained through the previous prongs (i.e., past, present, future) by providing her with experiences that ensure future successes.

During recent EMDR trainings, the order of processing the three prongs (i.e., past, present, future) and strategically identifying the touchstone event, *if any*, have been emphasized more dramatically. If you have not been trained in EMDR in the past year or so, pay particular attention to chapter 3 and chapter 4 of this Primer.

Why Is the Concept of Past, Present, Future so Important?

The foundation of the three-pronged protocol postulates that earlier memories are processed before current events, and current events are processed before future events. Why is it so important to process these events in this order? What is the effect on the overall treatment result if it is not processed in order of past, present, future? Earlier life experiences set the groundwork for present events and triggers. So it becomes necessary to clean up as much as possible of the historical associations to the triggers. Once the associations have been eliminated, many of the triggers will dissipate as well. Unfortunately, there still could be current triggers that exist outside of these channels of association that will need to be targeted and processed independently from the past events. Or there may be unprocessed material that surfaces when processing these triggers. These triggers will be the next targets to be processed.

The focus on the future template provides the client an opportunity to imaginally rehearse future circumstances and desired responses. This is yet another opening for unprocessed material to surface. This material is addressed through the use of the future template, providing the client a means of resolving as he rehearses encountering the material, such as anticipatory anxiety, in similar future situations. The three-pronged approach appears to be a bottom-up process in that the future is subsumed by the present and the present is subsumed by the past. It has been suggested that bypassing the three-pronged approach as part of the full EMDR treatment means obtaining only a fraction of the full treatment effect. Furthermore, if one does not do the full protocol and believes that the material is resolved because the past has been successfully reprocessed, the client may remain unprepared for being triggered in the present.

TARGETING POSSIBILITIES

Targets May Arise in Any Part of the EMDR Process

When a clinician instructs a client to focus on a target in EMDR, she is asking the client to tune into a specific memory, image, person, or event or the most disturbing part of it. The target or node then becomes the pivotal point of entry into the associated psychologically stored material. If a client's presenting issue relates to the way he responds to his mother-in-law when she first sees him, the target he selects may be the image of her hugging and kissing him as a form of greeting. Because the target image has a constellation of associated experiences around it, Dr. Shapiro (2001) calls it a *node*.

Throughout Dr. Shapiro's clinical books, she refers to several different targets that may arise in certain parts of the process. The past, present, and future targets referred to above are the primary focus in the EMDR training. Her text also introduces the reader to other associated words, such as node, channel, cluster, and progression. Figure 1.10 attempts to provide a better understanding of the relationship between these types of targets from a more visual perspective.

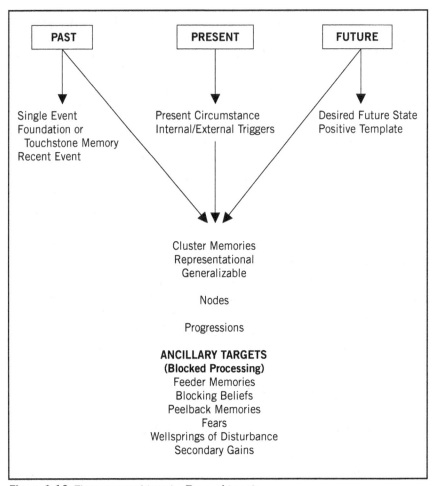

Figure 1.10 Three-pronged targets: Types of targets.

Types of EMDR Targets

As you think about your client sessions, do you recognize any of the types of targets, including the ancillary targets (i.e., other factors that may be contributing to a client's disturbance) listed in Figure 1.10? Are you aware under which prong of the EMDR protocol these types of targets might fall? The following definitions are provided as a refresher:

Targets From the Past
Touchstone Memory. A memory that lays the foundation for a client's current presenting issue or problem. This is the memory that

formed the core of the maladaptive network or dysfunction. It is the first time a client may have believed, "I am not good enough" or that this conclusion was formed. The touchstone event often, but not necessarily, occurs in childhood or adolescence. Reprocessing will be more spontaneous for the client if the touchstone events can be identified and reprocessed earlier in the treatment.

Example: As an adult, Mary Jane reported being uncomfortable engaging with large groups of people (i.e., 20 or more). She frequently experienced high levels of anxiety before and during office meetings, church, and social events. She was nervous and tentative, fearful and unsure because she could not trust herself to be in control. During the history-taking process, it was discovered that, when she was in the second grade, Mary Jane wet her pants often. She was afraid to use the restroom because she feared its "tall, dark stalls." Students often teased her, calling her "baby" and yelling out to the other students that she had wet her pants. What she came to believe about herself was, "I cannot trust myself." This belief carried over into her later life and caused her to react tentatively in group situations.

Targets From the Present
Circumstances. Situations that stimulate a disturbance.

Example: Getting summoned to the principal's office caused Jerry to flush with anxiety, even though he had been Teacher of the Year three times running and was a 25-year veteran in the public school system as a high school teacher.

Internal or External Triggers. Internal and external cues that are capable of stimulating dysfunctionally stored information and eliciting emotional or behavioral disturbances.

Examples: Sights, sounds, or smells may be triggers. A client reports becoming triggered by driving on or near a section of roadway where he was involved in a fatal crash in which his best friend was killed. Or a client becomes anxious and ashamed when being innocently questioned by a police officer, even though he has not done anything wrong.

Targets From the Future
Future Desired State. How would the client like to be feeling, sensing, believing, perceiving, and behaving today . . . and in the future? What changes would be necessary? The third prong of EMDR focuses on targeting a positive template that will assist in incorporating

appropriate future behaviors for the client or reprocessing future anticipatory events. This stage may involve teaching the client assertiveness skills, modeling good decision-making, or having the client imagining future situations, such as coaching people to help them respond more appropriately.

Example: Ryan had always been a passive guy who never could say, "No." "Peace at any cost" *was* his motto. The touchstone event identified with his conflict-avoidant behavior was a memory of his usually calm mother lunging at his father with a butcher knife during the heat of his father's verbal attack. Before the night was over, his father had beaten his mother so severely that she was hospitalized for 3 days. Once this memory had been targeted and reprocessed, Ryan felt more empowered but needed instruction on how to stand up for himself more assertively. After the training, he was able to imagine himself successfully interacting and responding appropriately in conflict-laden circumstances.

Positive Template (Imaginal Future Template Development). A process where the client uses the adaptive information learned in the previous two prongs to ensure future behavioral success by incorporating patterns of alternative behavioral responses. These patterns require a client to imagine responding differently and positively to real or perceived negative circumstances or situations or significant people.

Example: Joe came home from a business trip and found his wife in bed with his best friend. Joe and his wife had reconciled despite the obvious upheaval it had caused in their already shaky relationship. In the processing of this abrupt discovery, Joe had mostly worked through his reactions and feelings toward his ex-best friend, but he never wanted to interact with him again. However, both worked at the same firm; and it was inevitable that their paths would cross. What the clinician had Joe imagine was a chance meeting with this man and how Joe would like to see this encounter transpire from beginning to end.

Other Potential Targets
Node. In terms of the AIP model, a node is an associated system of information (Shapiro, 2001). It is "the biologically stored experience central to the memory network designated for therapeutic targeting" (Shapiro, 2008). A node could represent a cluster, a progression, or a feeder memory.

Example: Jeremy initially entered therapy because he had difficulty interacting professionally with his supervisor. Whenever his boss called or e-mailed asking him to come to his office, Jeremy felt like a small child being summoned to the principal's office. "What did I do now?" he thought. After a thorough investigation of his past and present, Jeremy related how he felt and reacted around his father. "I always felt as though I had done something wrong." Jeremy's father worked and traveled extensively and was not home very much. When he was, Jeremy could find his father in his office working steadily and mostly unaware of the rest of the family activities in their home. His father was gruff and matter-of-fact and never paid much attention to Jeremy. When he wanted something from Jeremy or would reprimand him for something he did, he would call Jeremy to his office. It was one of those memories that became the target for Jeremy's presenting issue.

Cluster Memories. These memories form a series of related or similar events and have shared cues, such as an action, person, or location. Each event is representational or generalizable to the other. These nodes are not targeted in the sessions in which they have been identified. The clinician usually keeps an active list of any nodes that arise during reprocessing and reevaluates them at a later date to see if further treatment is necessary.

Example: Anna between the ages of 7 and 10 was stung by a bee three different times. Each of these events has varying degrees of trauma attached, but each possesses a shared cue, the bees. These are cluster memories and can be grouped together as a single target.

Progression. A progression is a potential node. It generally arises in the course of the reprocessing of an identified target during or between sets (Shapiro, 2001). It is a more serious issue that cannot be pursued when it arises in the middle of an EMDR session.

Example: Tricia was targeting incidents related to her mother publicly humiliating her when the memory of how her mother acted at her grandfather's funeral arose. The clinician knew from previous sessions that Tricia had a close, loving relationship with her grandfather and that he was her primary advocate in the family. The clinician wrote down in her notes that her grandfather's funeral may need to be targeted in and of itself. When a progression (i.e., potential target) arises, it is important not to distract the client from her processing of the current target. Rather the clinician continues to allow the client to follow the natural processing of the present target and note any disturbance around this event that she may need to explore and target during a future session.

Feeder Memory. This type of memory has been described by Dr. Shapiro as an inaccessible, earlier memory that contributes to a client's current dysfunction and that subsequently blocks the reprocessing of it (2001). Unlike progressions, which typically arise spontaneously, feeder memories usually are discovered more by direct inquiry and are touchstone memories that have yet to be identified. If a client becomes stuck during reprocessing, this is a clue that there may be a feeder memory stalling the processing. Note: A feeder memory also differs from a progression in that the feeder memory is an untapped memory related to the current memory being processed. The feeder memory is treated before the current memory (i.e., EMDR within EMDR). This is unlike a progression, which is a new target (i.e., memory) that pops up during the processing of another traumatic incident (see above, under Progression). The progression is acknowledged and processed at a later time.

 Example: Brittany was in the midst of reprocessing a disturbing event involving malicious accusations by her mother (i.e., "You're a slut." "You must have brought it on somehow." "You deserved everything that happened."). These comments were made by her mother after Brittany at the age of 18 was nearly raped while walking home from school 2 months earlier. Following several sets of reprocessing and clinical strategies to unblock or shift her processing, Brittany's level of disturbance did not change. The clinician strategically asked Brittany to focus on the words "I am dirty," (her original negative cognition) and to scan for earlier events in her life that were shameful and humiliating. The memory that finally emerged was the memory of her brothers waving her dirty underwear out a second-story window of their home for all the neighborhood boys to witness. The memory of her brothers' cruel behavior is what is called a feeder memory.

Blocking Belief. A blocking belief is a belief that stops the processing of an initial target. Blocking beliefs typically show themselves when the clinician is evaluating the Subjective Units of Disturbance (SUD) or Validity of Cognition (VoC). In the desensitization phase, the SUD level will not move below a "1" and, in the installation phase, the VoC remains below a "7." Typically, when the clinician asks the client in the desensitization phase, "What prevents it (i.e., SUD) from being a '0'?" or, if the client is in the installation phase, "What prevents it (i.e., VoC) from being a '7'?" the client is able to respond with a negative belief and an appropriate, associative early memory. At this point, the processing on the initial target is stopped until the blocking belief memory has been targeted and reprocessed. Then, and only then, is the original memory retargeted and reprocessing continued.

Example: Heather, a sergeant in the military, returned home after sustaining injuries during a rocket attack while on a routine field mission in Iraq. Two of her fellow soldiers died from the blast. Heather was hit by flying shrapnel that literally left a hole in her leg. She required two subsequent surgeries, both of which were unable to remove all of the rocket shrapnel from her leg. During recuperation, Heather reported disturbing recurring dreams, flashbacks, and thoughts of the rocket attack, which were frequently accompanied by high levels of anxiety or a panic attack. While targeting the event utilizing EMDR, the sergeant's negative cognition was "I'm unsafe" and her positive cognition was "I can be safe." When assessing the sergeant's positive cognition during the installation phase, she reported a VoC of "6." After attempting to shift her response by changing the direction and speed of the bilateral stimulation with no success, Heather was asked by the clinician, "What prevents it (i.e., VoC) *from being a 7?*" Heather immediately responded with the blocking belief, "I can never be safe." Further questioning by the clinician revealed that, when Heather was 5, she had been digitally penetrated by an older cousin who had said to her, "If you tell anyone what happened, you will never be safe. I will find you. And I will kill you." This is also a feeder memory in that it contributes to the current dysfunction and blocked processing. This feeder memory is represented by the blocking belief, "I can never be safe."

Peelback Memory. A peelback memory usually occurs when a touchstone has not been identified and, during reprocessing, other associations begin to "peel back" to expose prior disturbing memories.

Example: After the processing of an earthquake, Taylor continued to exhibit symptoms of PTSD for which there seemed to be no reason. She continued to have many problems associated with the earthquake despite the fact that her house had remained intact, and she or others in her family did not sustain any injuries. Her initial intake showed no indications of previous trauma. Upon further processing of the earthquake, an early association "peeled back" a memory in her 20s when she was date raped, and then again to an even earlier time when she was molested by a neighbor in her adolescence. Her initial negative cognition, "I am out of control," may have helped to uncover these earlier memories. Unlike a feeder memory, which is an earlier disturbance that blocks the reprocessing of the event, a peelback memory emerges spontaneously during reprocessing and is similar in terms of the emotional, physical, or cognitive content of the memory being reprocessed.

Fears. Fear in the processing of targeted information can become a blocking mechanism. It stalls the process. Dr. Shapiro identified fears to include fear of the clinical outcome of EMDR or the process itself, fear of going crazy, fear of losing good memories, and fear of change. Fear of the process can be readily recognized whenever a client begins to identify elements of EMDR that appear to be problematic for her (2001). Also check to ensure that any expressed fears of the process are not related to secondary gain.

Example: It is not unusual for a client to express concern or fear that he is not "doing it" (i.e., the process) correctly or is afraid of extreme abreaction or that the clinician cannot handle the potential level of distress that he might express during the reprocessing.

Wellsprings of Disturbance. This phenomenon is indicative of "the presence of a large number of blocked emotions that can be resistant to full EMDR processing" (Shapiro, 2001) and is often caused by the existence of an extensive negative belief system. A wellspring is similar to a feeder memory in that both are feeding the emerging emotions. Clients who are resistant to therapy or who seek therapy involuntarily at the urging of someone else (e.g., therapy is court-ordered or requested by a persistent and threatening spouse) are most susceptible to this phenomenon. They are in therapy because of someone else and possess no desire to report or deal with any feelings (Shapiro, 2001).

Example: A man who is forced into therapy at the urging of a disgruntled spouse may possess the belief that "real men don't cry." This belief may be associated with an earlier traumatic memory and result in the client suppressing any high level of disturbance that might otherwise naturally occur under a current circumstance (e.g., dealing with his wife's raging episodes). The true level of affective disturbance is never reached by the client, and it is this same level that contributes to the client's present dysfunction. Earlier experiences taught him that men (or boys) are not allowed to express themselves emotionally. If there is no change in the client's imagery, body sensations, or insight but he continues to report a low level of disturbance, the wellspring phenomenon is probably in effect. When present, the clinician may need to provide additional EMDR strategies in order to access the blockage. See the formulas in Figure 1.11.

Blocking Belief = A negative belief about oneself that stalls EMDR processing

Wellsprings of Disturbance = Negative Beliefs + Unresolved (Early Memories) + Blocked Emotions

---

Figure 1.11 Difference between wellsprings of disturbance and blocking belief.

The distinctions between wellsprings of disturbance and blocking beliefs are important because the presence of either determines what course of action a clinician may take to resolve the blocking issues.

Secondary Gain. A secondary gain issue has the potential of keeping a presenting issue from being resolved.
Example: Typical examples involve—What would be lost (e.g., a pension check); what need is being satisfied (e.g., special attention); or how current identity is preserved (e.g., "If I get over my pain, I'm abandoning those who have stood by me since the war.").

Now that you have a clearer picture of what these targets are and how they are related, can you think of examples for each? Recollect targets from some of your EMDR sessions with clients to help you identify examples of each. Targets . . . *past, present, and future* . . . especially ancillary targets can emerge in any of the three prongs in the EMDR protocol. Refer to Figure 1.12 for assistance. It is important to be on the lookout for them through the entire process in order to ensure adaptive resolution of every aspect of the client's traumatic history.

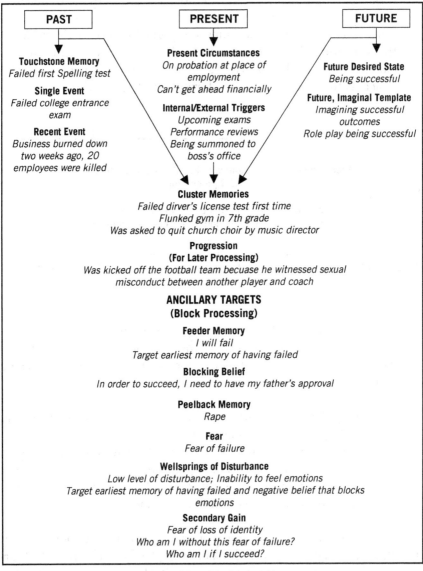

Figure 1.12 Three-pronged targets: Types of targets with examples.

DUAL ATTENTION STIMULATION

What Does It Do?

When Dr. Shapiro was in the early stages of developing the theory, procedures, and protocol behind EMDR, she thought that it was the saccadic eye movements or eye tracking that helped to activate the information processing system, which processes the dysfunctionally stored material around a traumatic event. It was subsequently found that alternating bilateral hand taps and auditory tones could also be utilized. Some clinicians use alternating bilateral instrumental music. The type of bilateral stimulation utilized is important in terms of what the client can best tolerate. A person with an eye disorder obviously might not be able to track a clinician's fingers well. Someone who does not like to be touched may not be able to tolerate being tapped by the clinician or the close proximity of the clinician to them. The type of stimulation chosen depends on the client. It is important to be able to offer more than one type of stimulation to accommodate the preferences presented by the client.

In the event that information during reprocessing is not moving or becomes stuck, it is important to have the client agree beforehand on two preferred directions (i.e., back and forth, up and down, or diagonal) or two types of modalities (i.e., eye movement, audio, tapping) from which the client can choose. Thus, if a need for change in direction or modality occurs, the client has agreed to his preferences in advance. Any time a change in bilateral stimulation is indicated, the clinician checks with or informs the client that a change is being made before implementing the change.

Preferred Means of Dual Attention Stimulation

Dr. Shapiro's preferred means of bilateral stimulation is eye movement. All the research involved in establishing the efficacy of EMDR was done utilizing eye movements. This type of stimulation also supports dual attention whereby the client can attend to both internal and external stimuli. The client processes using eye movement with his eyes open so that he remains aware of his present environment. Twenty studies have focused on investigating the role of eye movements in EMDR to date: (a) case studies (Montgomery & Ayllon, 1994; Lohr, Tolin, & Kleinknecht, 1995; Lohr, Tolin, & Kleinknecht, 1996; Acierno, Tremont, Last, & Montgomery, 1994); (b) clinical dismantling studies with diagnosed participants (Devilly, Spence, & Rapee, 1998; Renfrey & Spates, 1994; Boudewyns & Hyer, 1996; Pitman et al., 1996); (c) clinical dismantling studies with analogue participants (Carrigan & Levis,1999; Sanderson & Carpenter, 1992; Solomon, Gerrity, & Muff, 1992; Van Etten & Taylor, 1998); and (d) component action studies (Barrowcliff, Gray, MacCulloch, Freeman, & MacCulloch, 2003; Wilson, Silver, Covi, & Foster, 1996, Kuiken, Bears, Miall & Smith, 2001–2002; Christman, Garvey, Propper, & Phaneuf, 2003; Andrade, Kavanagh, & Baddeley, 1997; Kavanagh, Freese, Andrade, & May, 2001; Sharpley, Montgomery, & Scalzo, 1996; van den Hout, Muris, Salemink, & Kindt, 2001). See also Maxfield, Melnyk, and Hayman (2008) and Propper and Christman (2008) for further information on this important topic. No research presently exists to support having the client process with his eyes closed or for the other methods of stimulation (i.e., auditory tones, tapping).

Is Dual Attention Stimulation EMDR?

Dual attention stimulation, or bilateral stimulation as it is called most often, is but one component of EMDR. Stimuli, such as directed and accelerated eye movements, are used to activate the client's information processing system as he focuses on a past trauma, present-day trigger, or future event. Over the years, many beginning students of EMDR, consultees, and even seasoned veterans have referred to bilateral stimulation as EMDR. Bilateral stimulation is used when facilitating the sacred space exercise and with the calm (or safe) place and resource installation exercises (see Appendix B). Does this mean sacred space, calm (or safe) place, and even resource installation when coupled with bilateral stimulation are EMDR? EMDR is clearly identified as an eight-phase process. If one of the phases is eliminated or substituted with something else, it can no longer be called EMDR.

Shorter or Longer? Slower or Faster?

During the preparation phase, bilateral stimulation is originally introduced with the calm (or safe) place and any other resource enhancement or stabilization exercises deemed appropriate by the clinician prior to using EMDR and, then again, during reprocessing in the desensitization phase. There is a difference in the speed and number of bilateral sets of stimulation used in both. The recommended rate of speed is slower, and the number of round-trip passes is fewer (4–6), when using bilateral stimulation with resource, coping, relaxation, and stress reduction exercises and strategies.

While using bilateral stimulation when reprocessing, including installation, the speed is tolerably comfortable (i.e., much faster) for the client and number of sets is increased (20–30 round-trips). Faster and longer sets of bilateral stimulation are more likely to activate disturbing material and trigger associated channels of information. Slower and shorter sets are utilized in stabilization efforts so as to not activate any disturbing material prior to actual reprocessing with EMDR.

Although the purpose of the installation phase is to fully integrate a positive self-assessment with the targeted information, there is still the possibility other associations could emerge that may need to be addressed. The faster, longer eye movements facilitate the emergence of any lingering disturbing material related to the original targeted event. Remember, a completely successful treatment of the original target memory cannot be attained until the early memories that caused the blocking belief are reprocessed. There is little research regarding this widely practiced distinction. However, it is considered a guideline by many EMDR trainers, facilitators, and therapists.

IMPORTANT CONCEPTS TO CONSIDER

What Once Was Adaptive Becomes Maladaptive

Some behaviors are learned. Some serve us well and others do not. Some serve us for a period in our life and eventually become a nuisance. For example, a woman who was repeatedly sexually molested by a relative as a young child may have learned to dissociate during the molestation. This was her way of coping with the fear and pain of the trauma at the time of the abuse. Years later, as an adult, she may still find herself dissociating during stressful situations in her job. As a child, dissociation was the only way she knew to cope; and it worked well at the time. As a maturing adult, the dissociation begins to cause problems at home, at school, and/or at work.

State vs. Trait Change

Dr. Shapiro (2008) differentiated between a state and a trait change. She defined a state change as momentary or transitory, whereas a trait change reflected a permanent change. A state change is a change of mind. It instills a sense of hope in the client. A state change also requires the use of coping mechanisms to continue the change, whereas a trait change no longer requires use of any. With a trait change, the client changes how he sees or views the event and, as a result, can experience it differently. When a client changes his perspective about a traumatic event that he has experienced in his life and has the needed skills, he is able to function more appropriately. An example of a state change is the client saying, "I am able to soothe myself by breathing and using my safe place when my boss asks me to come to his office. I feel much calmer." A trait change may be, "I am no longer triggered when my boss asks me to come to his office." To simplify, "states are weather" whereas "traits are climate." "All traits are states" but "not all states are traits" (Shapiro, 2006).

Dual Awareness

Dual awareness or mindfulness or what Dr. Shapiro calls "dual focus of attention" (2001) allows the client to maintain a sense of present awareness and for the client's internal processes to function without interference during EMDR. In essence, it allows the client to be a nonevaluative observer with respect to whatever emerges during an EMDR session. One of the primary reasons to teach a client grounding and breathing skills and anchoring him in the present is to help him learn to keep one foot in the present while reprocessing something traumatic from his past. This provides him with a dual focus of attention and reduces the possibility or risk of a client dissociating, blanking out, and/or resisting. Teaching him these skills prior to the EMDR processing will help facilitate a smoother EMDR experience. It also allows the client to maintain a sense of safety in the present while accessing and stimulating negative information from the past. The clinician can solidify the client's connection to the present by utilizing verbal reassurances such as, "Good," "You're doing fine," "It's over," or "You're safe now." The clinician may also change the direction or speed of the bilateral stimulation. When a client is in an abreactive state, these types of clinical strategies are particularly important to help the client maintain an external focus (Shapiro, 2001).

Ecological Validity (i.e., Soundness)

In attempting to discern whether a client's target has been resolved, take a look at what resolution of this particular traumatic event would look like in the real world given the individual, the timing, and the situation.

To what degree does the current situation "fit" the circumstances? Ask yourself, "If a woman was processing a rape that occurred months before and the rapist was still on the loose, would it be appropriate for her to continue to feel fear and demonstrate vigilance around this event?" The answer depends on how her information processing system works. Is there a reason she may be or may think she is still in danger? Is her sense of vigilance and fear around the rapist emotionally appropriate under the circumstances? If the answer to these questions is, "Yes," there is ecological validity in this instance.

How does one recognize ecological validity? And how do you work with it within the EMDR framework? First, use Wolpe's Subjective Units of Disturbance scale (SUD; Wolpe, 1990; see Figure 1.13).

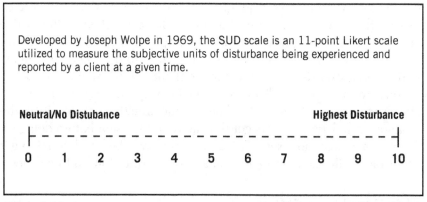

Figure 1.13 Subjective Units of Disturbance scale (SUD).

The SUD scale is an 11-point Likert scale utilized to rate the anxiety level of a memory being accessed by a client in the present. When you ask the client to focus on the original event (or incident) and again ask, on a scale from "0" to "10," "How disturbing does it feel *now*?" and the client says a "1," you need to check out what is blocking (i.e, blocking belief) desensitization of the original target by asking, "What keeps it from being a '0'?" In the case of a rapist, the client might respond, "He's still out there." Ask the client to "go with that" and continue to process to a more complete resolution. Do not assume that the client has reached the end of the channel just yet. Continue to process and check the SUD again before proceeding to the installation phase.

If the client still clings to the "1" and "he's still out there," you can consider this to be ecologically valid. Ecological validity is the only reason you may go directly to the installation phase without the client's SUD level getting down to a "0." The SUD scale will be discussed in more depth in chapter 2 and chapter 3.

A blocking belief may also arise in the installation phase when evaluating the Validity of Cognition (VoC), a 7-point Likert scale which measures the validity (i.e., felt sense of the trueness or falseness) of the client's stated positive cognition (PC). If the client reports a VoC of "6" or "6.5," use the same questioning used above when the SUD does not equal '0' (i.e., "What prevents it from being a '7?'") to discern for: (a) a blocking belief; or (b) ecological validity.

Dr. Shapiro has been known to say, "Forgiveness is like rain—it may or may not happen." If a person forgives someone who has hurt her, it doesn't mean she uses poor judgment with respect to that person (e.g., leaving the children with a past abuser). However, clients often arrive at forgiveness more quickly and more completely than they might with other forms of therapy. Clinicians must be alert to not use their own experiences or experiences of their other clients to determine "ecological validity" for any specific client. If processing stops at a certain place, first attempt to remove the block by changing the direction or modality of the bilateral stimulation. Always get the client's permission before doing so. Then do a couple more sets of bilateral stimulation before determining if it is ecologically valid for the person to move further toward forgiveness.

Side Benefits of EMDR

The primary goal of EMDR is to clear out any irrational, negative cognitions, emotions, and physical sensations associated with a trauma. It does not, however, have the power to clean out rational, negative sensations and cognitions related to a traumatic event. In the rape example above, it may be important to the client's stability that she maintains a healthy sense of fear and a high level of vigilance until after the rapist has been caught and her physical safety is ensured. Depending on the circumstance of the rape, it could be unlikely that her fear and vigilance will dissipate completely until the rapist is apprehended.

The EMDR process does not have the ability to clean out any negative thoughts, emotions, or physical sensations that are appropriate to the situation. For example, a client may hate his mother. His mother may have been abusive, neglectful, and distant. The client may have developed low levels of self-esteem and confidence as a result. EMDR may be successful in raising the client's self-esteem and other issues, but the client may or may not still feel hatred toward his mother after the EMDR work has been completed. EMDR does not have the potential for making you fall back in love with your significant other if you do not love him, attain a raise at your job if you do not deserve one, or make you the next race car champion of the Indy 500 if you do not have the ability to drive a race car. It cannot make the true untrue or the untrue true. It only has the ability to decompress the negative thoughts, feelings, and physical sensations from the client's internal system so that natural healing can take place.

Another side benefit of EMDR is the resultant learning that is possible. In addition, new insights may occur, behavior, perceptions, and attitudes can shift, and physical and emotional responses can change.

Holistic Nature of the Approach

Even though it has been around for 20 years, EMDR is very much a "cutting edge" therapy. One of the reasons that it continues to be cutting edge is because it appears to be a permanent means of flushing traumatic memories and the negative cognitions, emotions, and physical sensations that accompany them from the client's system in a way that talk therapy and some of the alternative therapies do not. It is a whole system approach. It can reach down into the depths of a client's despair, attach itself to every negative element connected to a traumatic event, and then flush it out.

Useful Train Metaphor

Dr. Shapiro prescribes the use of a train metaphor to help clients move along their processing "tracks." Reference to and use of this metaphor will be utilized frequently throughout this Primer. During the desensitization phase, this metaphor can be applied as a means of noticing, yet distancing the client from fear of the trauma. Dr. Shapiro favors this metaphor because it conveys a sense of movement and safety (Shapiro, 2006). The train metaphor may be used throughout the reprocessing as needed. It goes like this:

> In order to help you "just notice" the experience, imagine riding on a train and the feelings, thoughts, etc., are just scenery going by" (Shapiro, 2001).

During the reprocessing, the image of the train going down the track is also used to encourage the client to continue. The passenger is the client, and the scenery represents the dysfunctional information that she is reprocessing. The clinician might say, "It's just old scenery. Just watch it go by." This metaphor is a reminder to the client that the train passes the scenery as quickly as it appears.

Dr. Shapiro describes the processing as "metaphorically like moving down a train track" (Shapiro, 2006). From the point of origination to the destination, there are freight depot stops where passengers get off (i.e., dysfunctional information is unloaded) and new passengers get on (i.e., adaptive information is loaded). In between stops, linkage to adaptive networks can occur. See Figure 1.14 for a pictorial rendition of this metaphor. Again, the damaged material is unloaded and discarded at the freight depots found along the track during the stopping and starting of the bilateral stimulation. It is also at this freight depot where adaptive information is loaded. When the train finally reaches its final destination, the client has reached adaptive resolution.

Whether recommending the train or another example, the metaphor is an option being offered to a client if the trauma becomes too much to bear and distancing from it will allow reprocessing to continue. Installation is unnecessary.

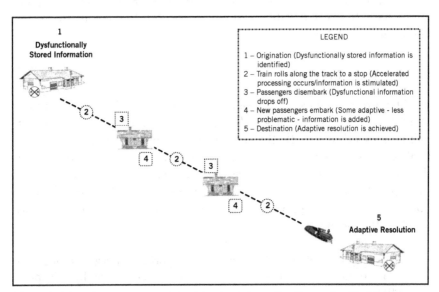

Figure 1.14 Train metaphor and the Adaptive Information Processing Model.

Dr. Shapiro also uses the train metaphor to describe information that moves adaptively from dysfunctional to functional. It is a common experience for a client's once vivid negative images, affect, and cognitions to become less vivid and less valid while the opposite happens to the positive images, affect, and cognitions. Can you visualize a train traveling down its track? Each time the dysfunctional information is stimulated or when accelerated processing takes place, the train moves down the track and stops. At each stop, the client drops off dysfunctional information and boards more functional or adaptive information. The train continues on this route until it reaches its final destination (i.e., adaptive resolution).

Another metaphor used by Dr. Shapiro (2001) is driving a car through a tunnel. In order to get through the tunnel as quickly as possible, the passenger will need to increase his pressure on the accelerator (i.e., *"You are in a tunnel. Just keep your foot on the pedal and keep moving"*). Remember, the processing of the dysfunctional information is accelerated by the bilateral stimulation. This metaphor is utilized to encourage the client to pass through the tunnel as fast as possible (i.e., keep moving his eyes quickly). If he eases up on the accelerator or chooses to stop during transit, the car moves slower; and it takes much longer to get through the tunnel. Or the person is left in the midst of unprocessed material.

PRACTICAL TIPS TO REMEMBER

Practice, Practice, Practice

Practice, practice, practice is this Primer's mantra. In the EMDR Weekend 1 and 2 trainings, you were introduced to EMDR—but, because of time limitations, you may not have fully integrated its substance and protocol into your own therapeutic paradigm. Learning EMDR comes from the *actual doing of it*. Even skilled clinicians who have conducted hundreds of EMDR sessions have the potential for learning something new about EMDR every time they execute the process with a client. It is only from practicing EMDR that excellence and expertise can be derived, so the mantra *practice, practice, practice* cannot be overly emphasized.

Follow the Script Verbatim

Newly trained EMDR clinicians are strongly encouraged to follow Francine Shapiro's script verbatim in the assessment phase. Dr. Shapiro has chosen every word for a specific reason, and these words have been tested and validated over and over again in one context or another in session after session with clients presenting various mental health issues. It is important for the reader to appreciate the wording of her famous protocol before implementing individual styles of eliciting the same information. Clinicians who learned the script in the early days of EMDR may notice how it has been refined throughout the past 20 years.

If you have been recently trained or have decided to finally put your EMDR training to use, sit with a copy of the EMDR protocol in your lap as you implement the assessment phase with clients (see chapter 3). Reading the script verbatim may feel unnatural at first, but you can expect to feel more at ease as you learn the procedural steps. Sitting with the pages in your lap and reading the script as it is written can also serve as good modeling for your client as he watches you work with something new on his behalf. As you become more familiar with the protocol and what words are required in each part, you will most likely develop your own style for setting up the EMDR protocol. The words absolutely necessary to optimize receiving the desired processing outcome have been underlined in subsequent chapters for your recognition and convenience.

Consider logging onto the EMDR Humanitarian Assistance Programs (EMDR-HAP) Web site and ordering the EMDR Progress Notepad. The monies contribute to a good cause, and the worksheets can assist you in being more consistent and successful from client to client. You may also consider purchasing the laminated SUD/VoC Scale Chart. These items may be purchased online at the EMDR-HAP Store (http://www.emdrhap.org). It is not an uncommon reaction for a client to look like a deer caught in the headlights when asked, "What words go best with the picture that express your *negative belief* about yourself *now*?" The laminated scale can save time and also help the client to distinguish a belief from a feeling and to select a negative belief appropriate to his situation.

Know Your Client

Before you begin using EMDR, it is important that you know your client well. Know his strengths and weaknesses. Know his abilities and his limitations. Know his ego deficits. Know his coping mechanisms and strategies. Know his support system—or lack of it. Some clients may not be appropriate or ready for EMDR trauma processing. There could be situations, however, where you will not have the luxury of waiting weeks to know your client before beginning reprocessing. Then it becomes imperative that you learn as much information as you can about your client in a brief period of time, particularly where situations or circumstances indicate a necessity of serious caution.

Stay off the Tracks

After completion of the assessment phase, the clinician is encouraged to be very limited in what she says, such as "Let it go" or "rest" or "blank it out" (i.e., meaning take a break or clear your mind). "Let it go. Take a deep breath." "What are you noticing *now*?" "Good." "Go with that." "Notice that." The clinician does not say much of anything else unless the client appears stuck in the process.

The most appropriate and easiest method to stay out of the way is by consistently maintaining a position of quiet neutrality. During the process, the clinician encourages the client by saying "Good" or "You're doing fine." Beyond this, the clinician must be careful not to physically or verbally express what he believes or thinks about a client's responses between sets of bilateral stimulation. It is imperative that the clinician allow the client to own the reprocessing of his traumatic event and not be encumbered by the therapist's interventions, comments, or questions.

Tracking the Client

It is important for the clinician to write down as much as possible of what the client says during the assessment phase, especially the exact wording of a client's negative and positive cognitions and key words from his descriptions of traumatic events. Why? Because it is important to use exact wording when activating what a client says. If a client provides a negative cognition, such as "It's my fault," and a clinician reframes it as "I'm responsible," the clinician may have inadvertently distorted what the client originally meant. In doing so, the clinician has also placed himself in the client's process. Because the clinician reframed it that way, the client may begin to interpret it as, "I'm responsible" simply because the clinician said it. "It's my fault" and "I am responsible" may or may not mean the same to the client. To the degree that it does not, it can alter the direction of processing. And, if writing down what the client says during reprocessing slows, interrupts, or hinders in any way the client's flow, stop writing and opt to listen and observe more closely what the client is experiencing in the moment.

Keep It Simple

In the early days of your EMDR experience as a clinician, try to keep it simple. Do not go straight from the training to your office and select the most challenging client to conduct your first session of EMDR. Select someone with a less complex trauma, such as a client who presents with a single-event trauma. Maybe someone has recently been involved in an automobile accident that relates to no other traumatic event in his life. As will be described in chapter 4 when the three-pronged approach is discussed, multiple-event traumas are more comprehensive, will take a longer timeframe to deal with, and require more skill than a client who presents with a single event. As a new EMDR clinician, you may not yet have the skill level required to deal with multiple-event traumas.

Then or Now?

One of the most emphasized words in the EMDR protocol is "now." Why? Because we are asking the client what he believes negatively about himself, what he wants to believe positively about himself, and what are the negative emotions and physical sensations that go with the event he is focusing on "now." How is he being affected in the present by something that happened to him 2 months, 2 years, or 20 years ago? How is he being affected now?

The clinician may need to repeat the "now" over and over to a client. A client may get confused between how she felt "then" about an incident and how she feels "now" and ask questions that indicate her confusion. "Do you mean then or *now*?" And she could say, "Then it felt awful, but *now* it does not feel so bad." If this happens during the assessment phase, the clinician may need to reevaluate whether or not the client has chosen an appropriate target. Remember, the clinician is looking to relieve the client of a memory that is charged with negativity. Use Figure 1.15 to help remember this important point.

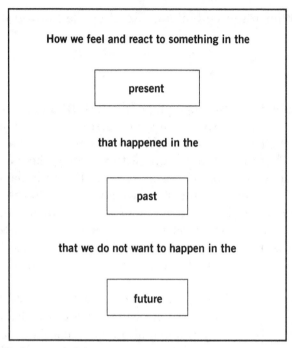

Figure 1.15 Past, present, future.

One More Time

A good rule to remember during EMDR reprocessing with a client is that, any time something is positively reinforced with bilateral stimulation, it strengthens the focus of reinforcement. So, when a client reports a positive direction in the reprocessing, "Go with that," just one more time before returning to target. After the client reaches the SUD of "0," VoC of "7," and a clear body scan, say, "Go with that," one or more times to reinforce the positive treatment effect and/or to allow deepening of the positive cognition (Shapiro, 2001, 2009). If the clinician is consistent with this rule, the success of the EMDR will be enhanced. In any case, it is important to continue bilateral stimulation as long as positive material continues to emerge or strengthen in any part of the client's reprocessing experience.

When reinforcing a positive effect during the desensitization, installation, and body scan phases, the bilateral stimulation will be faster and the length of the sets longer (i.e., 20–30 round-trip passes) than during the preparation phase when using the calm (or safe) place and other resource building exercises (i.e., slower 4–6 round-trip passes).

Solo Run

Client selection is an important part of the EMDR process but more so when a clinician is choosing clients for a first solo run. Clinicians may want to select clients with whom they have healthy client–clinician relationships. There is nothing wrong with selecting clients with issues that maximize a clinician being successful in the early days of usage. Pick the easiest cases. Imagine that the client is an onion and his layers of trauma are as the layers of the onion. How many are there? How thick? How thin? So, when looking at the onion, look for the one- or thin-layered skins. And go slowly. Do not expect to utilize EMDR on the most difficult client and for it to go without some frayed ends here and there.

If you are new to EMDR, select a client with more strengths than weaknesses, adequate coping mechanisms, and a supportive network of family and friends. Initially, you may also want to consider working with a client's lesser issues to build up your experience and the client's confidence in EMDR during your learning process. For example, Sharon entered therapy 3 weeks prior. She had been sexually abused over a long period of time by an older brother who had an intellectual disability. Because Sharon was new to therapy and the clinician was new to EMDR, it was decided that her first session of EMDR would focus on her fear of dogs. It turned out that Sharon had been bitten by a stray dog at the age of 5. Because the session was so successful, they were able to continue using the EMDR on the sexual abuse she experienced at the hands of her older brother.

Dr. Shapiro appears to favor first identifying the "touchstone" event when there may be one (2008). Before proceeding in this direction, however, one has to carefully discern whether or not it is possible for the client to attain successful processing of a touchstone event. This means that the client must be able to tolerate any level of disturbance that may arise. If the touchstone event is chosen for processing and the client becomes too frightened by the experience, much time could be lost by having to "undo" the client's newly created fear of the EMDR process. On the other hand, if you do not target the touchstone event and it arises as a feeder memory, it has the potential to be even more disturbing. The significance of completing a comprehensive history and obtaining informed consent becomes clearer here; that is, it is important for the client to be informed of the potential for accessing feeder memories during the reprocessing of any chosen target.

In this chapter, an attempt has been made to help refamiliarize the reader with basic concepts inherent in EMDR. Throughout subsequent chapters, case examples will be provided along with teaching points that attempt to explain the clinician's strategies or to point out techniques prescribed by Dr. Shapiro during reprocessing.

SUMMARY STATEMENTS

1 EMDR is an integrative psychotherapeutic approach and is guided by the information processing model. The AIP model "provides the theoretical framework and principles for treatment and an explanation of the basis of pathology and personality development" (Shapiro, 2001). As an integrative psychotherapeutic approach, EMDR is distinct from CBT, experiential, and psychodynamic approaches although it is not exclusive and may be informed by or used together with these approaches.

2 EMDR has eight distinct phases.

3 EMDR is a three-pronged approach addressing the past, the present, and the future.

4 Dual attention stimulation using bilateral stimulation is not EMDR. It is only one component.

5 EMDR is a fluid, dynamic approach that entails the clinician using all her clinical skills. It is neither mechanistic nor a cookbook approach.

6 The heart of EMDR is the AIP model. As such, it is critical that the clinician have a clear understanding of it in order to proceed with EMDR practice.

7 Practice, practice, practice. This is how to learn the model.

8 Know your client, inside and out.

9 Stay out of the client's way. The reprocessing is about the client, not the clinician.

2

Eight Phases of EMDR

Eye Movement Desensitization and Reprocessing (EMDR) is an eight-phase protocol—no less. Dr. Shapiro and the EMDR International Association (EMDRIA) are precise about what EMDR is and what it is not; and if you eliminate one of the eight phases, it cannot be called EMDR. The intention of this chapter is to touch briefly upon some of the eight phases and more extensively on others. An effort is made to enhance and expand on key areas that can assist the clinician in client selection, target selection, and adaptive resolution. Table 2.1 offers a short description of the goals and objectives of each phase as described by Dr. Shapiro (2001, 2008, and 2009).

PHASE 1: CLIENT HISTORY AND TREATMENT PLANNING

The client history and treatment planning phase has a threefold purpose. The data collection that occurs in this phase provides a client with all the information needed for informed consent. It drives the client selection process and helps a clinician identify potential treatment targets that emerge from examining the positive and negative events in a client's past, present, and future. This is the phase in which

Table 2.1

EIGHT PHASES OF EMDR

1	Client History – Take a general history from client and develop an appropriate treatment plan.	Has all the relevant client information been gathered? Has risk or crisis assessment on the client been performed? Has the client been evaluated for affect tolerance, trust, and self-regulation? Have the client's strengths and internal/external supports and resources been assessed? Has the client's selection and readiness been determined? Have potential targets and sequencing of targets (i.e., past, present, future) been identified? If appropriate, has the client's touchstone event(s) been identified?
2	Preparation – Introduce and prepare client for EMDR.	Has an appropriate relationship been established with the client? Are there medical considerations that need to be addressed? Has the client been formally introduced to EMDR? Has the client been educated about the EMDR process? Have the client's fears been assessed and addressed? Has informed consent been established via the client's verbal understanding and agreement to continue with EMDR? Has the client's stability been assured? Have coping strategies (i.e., stabilization/affect tolerance, train metaphor, stop signal, calm/safe place) been introduced? Has bilateral stimulation been introduced (i.e., type, speed, distance, seating arrangement)? Have timing considerations been taken into account (e.g., client has an important meeting; clinician is going on vacation)? Are there current life stressors in the client's life that may be exacerbated as a result of the EMDR?

(continued)

3	Assessment – Access target using three-pronged approach for EMDR processing and primary aspects of memory (NC, PC, VoC, emotions, SUD, and body sensations).	Has a target image been obtained? Have the negative and positive cognitions been identified? Has the validity of positive cognition been rated using the VoC scale? Have the relevant emotions been identified? Has the level of disturbance been rated using Wolpe's SUD scale? Has discomfort or other negative physical sensations experienced by the client been identified?
4	Desensitization – Reprocess selected targets (and all related channels of association) toward an adaptive resolution (SUD = 0).	**Be sure to:** Begin the reprocessing by bringing up the image, negative cognition, and location of negative physical sensations. Use a speed that is tolerably comfortable for client and in about 24–36 sets. Avoid talking, analyzing, summarizing, or clarifying. Return to target only after the end of a channel has been reached. Not interrupt a client's abreactive experience. Use strategies for blocked processing and cognitive interweaves sparingly and effectively. Ask for a SUD rating only when all channels of association have been completely cleared or when you are unsure if the client is moving. Determine if the desensitization is complete before moving on to installation. Check to see if ecological validity applies if SUD > 0 (i.e., greater than zero).
5	Installation – Re-check the validity of positive cognition. Integrate positive effects when linked to original target (VoC = 7).	Does positive cognition still fit? Can the client easily pair the original image and positive cognition? Are there emerging blocking beliefs or feeder memories? Is ecological validity appropriate?

(continued)

Table 2.1 (continued)

EIGHT PHASES OF EMDR

6	Body Scan – Complete processing of residual elements associated with traumatic memories by linking original event and positive cognition and checking for bodily discomfort (Completed treatment = clear body scan).	Is body scan clear? Are there unresolved negative physical sensations that need to be reprocessed?
7	Closure – Appropriately close a complete or incomplete session.	Has the client been briefed as to what to expect after a complete or incomplete session? Has the client's stability been ensured after EMDR processing? Has a log been requested from the client? Does the client need stabilizing using the Calm (or Safe) Place or other regulatory exercise?
8	Reevaluation and use of the EMDR Standard Three-Prong Protocol.	Has the successful completion of relevant material been determined? Has the client's log been checked? Has the client's SUD level been rechecked and image reprocessed, if necessary? Does client need to move to a new target?

the clinician begins to know the client. This phase of EMDR does not supplant the clinician's usual history-taking process but supplements that information gathering with history taking specific to EMDR.

Informed Consent and Suitability for Treatment

The process of informed consent begins here. That is, the client has given consent to the use of EMDR based on his appreciation and understanding of the facts and implications of possible treatment outcomes. In this first phase, the clinician begins to gather information pertinent to the client's readiness, willingness, stability, and ability to engage in the EMDR process. The clinician will take a complete and thorough client history using whatever methodology she is comfortable with, identify the presenting problems, and establish treatment goals in the same way she might for clients with whom she will not be using EMDR. The next step is to utilize this information plus valuable data collected from risk or crisis assessments, diagnostic and dissociative evaluations, and the presence of internal and external supports, along with the client's strengths and limitations, to assess a client's suitability for treatment.

To begin an initial assessment of the client's appropriateness for EMDR, the following questions need to be answered: Is the client ready for EMDR? Will the client benefit from EMDR? Is the client able to self-regulate? And finally, does the client consent to the use of EMDR? See Table 2.2 for the fourfold purpose.

Table 2.2

CLIENT HISTORY-TAKING AND TREATMENT PLANNING PHASE

FOURFOLD PURPOSE

- It is the result of the data collection that occurs in this phase that provides the client with all the information needed for informed consent. It drives the process by which a client's appropriateness for EMDR treatment is evaluated.
- It helps the clinician identify potential treatment targets that emerge from examining the positive and negative events in a client's past, present, and future.
- This is the phase in which we begin to *know the client.*
- Potential targets, including touchstone events, if available, are identified.

Client Selection Criteria

The client selection criteria are diverse and obtained from various sources. First, examine safety factors relevant to the client to assist in determining appropriate candidates for EMDR. For instance, does the client possess a sufficient level of trust? Before initiating EMDR, it is essential to ensure that there is an *adequate level of trust* between client and clinician. Remember that many clients have been abused in different ways, and their trust reserves are often depleted by the time they get to treatment. In addition, the clinician may be asking a client to share intimate details of her life. Facts that she has never shared with anyone may emerge during EMDR. Although clients are not required to share all details with the clinician, this may occur or could be helpful from the client's perspective. That is why it is important to build and establish adequate rapport with the client, sometimes in very short periods of time, to maximize the success of the EMDR processing. A client who has a history of severe abuse is screened more intensely than others to identify her appropriateness and readiness for this treatment because it is likely to be more difficult to really trust anyone. The goal is to trust enough to proceed safely with EMDR.

Client's Suitability and Readiness for EMDR

Check the client's stability. Can the client sustain high levels of emotion throughout the EMDR process? As the client's needs and reactions to the treatment become different after each session, the clinician needs to constantly reevaluate suitability and readiness, as well as the benefits. This evaluation is a process, not a one-time event.

In addition, the clinician also needs to take into consideration the client's responses to the following questions:

- Does the client have a medical condition that might preclude her as a candidate for EMDR (e.g., epilepsy, heart condition, high-risk pregnancy)?
- What is the age of the client?
- What medications does she take that may contraindicate success with EMDR?
- Is the client inpatient or outpatient?
- Is there a history of neurological impairment that may prevent the client from succeeding with the EMDR process?
- Is the client physically able to sustain intense emotion?
- Has the client been in counseling before? With whom? Why? How long? Does the client have a history of treatment failure?
- Does the client have a history of alcohol or drug abuse? Is the client actively using alcohol or drugs or recently entered recovery?
- Does the client have impending legal proceedings that need coordination with an attorney?
- Does the client have eye problems or difficulties (e.g., eye pain) that might prohibit the use of eye movements?
- Does he or she have ear problems that might complicate the use of auditory bilateral stimulation (BLS)?

In addition, the clinician may want to assess previous therapy that the client may have had (i.e., reason, focus, length, quality), previous losses, and present relationships with significant others and children (Shapiro, 2006). See Dr. Shapiro's (2006) *EMDR: New Notes on Adaptive Information Processing with Case Formulation Principles, Forms, Scripts, and Worksheets* for further assistance in taking a more thorough history of the client. Included as part of the booklet is an Intake Case Conceptualization Form with questions that she suggests be incorporated into the history-taking phase to aid case conceptualization and management. This booklet can be purchased from the EMDR-Humanitarian Assistance Programs (EMDR-HAP; see Appendix E for more information on EMDR-HAP).

Screening for Dissociative Disorders

Before preparing a client for EMDR, it is important to screen him for a dissociative disorder. Familiarize yourself with the clinical signs of dissociative disorders and use of the Dissociative Experiences Scale (DES). See Appendix E for signs and symptoms of dissociative disorders and information on the DES. Screen every potential EMDR client for dissociative disorders as special preparation is needed for dissociative clients to stabilize them. This screening will take into consideration the number of years the client was involved with unsuccessful psychotherapy, past episodes of depersonalization and/or derealization, history of memory lapses, occurrence of flashbacks and intrusive thoughts, existence of Schneiderian symptoms (i.e., audible thoughts, hallucinated voices, thought broadcasting, thought insertion, thought withdrawal, delusion perception, and somatic passivity), and presence of somatic symptoms. Also, if these symptoms are present, it will be necessary to lay special groundwork to aid in accessing the dysfunctionally stored material. See the cautionary note in Table 2.3 about dealing with special population clients with whom you have no expertise.

Table 2.3

CAUTIONARY NOTE

If your areas of expertise do not match the diagnoses or the age of the clients that present as possible candidates for EMDR, it is your ethical responsibility to refer them on to someone who specializes in EMDR and those particular diagnoses or age groups (i.e., children). EMDR is meant to be a treatment for the types of clients with whom you normally see and does not make you an expert in areas beyond your specialization. If a clinician does not possess training in specialized populations, such as dissociation, eating disorders, children, or addictions, these clients should be referred to someone who has that specialized training.

Client Willingness to Do EMDR

Once the answers to the above questions have been fully investigated by the clinician, assess the client's willingness to continue treatment utilizing EMDR. "Is EMDR something that you might like to consider as a course of treatment?" In cases where an adequate level of trust has been established with the client and the clinician, EMDR may be initiated early in the therapeutic relationship. It is optimal that the client also possesses a high level of comfort with the clinician. So ask, "Are you comfortable with our doing the EMDR at this time?" If the answer is affirmative, the clinician may move forward with the scheduling. It is also important for the clinician to be available for support and follow-up immediately after beginning EMDR.

Be careful about initiating EMDR with a client and then leaving town, let alone the country, for an extended length of time. It may be best that the client not be engaged in extended trips shortly after beginning trauma processing. The clinician can also ask the client to select a time for processing in which there is nothing particularly demanding on her schedule following the session.

Assessment

In the treatment planning stage of Phase 1, a closer look at the client's presenting problems is undertaken. Once the client's suitability for EMDR has been established, the clinician can better identify the negative events in the client's past, present, and future that need targeting. The questions below are typical of what a clinician may want to consider before implementing EMDR with a client.

- What targets appear to have set the groundwork for the client's presenting issue?
- What negative reactions does the client possess in the present that can be traced to experiences in her past?
- Which of these targets appear to have potential to fill in deficits in the client's life and optimize a healthier level of functioning?
- Is the client able to access these identified experiences and process them to successful resolution?

In Phase 1, the clinician is attempting to complete the client's clinical picture by investigating and including all pertinent details before initiating processing of her traumas using EMDR. Once a solid outline of these pictures begins to emerge, the clinician can begin to set targets for the treatment planning stage to determine possible interventions.

Treatment Planning in EMDR

EMDR treatment planning may be simple in the case of a single-event trauma, or it may be more complicated. A single-event trauma can be the easiest to process and often the most successful. It could be considered to be a one-layered onion. A multiple-event trauma is more comprehensive. This entails identifying the earliest dysfunctional memories associated with the client's presenting problems or issues or what are called *touchstone memories*. In either case, the clinician also needs to identify present situations and experiences that trigger the dysfunction and the alternative future behaviors that ensure the success of therapy.

In the manual for Part 1 training (2005), Dr. Shapiro presented a worksheet for the clinician to use as a checklist to ensure that necessary criteria have been evaluated before pursuing EMDR with a client. A modification of this worksheet appears below in Table 2.4.

These questions will not be answered as briefly as the table might suggest, but be aware that all of them need to be considered in some fashion. It is up to the clinician to decide whether to simply check off each criterion met above by the client. Alternatively, the clinician can rate each item on a scale of 1 to 3 to record the client's level of appropriateness for EMDR in each criterion. In either case, this can be a valuable tool.

Table 2.4

EMDR SELECTION CRITERIA

CRITERIA	PROBLEM IDENTIFIED	CONSULTATION NEEDED	FAVORABLE FOR EMDR
Client–Clinician Relationship Adequate trust exists between client and clinician. Client is willing to be truthful. Client is willing and able.			
Clinician Presentation Client is stable and has the ability to manage stress. Client has been screened for dissociative disorder (use Dissociative Experiences Scale [DES]).			

(continued)

Table 2.4 (continued)

EMDR SELECTION CRITERIA

CRITERIA	PROBLEM IDENTIFIED	CONSULTATION NEEDED	FAVORABLE FOR EMDR
Secondary gain issues have been identified and appropriately addressed. Severity of possible newly activated issues considered.			
Stabilization Adequate stabilization/ self-control strategies are in place. Client has adequate life supports. System issues that might endanger the client have been identified and addressed. Client is able to call for help if indicated.			
Medical Considerations General physical health, medical condition, and age have been considered. Medications. Inpatient care has been considered or arranged. If needed, eye movement has been cleared by physician. Any other neurological impairments or physical complications have been identified and addressed.			
Timing Considerations and Client Readiness Treatment has been timed around client's projects, demands, work schedules. Availability of both clinician and client for support and follow-up has been ensured. Willingness and ability of the client to continue treatment has been assessed. Ninety-minute sessions, if possible, have been arranged. Legal obligations are considered.			

Elements Pertinent to EMDR

There are other factors the clinician may also want to take into account during the history-taking phase of EMDR. The clinician may want to consider previous therapy the client may have experienced. What was her reason for seeking therapy? How long did the therapy last, and what was the outcome? There may be a need to seek more information concerning the past and current state of the client's relationships with the significant individuals in her life—parent, lover, spouse, boss, coworkers, children, and friends. How does the client self-soothe (e.g., relaxation, exercise, meditation, drugs and alcohol)?

Table 2.5 provides a list of pertinent questions specific to EMDR.

Table 2.5

HISTORY TAKING

ELEMENTS PERTINENT TO EMDR

CRITERIA

What are the specific symptoms (i.e., negative emotions, cognitions, behaviors, and somatic complaints) reported by the client? Have the symptoms changed?
What set the disturbance in motion? What was the initial cause or incident associated with the symptoms?
Does the client report or describe a specific internal picture, cognition, or feeling?
Are there current triggers? If so, what are their frequency, timing, and locations?
How long has the client been aware of the presenting problem/issue?
Does the client report past occurrences of a similar event?
Is this a part of the bigger trauma/complex/ multiple trauma?
Does the client remember the first time she felt this way?
Are there other similar events that might be clustered in this same group of events?
Does the client allude to or report alternative complaints, such as substance abuse, eating disorders, relationship problems, or somatic problems?
How is the client being affected at present?
What is the client's desired state? How does the client want to feel?
Does the client have secondary gain issues?
Does the client have a good support system in place?

Candidates for EMDR

Not everyone who walks into your office is a potential candidate for EMDR. In looking at both clients below, Sally and Marie, as candidates for EMDR, the clinician might want to consider the criteria specified by Dr. Shapiro before proceeding to the processing stage.

Keep in mind that as a clinician seeks answers to these questions, she is looking for patterns—clusters of similar events, responses, and other parallels between the client's past and present.

CASE EXAMPLE 2A: SALLY

Sally came into the clinician's office and stated that she was extremely disillusioned with her marriage and wanted to decide what to do about it. She stated that she "loved" her husband a great deal and that he was a wonderful man, but she was no longer "in love" with him. In her most recent past, she had become enamored and eventually became sexually involved with one of her male coworkers. She alleged no abuse in her childhood or her marriage. The rest of her history appeared unremarkable in terms of other traumatic events. She simply no longer loved her husband and longed for something more with another man.

Is Sally a candidate for EMDR? Consider the following:

1 **Symptoms:** When Sally arrived, she was rushed and breathless. She was extremely apologetic for being late for her first appointment and talked hurriedly as she explained the situation with her husband and current lover. She stated that she was confused and frustrated and no longer loved her husband and was in a quandary as to what to do about it. She did not want to hurt or leave him but was opposed to living with a man with whom she could no longer experience emotional and sexual intimacy in the ways she did when they were younger.

2 **Initial cause:** It was not until she initiated a friendship with a coworker that she realized how isolated and lost she was in her marriage. She felt more like she was living with her brother than her husband.

3 **Past occurrences:** After starting up the friendship, Sally realized that she had been unhappy in her marriage for a long time.

4 **Other complaints:** Sally's infidelity was a one-time occurrence for which she felt remorse.

5 **Constraints:** Sally continues to be unhappy in her marriage, confused as to what to do, and remorseful for her infidelity.

6 **Desired state:** Sally wants to be happily married.

Sally did not appear to be an immediate candidate for EMDR. After exploring her many options, the clinician and Sally entered into the problem-solving process to find out what had occurred in her marriage over the years that made her "fall out of love" with her husband and what could be done to light a new fire under it. After a few weeks of therapy, Sally was asked to bring her husband, Ralph, to therapy with her. He had no idea she was in therapy, nor did he know that she was unhappy in their marriage. After a few months of counseling, their relationship was renewed and moved to a more intimate level. As you can see, EMDR did not appear to be an appropriate intervention with this particular client or her husband. (Note: EMDR might have been used with either of the two to focus on issues that caused them to feel "separate and isolated" from one another later on in their therapeutic process).

CASE EXAMPLE 2B: MARIE

Marie had been involved in a car accident 2 months earlier. Since then, she had not been able to get behind the wheel without experiencing feelings that she associated with loss of control.

1 **Symptoms:** Marie reported feeling depressed and anxious. She had been medicated for anxiety and depression for as long as she could remember. A history of both was evident from her other comments, but they had become "more exaggerated after the accident." She stated that she was often nauseous and light-headed even at the thought of driving a car. As a passenger, she reported being agitated and hypervigilant. She cannot ride in a car for long periods of time or tolerate busy intersections without inducing a near panic within her. Whoever drives her has to take long and complicated detours to avoid major intersections along their route. Currently, the client only gets into the passenger side of the car if she has to go to the doctor. She will not enter a car for any other reason. As a result, she has not been able to work.

2 **Initial cause:** When she was 10 years old, Marie was involved in an accident in which her mother and younger sister were killed. This is the touchstone memory.

3 **Past experiences:** When she was in college, a fire broke out in one of the lower floors in her dorm. Marie was trapped on the seventh floor of the dorm for 4 hours before it was safe for her to take the elevator to the dorm's lobby.

4 **Other complaints:** Since the accident, Marie becomes anxious and agitated if she does not feel in complete control, especially while riding in a car.

5 **Constraints:** None.

6 **Desired state:** She sought self-empowerment and peace behind the wheel.

Marie's trauma was appropriate for EMDR. She had a history of previous events during which she felt out of control. The clinician initially processed the automobile accident in which her mother and younger sister were killed and then the subsequent occurrences where she similarly felt out of control. Many of her present symptoms and dysfunctions disappeared after these events were fully processed. Marie had been experiencing residue from these events every time she entered a busy intersection. After several months of successfully processing the car accident, dorm incident, and other disturbances where she previously felt out of control, Marie terminated and began living a more secure, stable existence.

PHASE 2: PREPARATION

While history taking and treatment planning lay the groundwork for EMDR, the preparation phase sets the therapeutic framework and appropriate levels of expectation for the client (Shapiro, 2001). In this phase, the primary goal is to prepare the client to process a disturbing target utilizing EMDR. Over the past few years, client preparation has been emphasized more heavily in trainings. It is often a "make or break" aspect of successful EMDR.

Setting the Stage for Effective Reprocessing

It is during the preparation phase that the clinician begins to set the stage for effective reprocessing. There are specific tasks identified by Dr. Shapiro that the clinician does before initiating the reprocessing of disturbing material with the client: (a) the safety within the therapeutic relationship is ensured; (b) the EMDR theory is explained and the model is described; and (c) the potential concerns, issues, and emotional needs are addressed. These tasks are identified in Table 2.6.

Maintaining a Safe Therapeutic Environment. Establishing sufficient rapport, trust, and safety are essential in the therapeutic relationship. The same is true of EMDR, but often the clinician may only have a very short time to form this kind of bond with the client. As a result, a clinician's demonstration of flexibility, respect, and accommodating attitudes toward the client's sense of safety and need for reassurance becomes more pronounced. Because clinicians may implement EMDR

Table 2.6

CLIENT PREPARATION

SETTING THE STAGE FOR EFFECTIVE REPROCESSING

A safe therapeutic relationship is established.	A clinical stance is adopted. A bond is formed with the client. Rapport, trust, and safety have been established.

The process and its effects are explained in detail.	Preparing the client in terms of education and informed consent is assured (see Appendix D).
	    The theory behind EMDR is explained.
	    The AIP model is briefly described.
	Eye movements (or other form of bilateral stimulation) are introduced, demonstrated, and tested.
	Medical considerations are taken into account.
	The client's stability has been assessed, and coping strategies have been introduced.
	The client is able to create a safe place.
	Timing is appropriately planned.

The client's concerns and potential emotional needs are addressed.	Expectations are set. Client fears are evaluated. Current stressors are identified.

Adapted with permission of Guilford Press from Shapiro, F. (2001). Eye movement Desensitization and Reprocessing: Basic Principles, Protocols, and Procedures. NY: Guilford Press.

after a few weeks of first meeting a client, a sufficient level of trust and adequate bonding must take place before EMDR is attempted.

Explanation of the EMDR Process and Its Effects. The importance of providing the client with a descriptive and informative explanation of EMDR during this phase cannot be stressed enough. Unfortunately, many EMDR-trained clinicians do not say more than, "I just learned this new technique. Let's try it." And, without hesitation, they lead the client into setting up the procedural steps outlined in the assessment phase without telling the client what the acronym EMDR stands for or providing an adequate explanation of what is involved.

The client is provided with a simple, general understanding of the theory behind EMDR and how his brain originally stores information. The amount of information supplied varies with the age of the client (i.e., children need far less information) and the expressed desire of the client for more or less information. EMDRIA sells a pamphlet called *EMDR Brochure for Clients,* which can be used as an option for this process. It is also printed in Spanish and French (see Appendix E for more information on EMDRIA).

Because clients frequently report feeling "stuck" in terms of emotions or body sensations, Dr. Shapiro's (2001) explanation of how trauma gets locked into the central nervous system, gets triggered by internal and external stimuli, and results in a flood of intense emotional and physical sensations, can support their understanding. In addition, it can be helpful to elaborate on how BLS helps to free the "stuck" information and allows the locked information to emerge to the surface, integrate, resolve, and flush out. However, this may be too much information for some clients. Use clinical judgment as to how much psychoeducation to provide.

Dr. Shapiro (2001) also suggests describing the model in terms of connecting the target with adaptive networks. Figure 2.1 presents a graphic understanding of the theory about how the brain stores a disturbing event: (a) when a traumatic event occurs, the brain stores it in an isolated memory network and prevents it from linking up with more adaptive information. As a result, no learning can take place; (b) once the EMDR reprocessing has been initiated, appropriate links between the maladaptive and adaptive information occur and shifts begin to emerge that allow learning to take place; and (c) if EMDR has been successfully completed, all necessary links between memory networks have been addressed, learning has taken place, and the event is no longer disturbing.

It is important for the clinician to spend an adequate amount of time explaining to the client the possibilities and options regarding BLS. Several methods of BLS have been developed over the years, such as tapping, sounds, or even the butterfly hug (Boèl, 1999, 2000; Artigas, Jarero, Mauer, Lopez Cano, & Alcala, 2000; Jarero, 2002; Artigas & Jarero, 2005). (Note: The butterfly hug involves the client crossing her arms over her chest and lightly and alternatively tapping her upper arms.) Because *all* the research to date has been done using eye movements, it has become the preferred means of BLS for most clinicians. Thus, it is important to inform the client of this as other options may be explored.

When assessing for the appropriate type of BLS to utilize with a client, it is optimal to assess and monitor her physical limitations. Does

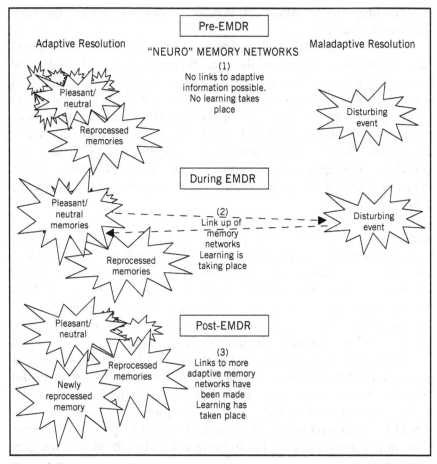

Figure 2.1 How the brain stores a disturbing event.

she suffer from a hearing deficit? Does she wear glasses? Does she have problems moving her eyes back and forth (i.e., side to side) in a brisk movement? Does she have mobility in her body to tap her own knees or shoulders? Because different types of BLS are used, check to see if the client can tolerate eye, audio, or tactile movement. Remember to take these options into consideration when assessing the proper stimulation for each client.

Make sure the client is comfortable with whatever option is chosen. If the client prefers eye movements, model the "two-ships-in-the-night" seating arrangement and demonstrate centerline-to-centerline movement of fingers while also testing for distance, range, direction, and speed variance.

What effect does the dual activation stimuli have? Although the mechanism of action is unknown at this time, there is a great deal of informed speculation as to how it works. What happens when we intentionally shift our focus back and forth at an increased rate of speed? Does it cause us to process information, experiences, or trauma more efficiently? With more advanced computer technology becoming available, such as information from single photon emission computed tomography (SPECT) and computed axial tomography (CAT) scans, we are able to gain clearer understanding of how the brain works and how it may respond to BLS during EMDR processing.

Calm (or Safe) Place and Other Coping Strategies. Although these techniques will not be covered in depth in this Primer, there are various calming, soothing, relaxing, containing exercises with which the clinician may want to be familiar. Several are described in the EMDR literature, and there are myriad options available to the clinician, including different breathing techniques, hypnosis, and muscle relaxation exercises. These maximize the likelihood that the client will be able to handle the level of disturbance which could arise before, during, or between EMDR sessions. Some of these techniques may also be useful when closing down incomplete sessions. It is optimal for clients to be trained in some of these self-control techniques prior to implementing EMDR. It is also recommended that EMDR not be pursued if a client does not respond or is unable to use guided visualization or imagery techniques.

At the very least, it is strongly recommended that the clinician teach the calm (or safe) place exercise (see Appendix B), a mechanism for self-regulation. Once created by the client (with assistance or guidance from the clinician), the clinician can encourage the client to return to it before, during, or after an EMDR session, especially if she is experiencing a high level of emotional disturbance. With more complex clients who display affect dysregulation, Resource Development and Installation (RDI; Leeds, 1998; Leeds & Shapiro, 2000) is suggested. Clinicians can experiment with various techniques listed below until it is determined that a client can tolerate or reduce levels of disturbance caused by the dysfunctionally stored material in her central nervous system. Although all clients need to be familiar with and use self-regulation techniques, some clients may be able to do it more easily on their own, so a limited number of these techniques may be necessary for stabilization.

The following techniques aid in the goal of successful processing and can also be used by clients in session or between sessions for symptom reduction and relaxation:

1   Lightstream technique (Shapiro, 1991)
2   Emmett Miller's audiotape (now available in CD), *Letting Go of Stress* (1994)
3   Container and conference room techniques
4   Grounding, diaphragmatic breathing, and anchoring in the present exercises (see Appendix B)
5   Calm (or safe) place (see Appendix B)
6   Sacred space (see Appendix B)
7   Breathing shift (see Appendix C)
8   Spiral technique (see Appendix C)
9   Visualization
10   Guided imagery
11   Self-control and relaxation exercises
12   Four elements stabilization technique formulated by Elan Shapiro for use with terrorist victims in Israel (Shapiro, 2006)

Calm (or Safe) Place

Dr. Shapiro (2001) prescribes the use of the calm (or safe) place exercise throughout the EMDR process. It assists in preparing a client to process traumatic events, to close incomplete sessions, and to help equalize or stabilize a client's distress in session if the information that emerges is too emotionally disruptive. It has been redesignated a calm (or safe) place over the years because it was found that some clients have been traumatized to such a high degree that it is ecologically impossible for them to imagine that a "safe" place can exist. The clinician has the client create a calm place instead. This exercise also serves to introduce the client to BLS in a comfortable way before it is used with disturbing material. If necessary, and according to the strengths and needs of the client, the clinician may suggest or name the type of place the client may create, such as a place of courage, a peaceful place, or a place for time out.

As with any technique utilized with a client, it is important to use caution. Listed below are cautionary elements with which the clinician needs to be aware when using the calm (or safe) place for self-regulation, symptom reduction, or relaxation (Shapiro, 2001).

1 The initial development of a calm (or safe) place may be disturbing to the client and increase her levels of distress. If this does occur, reassure the client that it is not unusual for this to happen. Then assist the client in developing another calm (or safe) place or initiate another self-regulating exercise.

2 Pairing the BLS with the development of the calm (or safe) place has the ability to bring some clients to high levels of negative affect very quickly. For example, the client may be in the process of developing a calm (or safe) place in a meadow and suddenly the image of the rapist appears as a dark figure overshadowing it. In a case like this, try again to develop a place that continues to be calm and/or safe to her, probably a different place, as the current image has been "intruded" upon by distressing material.

3 Negative associations may also emerge when the calm (or safe) place is developed and the BLS is introduced. For example, a client who happens to be a police officer is preparing to reprocess a memory of seeing her partner shot in a shoot-out with a gang member. Upon introducing BLS to her newly developed calm (or safe) place, a memory emerges of exchanging gunfire with a group of marauding student protesters. When this happens, the clinician can assist the client in developing another calm (or safe) place.

During the preparation phase, the clinician routinely reassesses the client's stability and provides coping strategies to enhance and strengthen a client's sense of safety before, during, and between EMDR sessions. Calm (or safe) place and relaxation exercises, metaphors, anxiety-control skills, stress-reduction strategies, and other resources can provide calm and safe means to assist a client in processing his most traumatic experiences. For more complex trauma presentations, the use of RDI is recommended (see below).

Resource Development and Installation, Dissociation, and Ego-State Therapy

Although not covered at length in this Primer, a discussion of the preparation phase also needs to include RDI, dissociation, and ego-state therapy. A brief description of each follows. Additional resources on these topics can be found in the resource section (see Appendix E, EMDR and Trauma-Related Resources).

RDI. Clinicians use RDI as a prerequisite to prepare clients with more complex affect dysregulation (i.e., limited capacities to emotionally self-regulate) for EMDR. RDI (Leeds, 1998; Leeds & Shapiro, 2000; Korn & Leeds, 2002) was developed as a means of enhancing a client's ability to alter her affective and behavioral states adaptively by heightening her access to functional memory networks. RDI provides a debilitated client who exhibits unstable behaviors (e.g., dissociation, mutilation or other self-injurious behaviors, addictions, eating disorders) a means of developing introjects and increasing affect regulation. Guidelines and protocol for EMDR RDI can be located in Appendix A in Dr. Shapiro's (2001) basic text. Before proceeding to the assessment phase, consider how much time is needed to stabilize the client.

What is Dissociation? Realizing that you do not know how to recognize dissociation or deal with it adequately when it occurs in session with a client is as important as knowing what dissociation is. Simply stated, dissociation is disconnection from the memories of an event and the attached emotion and/or physical pain that happened as a result of a past or presently occurring event. Clients can and often do dissociate during traumatic events. Dissociation is a valid and often critical defense mechanism during a traumatic event but can be problematic if it occurs during an EMDR session, particularly if the clinician does not recognize that it is transpiring or does not know how to ameliorate its occurrence. Along with a thorough clinical assessment, it is highly suggested that before initiating EMDR with a client, the clinician administer the DES (Bernstein & Putnam, 1986). For some highly dissociative clients, more robust clinical instruments, such as the dissociative disorders interview schedule (Ross et al, 1989), may be necessary as a more thorough diagnostic tool.

Ego-State Therapy. Ego-state therapy can be utilized in EMDR with clients who have complex posttraumatic stress disorders, dissociative disorders, performance enhancement difficulties, and problems associated with serious illness. Some clients enter therapy with dissociated parts that are unable to cope with the symptoms that have emerged as a result of their traumas. So it becomes imperative in the history taking to identify a client's fragmentation and alienation. Then define the appropriate ego state and select the somatosensory and affect management strategies to help these challenging clients. Integrating ego-state techniques with ego-state therapy can be highly useful and successful with clients possessing dissociative disorders (see Table 2.7).

Table 2.7

CAUTIONARY NOTE

Dissociation is not a simple state, and clinicians who have not been formally and adequately trained to treat dissociative disorders or dissociative symptoms when they arise in sessions should immediately seek supervision or refer the client to someone who does have this training. EMDRIA-approved basic trainings do provide an overview of dissociation, but time constraints do not permit in-depth discussion. Note that many of the advanced EMDRIA-approved trainings do concern themselves with the subject of EMDR and dissociative disorders.

Addressing the Client's Fears and Expectations

Client Expectations. The client can expect to be able to maintain a sense of safety and of being in control. These are critical for safe processing. If, during the reprocessing effort, the client indicates that he wants to stop, the clinician needs to honor his request. To do otherwise might seriously undermine treatment effects and the integrity of the therapeutic relationship. The clinician assists in helping the client maintain that dual awareness, reassuring him that the surfacing emotions and memories are transient and that he is in no real danger in the present.

Client Fears. It is in the preparation phase where the clinician addresses fears the client may have about the process and instills hope, however thin and tattered they may have perceived it to be. And it is this shred of hope that sets up the client's potential for success in the EMDR process.

After an explanation of EMDR theory, the clinician is encouraged to introduce metaphors (e.g., train or video) or analogies that may be used during the actual reprocessing of the client's disturbing material. The client can then have familiarity with those metaphors if the clinician references them during the ensuing session. Other concerns or fears may be addressed at this time.

In summary, the clinician informs the client about the nature of EMDR and what he might expect as a result of EMDR, establishes an adequate therapeutic relationship through bonding, rapport, and honesty, and ensures client safety, stability, and the client's ability to maintain his control over the process.

PHASE 3: ASSESSMENT

As target selection has been accomplished in previous phases, assessment is simply the measurements and amplification of the targets already selected. This is the phase where a client identifies the components of the target and baseline measures of his reaction to the process as its simplest explanation. The order of the EMDR components (i.e., image, negative cognitions [NC] and positive cognitions [PC], Validity of Cognition [VoC] scale, emotions, Subjective Units of Disturbance [SUD] scale, and body sensations) is specifically designed to access and stimulate dysfunctional target material. This is why a client's level of distress may become increasingly more agitated during the process, and the clinician needs to be prepared to activate processing soon after completion of the assessment to ease his disturbance.

Identify, Assess, and Measure

The three words that Dr. Shapiro uses to represent this phase are *identify, assess,* and *measure* (2001). The clinician assists and supports the client in *identifying* a specific pivotal picture and *assessing* its toxicity. This is accomplished by determining the NC, PC, and specific negative emotion(s) and body sensation(s) associated with the event. Then baseline *measurements* of the client's reactions to and progress within the phase are established and monitored (see Table 2.8).

Table 2.8

ASSESSMENT		
IDENTIFY	**ASSESS**	**MEASURE**
Target	Negative Cognition Positive Cognition/ Desired State Specific Emotion(s) Body Sensation: "Where do you feel it (i.e., the disturbance) in your body?"	VoC (1–7) of desired cognition. "When focusing on the event/ incident, how true does the positive cognition feel to you *now?*" SUD (0–10) "When focusing on the event/incident, how disturbing does it feel to you *now?*"

Identifying the Target. The memory selected for processing is identified in the first two phases of EMDR (see chapter 3 and chapter 4 for more information about target possibilities).

Assessing the NC and PC and Emotional and Physical Sensations. Along with the memory to be identified and treated (i.e., the target), the clinician assists the client in identifying the negative self-belief or statement (i.e., NC), the desired direction of change verbalized by the client, and emotional and physical sensations associated with it.

a. When a client voluntarily or involuntarily stimulates stored information associated with a specific traumatic event, perceptions may come to the surface that could distort what a client perceives in the present. These perceptions are explicitly expressed in an NC identified by the client (e.g., negative, self-referencing, generalizable, irrational, dysfunctional, and possessing emotional resonance). For example, shame and self-hatred can be explicitly expressed in the NC, "I am not good enough."

b. The PC is a positive reflection of what the client would like to believe about herself (i.e., desired direction of change) as she focuses on the targeted event and on the opposite side of a personal issue or theme indicated by the NC. For example, "I am a failure" versus "I am able to succeed."

c. As a client focuses on the targeted event, she is asked to name the specific *emotional sensations* that also emerge (i.e., the shame and self-hatred described above).

d. The clinician asks the client to initiate a body scan to determine *physical sensations* associated with the disturbance. For example, "Where do you feel it in your body?"

Measuring the VoC and the SUD. The VoC scale is used to measure the PC for validity and to ensure that it is attainable and not a result of wishful thinking on the part of the client. It is rated to provide a baseline measurement as to how true (i.e., "How true do those words feel?") and how believable the cognition feels to the client (i.e., Is it wishful thinking on the part of the client?). The VoC scale is shown below on Figure 2.2.

The SUD scale is a measurement for the level of *emotional disturbance* being experienced by the client. The SUD scale is in Figure 2.3.

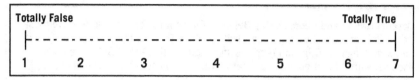

Figure 2.2 Validity of Cognition (VoC) scale.

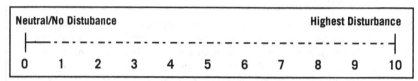

Figure 2.3 Subjective Units of Disturbance (SUD) scale.

These scales benefit both clinician and client in that they provide an indicator of the client's progress during the EMDR process.

The components of the assessment phase are considered to be the stepping stones to adaptive resolution, and chapter 3 has been entirely dedicated to stressing its importance.

PHASE 4: DESENSITIZATION

When Does It Begin?

The (*reprocessing* and) desensitization phase begins when the clinician instructs the client, "Concentrate (or "Focus") on that picture and those words, (client's NC). Notice where you feel it in your body, and follow my fingers." (Note: The clinician does not refer back to all aspects of the assessment phase—the PC, VoC, SUD, or emotions.) Once these instructions are given, the reprocessing is initiated and continues with subsequent sets of BLS until the SUD is 0, VoC is 7, and body scan is clear.

There are two important aspects of the desensitization phase (i.e., returning to target and checking the SUD level) that are implemented some time after the initial reprocessing begins. Figure 2.4 provides a simplified flow of the desensitization phase of EMDR.

Desensitization and Reprocessing Begins. "Concentrate on that picture and those words, (client's negative cognition). Notice where you feel them in your body and follow my fingers." Clinician reprocessing begins with a set of BLS. She ends each set with, "Let it go. Take a breath. What do you get now?" The client reports what he is noticing. Go to **A.**

A   **Continue with additional sets of BLS and more questioning.** If something new or distressing surfaces, repeat **A.** If nothing new or distressing surfaces or client's reports are neutral or positive for more than two consecutive sets of BLS, go to **B.**

B   **Go back to target.** Ask the client, "When you go back to the original experience, what do you get now?" The client reports what he is noticing. Say, "Go with that," and implement another set of BLS. Go to **A.** It may be necessary for the client to return to target several times before all the negative associated material has been accessed and reprocessed. If, after going back to target and doing another set of BLS, the client reports nothing new or distressing, go to **C.**

C   **Check the SUDs.** Ask the client, "When you bring up the experience, on a scale of 0 to 10, where 0 is no disturbance and 10 is the highest disturbance you can imagine, how disturbing does it feel to you now?" If the client's SUD = 1 or greater, go to **D.** If client's SUD = 0, go to **E.**

D   **Implement another set of BLS.** If still no change, ask the client "Where do you feel the '1' in your body?" and implement an additional set of BLS. If still no change, ask the client, "What keeps this from going to a 0?" If still no change, the clinician should be alerted to check for ecological soundness or validity. If client's SUD = 0 or ecological soundness has been established, go to E.

E   **Implement another set of BLS.** If SUD continues to equal 0, proceed to the installation phase.

Figure 2.4 Desensitization flow chart.

What About Reprocessing?

The title of the desensitization phase may prove inadequate as it does not describe all that it entails. It may be more appropriate to consider this the desensitization and reprocessing phase. Desensitization or removal of the disturbance associated with the initial target is actually only a side benefit of this phase. The PC restructuring (e.g., "I am bad" to "I am good"), integration of perception (i.e., from that of the 3-year-old who experienced the original trauma to that of the 30-year-old who is processing the trauma), new insights or "Aha" experiences, and positive changes in previously reported emotional and physical sensations are significant as well. The typical outcome of the desensitization represents the removal of the disturbing material, whereas reprocessing is the actual reprocessing of the material. Resultant restructuring of the cognition, spontaneous emergence of insights, and other positive shifts usually do not occur without this important component.

Purpose of Desensitization Phase

The primary purpose of this phase of the EMDR treatment protocol is to: (a) identify, reprocess, and flush out the dysfunctionally stored material associated with the original target and all channels of association (i.e., images, cognitive, emotional, or physiological nodes that link with other past experiences); and (b) desensitize the emotional impact of the memory. As the processing of the information unfolds, the clinician can observe shifts in client awareness, progression of insights, and noticeable changes in the original target information in terms of the image, affect, thoughts, sounds, sensations, or beliefs.

Associative Processing

Clients may report different aspects of reprocessing. They may mention changes in imagery (e.g., an angry face changes to a happy face). A new memory could emerge. A change in the presenting image can occur, details in the presenting image may unfold (e.g., the most terrifying moment of the traumatic event being targeted emerges), or a single image that represents a disturbing aspect of an event may change (e.g., intrusive thoughts, flashbacks, recurring nightmare images). Clients sometimes notice auditory and cognitive changes. They may also experience a diminishing negative emotion, indicative of the memory becoming less toxic and thus desensitized. Each of these shifts is processed completely as it emerges. Once fully processed, the client can be instructed to reaccess the original target.

The general tendency during the course of the reprocessing, whether the client is reporting new or shifting information, is for the disturbance to be less disturbing with each successive set. Even if this is not the case and the disturbances increase instead, reprocessing can still occur. The client may have accessed or experienced another aspect of the memory, and it is being metabolized at a different level. It is a safe assumption that, as the disturbance lessens progressively from set to set, the targeted channel is being cleared of dysfunctional debris.

In between sets of BLS, it is imperative that the clinician listen carefully to what the client reports so that the next focus of processing can be adequately identified, and the clinician's next intervention can be strategically orchestrated. When one channel of association has been addressed and exhausted, the client is instructed to return to the original target to discern the presence of new channels needing processing. Each of these channels is linked psychologically to the other. Although the client focuses on the target, the information can be shifted in different ways. It may be linked by shifting images, thoughts, sounds, tastes or smells, insights, sensations, or beliefs. New memories, emotions, and changes in body sensations may also shift the information in various ways. This is what Dr. Shapiro (2001) calls *associative processing*. Depending on which of these manifests will determine what action the clinician may take. Remember, desensitization of these channels cannot be completed until the dysfunctional material associated with the targeted event has been eliminated. Table 2.9 provides an outline of the possible changes in focus between sets identified by Dr. Shapiro (2001), examples (where applicable), and the clinician's response under the circumstances.

Assessment of the Channels of Association

In the desensitization phase, each line of association that emerges during the reprocessing of the client's disturbing material may be assessed on several levels. Is the progression or sequential processing that is occurring therapeutically relevant? When can a clinician assume that a channel has been cleared out? What does the clinician need to do when it is determined that an end of a channel has been reached? What happens after retargeting the original incident and no new associations, emotions, sensations, or images emerge? Table 2.10 is designed to answer these questions and more.

End of Channel?

When associations appear to have reached the end of a channel or when nothing new or disturbing appears after two or more successive sets of BLS, the clinician redirects the client back to the original target. "Think of the incident. What are you getting *now*?" (Or "What are you noticing *now*?") A new set of BLS is initiated regardless of whether the client reports negative or positive associations. If the client reports positive

Table 2.9

ASSOCIATIVE PROCESSING

CLIENTS TEND TO REPORT THEIR EXPERIENCES IN TERMS OF CHANGES IN IMAGERY, TASTES OR SMELLS, SOUNDS, SENSATIONS, AND EMOTIONS.

CHANGE IN	EXAMPLE	IF THEY EMERGE . . . WHAT DO YOU DO?
TASTES OR SMELLS.	(The smell of aftershave or the taste of tobacco, left behind after father's molestation of daughter.)	Target the taste or smell. If it fades, return to original target.
IMAGERY.		
New memory		
One memory.	(The memory of her father opening the door.)	Target the memory.
Several memories.	(The memories of the molestation and breakfast with the family the next morning.)	Target most disturbing memory.
All memories are equally disturbing.	(Both memories above are highly disturbing.)	Target last memory to appear.
Endless stream of associated memories (i.e., 10–15).	(Bits and pieces of multiple molestations stream through client's consciousness.)	Return to original target after each shift.
Transient memory.	(Memory of her first sexual encounter with a boyfriend.)	If needed, retarget after presenting memory has been completely reprocessed.
Image changes		
Negative image emerges.	(Father yelling.)	Target the negative image.

(continued)

Table 2.9 (continued)

ASSOCIATIVE PROCESSING

CLIENTS TEND TO REPORT THEIR EXPERIENCES IN TERMS OF CHANGES IN IMAGERY, TASTES OR SMELLS, SOUNDS, SENSATIONS, AND EMOTIONS.

CHANGE IN	EXAMPLE	IF THEY EMERGE ... WHAT DO YOU DO?
Neutral or positive image emerges.	(Father singing softly to himself while gardening or sitting silently on his rocking chair in the evenings.)	Early in session: Target a set or two to see if it strengthens; readdress the original issue as soon as possible. Later in session: Continue until strengthening ceases.
Two images emerge, one positive, one negative.	(Father singing and yelling.)	Target the negative one.
Incident unfolds	(Frame-by-frame scenes of the molestation emerge chronologically.)	Client focuses on each scene in separate sets until resolution is achieved.
Appearance changes		
Image itself changes in appearance.	(Father appears to be getting bigger and bigger.)	Target the changes in appearance. If client states the image is "blurry," ask the client to concentrate on it.
Image disappears, disturbance remains.		Tell the client to, "Just think of the incident" and concentrate on physical sensations. Continue the sets until the disturbance is resolved.
SOUNDS AND THOUGHTS		
Negative statement or idea	("I am a total failure.")	Ask the client, "Where do you feel it in your body?" If thought persists, implement proactive version of EMDR (e.g., cognitive interweave).

Mismatch		
Client deliberately brings something to consciousness.	(Client reports thinking of something funny.)	Determine whether client has deliberately attempted to bring something to consciousness that is inconsistent with the elements associated with the original target. If the determination is positive, ask the client, "Are you doing or saying anything deliberately?" If so, instruct the client to stop and to "Just let it happen, without judging or trying to force anything to happen."
Positive thought		
If positive thought emerges.	("I am a success.")	Target positive thought.
If no change in positive thought.		Return to original target.
If positive thought strengthens.		Initiate additional sets.
If both a positive and negative thought emerge at once.	("I am a failure." "I can be successful at some things.")	Focus on the negative thought.
Insights		
Become progressively more adaptive.		The clinician instructs the client to, "Think of that."
SENSATION AND AFFECT		
New emotion	("I am feeling unusually sad.")	The clinician will ask the client, "Where do you feel it in your body?"
Shifting body sensations	("My stomach is beginning to cramp.")	Target the physical sensations.

Adapted with permission of Guilford Press from Shapiro, F. (2001). Eye movement Desensitization and Reprocessing: Basic Principles, Protocols, and Procedures. NY: Guilford Press.

Table 2.10

ASSESSMENT OF ASSOCIATIONS

IDENTIFY, ASSESS, MEASURE

Assess associations for . . .
Progression (i.e., disturbance is more or less disturbing).
Other aspects of the memory being experienced.

A channel of association has been cleared when . . .
The client becomes less disturbed;
The associations have reached a reasonable stopping point; or
Nothing new emerges after two successive sets of BLS in different directions.

When enhanced associations cease . . .
Instruct client to retarget the original incident by saying, "Think of the incident.
What do you get?" Wait for client's response and then initiate another set.
Process emerging channels.
After each channel has been reached, instruct the client to return to the
original target.

When the original incident has been retargeted and no new associations,
emotions, sensations, or images emerge . . .
Recheck the client's SUD level.
If the client reports a SUD equal to 0, it is considered to be desensitized and
the installation of the positive cognition may begin.
If the client reports SUD greater than 0, the clinician asks, "What emotion(s)
are you feeling?" If the client reports feelings of calm or well-being,
instruct him to only focus on disturbing feelings and recheck the SUD.
If the client reports low-grade negative feelings, the clinician asks,
"What prevents it from being a 0?"
If a response indicates the presence of a blocking belief (e.g., "If I get
my hopes up too high, the other shoe will drop.") implement a full
EMDR treatment on the corresponding memory.
If the client's response seems appropriate given the circumstance
(e.g., "It's difficult to feel totally safe knowing the rapist is out on
bond."), initiate the installation phase.

If the client has arrived at the end of a target and time is running out . . .
Go directly to the closure phase. A new target is not to be opened up.

If the client makes a statement that seems to limit further progress . . .
Acknowledge the statement and do at least two sets of BLS before accepting
the limiting statement as accurate.
Accept limitation only if it appears reasonable and if the additional sets of
BLS have proven inadequate.
Before advancing to the installation phase, examine all SUD levels higher
than 0 for ecological validity.

Adapted with permission of Guilford Press from Shapiro, F. (2001). Eye movement Desensitization
and Reprocessing: Basic Principles, Protocols, and Procedures. NY: Guilford Press.

images or reports "nothing," which is quite often the case, continue the BLS. It is not unusual for unexpected channels of association to open up at this point in time. If this happens, simply reprocess the material in the usual manner and redirect the client once again to the original target after the channel appears to have been completely cleared of dysfunctional material.

Only when the client reaches a point in which no new associations, images, sensations, or emotions come to the forefront will the clinician ask the client, "Focus on the original event (or incident) and tell me on a scale of 0 to 10, how disturbing does it *feel* to you *now*?" If the client answers, "0," the original target is said to be desensitized. Transcripts of client sessions, which include the desensitization phase, are provided in chapter 6

What happens if the reported assessment by the client is more than 0? Consider the following:

Clinician: From 0, which is neutral or no disturbance, to 10, which is the worst disturbance you can imagine, how disturbing does it <u>feel</u> to you <u>now</u>?
Client: It feels like a 2.

The clinician implements another set of BLS.

Clinician: How disturbing does it <u>feel</u> to you <u>now</u>?
Client: It's the same.
Clinician: Where do you <u>feel</u> the 2 in your <u>body</u>?
Client: In my head.
Clinician: Where in your head?
Client: My forehead.

It does happen that a client will report a sensation in her head that is not necessarily of a physical nature. Instead of questioning whether it is cognitive or physical, just ask the client the same question as above. You do not risk leading the client away from an important component of her processing in asking this question. Do not try to lead a client during reprocessing. Remember that what is being processed is about her, not you.

Clinician: Go with that. (Set of eye movements—change direction of eye movements.) Let it go. Take a deep breath. (Pause) What comes up for you now?

Client: It's the same.
Clinician: What emotions are you feeling?
Client: I'm feeling a little wary.

The client has reported a low-grade negative emotion. If the client had reported a more positive emotion at this time, the clinician could redirect the client to assess negative emotions if they remain.

Clinician: What keeps it from being a 0?
Client: If something good happens to me, something bad will follow.

The client's response has revealed what is called a *blocking belief*. If this particular response appears to be appropriate under the client's particular circumstance, the installation could be carried out in the normal manner. If not, this information will need to be carried over to another session and be targeted with an associated memory for the full EMDR treatment.

Clinician: Go with that. (Set of eye movements—change direction of eye movements.) Let it go. Take a deep breath. (Pause) What are you getting <u>now</u>?

If the client still reports no change, the clinician will need to check for ecological soundness. The clinician does not proceed beyond the desensitization phase of EMDR unless the client's SUD is 0 or ecological soundness has been validated (see chapter 1 for explanation of ecological soundness).

When to Return to Target?

Table 2.11 provides guidelines for returning to target (i.e., the original incident or event) and taking the client's SUD level.

How Long Does It Last?

The desensitization phase in some instances may last no longer than 10 minutes or span over numerous sessions. Some sessions can move smoothly from start to finish without the clinician saying anything more than, "Let it go. Take a deep breath. What are you noticing <u>now</u>?" or "Go with that" or words of encouragement, such as, "Good. You're doing fine." This is what is called *spontaneously reprocessing*. At times, you may experience other sessions that are full of verbal and nonverbal cognitive

Table 2.11

DESENSITIZATION PHASE WHEN TO ...	
Return to original target if . . . An end of channel is identified by repeated neutral or positive responses by the client.	**Take a SUD (0–10) if . . .** After returning to target and doing another set of bilateral stimulation, the client still reports neutral or positive material.
After at least two consecutive sets of bilateral stimulation, the client reports no change.	Client's progress is being checked. The end of the desensitization is identified (SUD equals 0).
The associations reported by the client are too vague or unrelated to the original target.	The client reports a SUD greater than 0, then do the following in order: Focus on client-reported body sensation and add BLS. Ask what prevents it from being a 0. If identified, do BLS. Search for blocking beliefs using direct questioning, floatback or affect scan. Consider ecological soundness.
Change characteristics of bilateral stimulation if:	
Client reports a headache, dizziness, or nausea.	Differences need to be accommodated.
No shift in information is reported or observed.	
. . . then change direction.	**. . . then change length and speed.**

interweaves (see chapter 5) along with words of encouragement every step of the way. Just like every client, each session is unique. Anything can and will happen. Go with the flow, keep out of the way, and let whatever happens, happen. This is a good EMDR mantra for both the clinician and the client.

When to Proceed to Installation Phase?

Remember, the rule of thumb for this stage is that the SUD level is reduced to a 0 before proceeding to the installation phase. Does this always happen? Not necessarily. We need to allow for ecological validity in some instances. What keeps it from being a 0? In others words, is this response most appropriate for this client under her particular circumstances? See Figure 2.5 for a graphic picture of the desensitization phase.

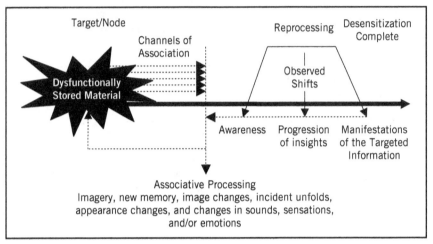

Figure 2.5 Desensitization phase.

Taking a Break

At the end of a set of BLS, when the clinician says, "Let it go" (or "Rest." or "Blank it out.") and "Take a deep breath," the clinician stops the eye movement (or other forms of BLS) and asks the client, "What are you getting <u>now</u>?" or "What comes up for you <u>now</u>?" or something similar. This is done for several reasons: (a) during BLS, information pertinent to the targeted traumatic event is stimulated. Stopping the processing allows time for the dysfunctional information to drop off and adaptive information to be consolidated; (b) this brief interruption allows the clinician to reevaluate the client's progress and to judge if reprocessing has taken place; (c) during this break, the client's concentration and intensity of focus is interrupted, and the client is given permission to rest, reorient, and verbalize what happened during the set. It also provides the client with a sense of empowerment; and finally, (d) it provides the client with an opportunity to verbalize her internal process and understand whatever changes have taken place more readily (Shapiro, 2001).

PHASE 5: INSTALLATION PHASE

What Occurs?

When all channels of association revealed throughout the reprocessing are completely cleared (i.e., SUD = 0), the clinician can embark on the installation phase. It is during this phase that the PC is linked to the original image (i.e., memory, picture, or incident). Installation occurs when the positive self-assessment established by the client is fully integrated with the targeted information. To allow this, the clinician rechecks the current *appropriateness*, *applicability*, and *validity* of the PC reported in the assessment phase.

Evaluate Appropriateness of Original Cognition

Because so much baggage is shifted or lost and new insights are being boarded at the various stops during the train ride, what the client originally wanted to believe about herself may now be different. She may need a stronger PC to complete the process. It may have gone from, "It's over. I am safe" to "I am a powerful person."

To provide the client with an opportunity to evaluate the appropriateness of the original PC, the clinician asks, "When you bring up that *original* incident, do the *words* (e.g., 'I am competent.') *still fit*, or is there another positive statement you feel would be more suitable (or appropriate)?" It is imperative that the client choose the cognition that resonates the most with her as she focuses on the original target. If you help the client to identify a PC at this stage, do so cautiously. Remember, the process belongs to the client; and we need to keep our distance from the moving train. We do not want to impede or derail the "train" with our attempts to be helpful.

Validity of the Positive Cognition

During this phase, the positive effects of the cognition identified with the initial target are being linked and can be fully integrated. Imagine that the client chooses the original PC. The baseline measurement has already been established. Has the VoC changed? To assess, the clinician asks, "As you think of the incident, how <u>true</u> do the words (e.g., 'I am competent.') <u>feel now</u> on a scale of 1 to 7, where 1 is completely false, and 7 is completely true?" If they do not link and the VoC does not increase, the PC will need to be rechecked and, possibly, a substitute will be considered.

Link to Original Target

Once an appropriate PC is chosen, it is linked with the original target. At this stage of the process, the original target can be a mere image of what it was when reprocessing began. Clients often describe it as cloudy, in the distance, untouchable, foggy, unclear, or far way. The client is asked to hold the event in mind while repeating the PC silently to herself in this way: "Think of the event, and hold it together with the words (e.g., 'I am competent.')." Successive sets of BLS follow.

When Is Installation Complete?

Like desensitization, installation continues until there are no longer changes and the VoC continues to be a 7. Continue to do BLS as long as the VoC of 7 continues to strengthen and becomes more adaptive. When it is a 7 and further BLS no longer causes it to shift in a functional way, the clinician then implements the body scan.

How to Discern the Presence of a Blocking Belief

If the VoC does not rise to a 7, it is a signal for the clinician to look for blocking beliefs or emerging associations that need to be addressed, such as, "If I don't have this problem, I won't know who I am." The clinician checks for a blocking belief by asking the client, "What keeps this from going to a 7?" Or "What is the worst thing that would happen if this went to a 7?" If a blocking belief arises, implement another set of BLS and say, "Go with that."

If the client insists on sticking with his blocking belief and it seems without much content, the clinician can proceed to the body scan. If the blocking belief has some punch and does not improve with successive sets of BLS, the clinician will need to assess for ecological soundness (see chapter 1 for definition of ecological soundness). There are occasions when the blocking belief becomes a target for the full EMDR session. It is not until the earlier memories behind the blocking belief are successfully reprocessed at the next session that the reprocessing of the original target can be called complete. Once the earlier memory has been successfully processed, the clinician needs to reevaluate the original target and complete the installation.

PHASE 6: BODY SCAN

Dysfunctionally stored material often manifests itself somatically. After having successfully installed the client's PC, the clinician asks her to reassess her body from head to toe for residual body tension, tightness, unusual sensations, or even positive changes that might still be present. In implementing a body scan at this juncture, the clinician is looking for residual blocking beliefs or other materials (e.g., major areas of resistance, associated networks containing dysfunctional information that might not be fully integrated). The amelioration of the cognitive, emotional, and physical sensations will increase the probability of a positive treatment effect.

The client is asked to focus on the original targeted event, her PC, and the identified physical discomfort. The clinician continues with successive sets of BLS until the tension has been lifted. This is what the clinician says to initiate a body scan: "Close your eyes and keep in mind the original memory and the words (e.g., 'I am competent,'). Then bring your attention to the different parts of your body, starting with your head and working downward. Any place you find tension, tightness, or unusual sensation, let me know." If positive sensations arise, use BLS to strengthen. If negative sensations arise, use BLS to decrease them and continue to reprocess until they subside or disappear. With standard sets of BLS, the client is able to decrease or eliminate negative sensations or increase positive sensations that are identified.

If the physical sensations do not dissipate, another channel or other associated networks of information may be present and will need to be processed before the current session will be considered complete. Positive sensations that emerge are reinforced with short sets (i.e., 4–6) of BLS.

It is not unusual for a client to report an obvious injury when scanning her body (e.g., pain in the back from a ruptured disk or upset stomach from something she had for lunch). When these types of bodily discomforts are reported, continue the body scan in the prescribed manner. There may be chronic or acute problems showing up physiologically that are affecting her psychologically as well. In these instances, three things can happen: (a) the discomfort may dissipate or remit completely; (b) the client may remember another incident that had not been anticipated by either the clinician or the client, which will need to be reprocessed at the next session (e.g., a pain in the lower back may cause a memory of being molested at age 5 to emerge); or (c) there is no change, because the bodily discomfort is unrelated to the current processing.

The key point to remember during the body scan is that the reprocessing of the dysfunctional material is not considered complete until the body scan is clear (i.e., free of residual negative associated sensations). Do not proceed to the next target until it is clear. If there is not enough time in the session to ensure the completion of this phase, either extend the session or close it down and address anything that is not completed at the next session.

PHASE 7: CLOSURE

Levels of Closure

The closure phase of EMDR refers to either properly shutting down an incomplete session or ending a completed session. This phase also includes debriefing the client after each session, instructing the client to maintain a log between sessions, and giving guidelines for in-between sessions. Regardless of whether the session is complete or incomplete, the primary goal of this phase is to ensure that the client is returned to "a state of emotional equilibrium" (Shapiro, 2001) by the end of the session.

Strategies for Closing Sessions

Strategies for closing down completed and incomplete sessions are different.

Completed Session. A session is complete when SUD = 0, VoC = 7, and the body scan is clear (see Figure 2.6). When a session has been successfully completed, the clinician indicates to the client that it is time to stop and provides encouragement and assurance by saying, "You have done very good work today. How are you feeling?" In addition, the clinician debriefs the client by further asking, "As you review your experience in our session today, what positive statement can you make to express what you have learned or gained?"

Incomplete Session. As Figure 2.6 depicts, a session is considered incomplete if one of the standard procedural steps has not been completed (i.e., SUD is greater than 0, VoC is less than 7, or no clear body scan). When it is necessary to close down an incomplete session, do not: (a) recheck the SUD or VoC levels; (b) refer back to the PC; or (c) do a body scan. If the clinician feels that she is at a good stopping point, she notifies the client, asks the client's permission to stop, and tells the client why. For instance, "We are near the end of our time together, so we need to stop. Are you okay with that?" It is at this juncture that the clinician may suggest containment, stress reduction, progressive breathing, relaxation exercises, or the lightstream technique to help return the client to her normal functioning. Remind the client of her calm (or safe) place. As additional processing may take place between sessions, it is important that the client be stabilized before leaving the clinician's office. Assure the client that she can call between sessions, if needed. Once the client is stabilized, encourage and debrief the client in the same manner described above for completed sessions.

Completed Target Session =

$(SUD = 0) + (VoC = 7) + (Clear body scan)$

Incomplete Target Session =

SUD is greater than 0
$(SUD = 0) + (VoC less than 7)$
$(SUD = 0) + (VoC = 7) + (No clear body scan)$

Figure 2.6 Formulas for completed and incomplete target sessions.

Assessment of Client's Safety

Regardless of whether the session is complete or incomplete, Dr. Shapiro (2001) suggests that the clinician remind and instruct the client in these key points as she leaves an EMDR session:

1   Stop the processing using safe place, lightstream, or other containment strategies to return the client to a more functional state of mind.

2   Additional processing may occur between sessions; additional disturbing material in the form of images, thoughts, or emotions may arise.

3   It is important to instruct the client to keep a log or journal of negative material (i.e., situations, thoughts, emotions, dreams) that may arise between sessions. The act of writing provides the client with an emotional distancing technique. The negative material collected in the log may serve as targets for future sessions (see Appendix C under TICES Log, [i.e., target = image,

cognitions, emotions, and sensations]). Although having a client keep a log between sessions is an ideal practice, some clients may be resistant. Just remember, it is neither necessary nor critical to the rest of the process.

4   To ensure client stability, encourage the client to utilize visualization and relaxation techniques between sessions. If she needs to write down something disturbing in the TICES log in between sessions, instruct her to use one of the self-control techniques that she was taught. Once she has written something in her log, it helps her to externalize it.

5   It is important for the clinician to provide the client with reasonable and realistic expectations of what might be the negative and positive reactions that a client could encounter before, during, and after a session.

What Can Happen After a Session?

Dr. Shapiro (2001, 2009) sums it up in this statement to the client, "Processing may continue after our session. You may or may not notice new insights, thoughts, memories, physical sensations, or dreams. Please make a note of whatever you notice. We will talk about that at our next session. Remember to use one of the self-control techniques once a day and after each time you write something in your log."

PHASE 8: REEVALUATION

What Has Changed and What Is Left to Do?

In this phase, the clinician elicits information as a follow-up to the client's previous EMDR processing (i.e., in the next scheduled session). What has changed? What have you noticed since your last EMDR session? What images, emotions, thoughts, insights, memories, or sensations have emerged, if any? Have you noticed changes in behaviors? What were your responses to these changes? Have new dreams or other material surfaced as a result?

In addition to reevaluating what has changed in the client's life since the previous EMDR session, the clinician will also reassess the work that was done. Has the individual target been resolved? Instruct the client to bring up the memory or trigger targeted in the previous session and say, "What image comes up? What thoughts about it come up? What thoughts about yourself? What emotions? What sensations? And, on a scale of 0 to 10, how disturbing is it to you *now*?" Once these stages are completed, the client is ready to tackle the next traumatic memory or trigger.

The clinician is encouraged to ask the client these questions regardless of whether the previous session was complete or incomplete. The questions are solicited in this way to ensure the resolution of the primary issue, the presence of ecological validity, determination of whether associated material has been activated that must be addressed in the present or subsequent session, and the existence of resistance on the part of the client.

Resuming Reprocessing in an Incomplete Session

If an event from the previous session was not fully processed (i.e., SUD = 0, VoC = 7, or a clear body scan), the clinician will resume the processing of the unfinished target (see Table 2.12).

Table 2.12

RESUMING REPROCESSING IN AN INCOMPLETE SESSION

Use when clinician did not report SUD = 0, VoC = 7, or clean body scan from previous session:

Reidentify the image
Clinician: Bring up the original incident (e.g., your brother threatening you with an axe).
When resuming the processing of an unfinished target from a previous session, the clinician is not required to identify the negative and positive cognitions or the VoC.
Client: Okay.

Identify the current level of disturbance (i.e., SUD)
Clinician: On a scale of 0 to 10, how disturbing does this incident feel to you *now*?
Client: It's about a four.

Identify physical sensations associated with the incident
Clinician: Where do you feel it in your body?
Client: In my chest.

Resume Desensitization and Reprocessing
Clinician: Focus on that image and where you feel the sensations in your body. (Implement bilateral stimulation of choice.)
Continue EMDR phases 4 through 6. When the clinician can report SUD = 0, VoC = 7, and a clean body scan, processing is complete.

Reevaluation of Treatment Effects

Have new aspects of the memory or other earlier associated memories emerged during the interim between this session and the last that need to be addressed? This is also the time to refer to the client's log or journal to assess changes in behavior or the way he is responding to the world.

Reevaluation of treatment effects takes place after each EMDR session. After a brief evaluation of changes in how the client acts, feels, senses, or believes, instruct the client to focus on the finished target from the previous session to see if treatment has held and ask, "On a scale of 0 to 10, how disturbing is it to you now?" If the treatment effect appears to have held (i.e., SUD = 0), proceed with processing other appropriate targets. If the client reports something other than a 0, the reprocessing of the disturbing material is in order, unless there is ecological validity.

Reevaluation and Treatment Planning

Reevaluation focuses on integrating each EMDR session into the client's full treatment plan by assessing how the treatment effect has impacted the client's associated internal factors and behaviors, how the treatment effect has, in turn, directly affected individuals with whom the client interacts, and what attention needs to be given to the client's interpersonal system issues as a result.

The reevaluation phase is much more than just a reassessment of previously targeted material to see if treatment has held or additional processing is required. Reevaluation also requires the clinician to actively integrate each targeting session within the client's overall treatment plan and calls for the clinician to assess appropriate targets and outcome in terms of the three-pronged approach (i.e., the client's past, present, and future). In this regard, Dr. Shapiro (2001) states that attention must be paid to four factors: (a) resolution of individual target; (b) addressing associated material that may have been activated within a target; (c) reprocessing of all necessary targets in all three prongs; and (d) adequate assimilation accomplished within a healthy social system.

Reevaluation of Targets

Not only do individual EMDR sessions need to be reevaluated, the clinician also needs to reassess whether the appropriate targets and subsequent outcomes have been attained in relation to the three-pronged protocol (i.e., past, present, and future). A treatment plan structured with EMDR is not complete until all childhood trauma has been processed utilizing all three stages of the protocol. Whether working on past, present, or future targets, or single- or multiple-event targets, the clinician is constantly reevaluating the successful processing of targeted material to ensure that all dysfunction has been reprocessed and that treatment effects continue to be maintained.

Final Stage Reevaluation

The final reevaluation stage of EMDR will conclude with whatever follow-ups are necessary to determine when it is appropriate for a client to terminate therapy. It is important to remember the treatment effect may not have generalized to every possible disturbance experienced by the client. It is possible other issues may arise in the future and that clients may come back to therapy at a later date in an attempt to resolve these issues. Then there

Table 2.13

SUMMARY OF REEVALUATION PHASE	
Reevaluate the state of the client's life since the last session.	What has the client noticed since the last session? What has changed?
Reevaluate targeted material processed during the previous session.	Reassessment of previously targeted material: Has the primary issue been resolved? Does it require further processing? Has the new information been appropriately and adequately integrated by the client? Have additional targets emerged as a result of previous processing? Have other memories or negative cognitions arisen that were not identified in the history-taking phase?
Reevaluation occurs during critical or pivotal points in treatment.	Have all appropriate targets and their subsequent outcomes been attained in terms of past, present, and future? Have feeder memories that emerged need to be processed?
A final reevaluation will end with an extensive follow-up period.	Is the client ready to conclude therapy?

Adapted with permission of Guilford Press from Shapiro, F. (2001). Eye movement Desensitization and Reprocessing: Basic Principles, Protocols, and Procedures. NY: Guilford Press.

is what Dr. Shapiro (2001) calls a *natural unfolding process,* which may indicate that the process continues even after therapy has concluded. When this happens, it is not an indication that the EMDR treatment process was a failure. The unfolding of new disturbing material is an opportunity for learning at a different level. Life is a dynamic process, and learning takes place on a minute-by-minute basis even after therapy has concluded.

Pivotal Points in the Reevaluation Phase

Table 2.13 presents a summary of pivotal points that Dr. Shapiro (2001, 2008, 2009) has identified for reevaluation to take place. Reevaluation is a dynamic and continuous process.

Reread chapter 4, chapter 5, and chapter 6 in *Eye Movement Desensitization and Reprocessing: Basic Principles, Protocols, and Procedures, Second Edition* (2001) by Francine Shapiro.

SUMMARY STATEMENTS

1   EMDR is an eight-phase integrative treatment approach . . . not one or two—eight.

2   Know your client. Know your client well.

3   There must be an adequate level of trust between the clinician and client for EMDR processing to be successful.

4   If your areas of expertise or specialization do not include the client's diagnosis, it is the clinician's ethical responsibility to refer the client to a professional who is appropriately trained. This applies if the client is new. If not, get the appropriate supervision.

5   It is not necessary for the clinician to know all the details about a client's trauma. What is important is that the clinician allows the client to process the trauma without interference. Stay out of the client's way. Stay out of their process.

6   If a sufficient level of trust or bonding has not been established, do not undertake EMDR.

7   The explanation of the model that supports the use of EMDR is presented in a way that instills hope and understanding in terms of how a client begins to understand his coping and defense mechanisms.

3

Stepping Stones to Adaptive Resolution

ASSESSMENT PHASE

Back to Basics

It is only after the clinician has obtained an adequate history, determined that the client is an appropriate candidate, and has prepared the client for Eye Movement Desensitization and Reprocessing (EMDR) that the assessment phase can begin. This phase entails two elements. First, the clinician and client confirm the previously selected target memory (i.e., an issue as part of the overall treatment plan), identifying the image or picture, and its cognitive, emotional, and physical components. Second, baseline measurements are established in terms of total disturbance and the credibility of the positive cognition (i.e., How possible is it given the circumstances?).

The components of the standard EMDR procedure remain consistent whether we are targeting single- and multiple-event traumas, past traumas, present triggers, and future events. In all cases, the clinician will be trying to identify targets that encompass the past, present, and future.

Variations of the EMDR procedural steps are used in specific and special situations (e.g., phobias, obsessive–compulsive disorder [OCD], chronic pain). These variations, however, still incorporate the main ingredients of the EMDR procedural steps. Many of these protocols can be found in Dr. Shapiro's book *Eye Movement Desensitization and Reprocessing: Basic Principles, Protocols, and Procedures, Second Edition*. We will not be covering these variations at this time. Instead, this Primer will be focusing on the standard EMDR protocol to ensure that you have a grasp of all that it entails. Scripted protocols for basics and special situations (Luber, 2009a) and special populations (Luber, 2009b) are now available as well.

How Much Do You Need To Know?

After completion of the first two phases (history taking and preparation), the clinician then proceeds to assessment, desensitization, and reprocessing. A common question that clinicians may ask is, "How much detail do I need to know about the client?" The answer is that the clinician needs to know only what the client wants to reveal or even less. This is the beauty of EMDR. The clinician is not required to know all the painful details of a traumatic event in order for the process to be successful. The clinician can encourage the client to provide only a brief description of the disturbing event (e.g., "My uncle chased me with a dead bird."), explaining that it is not because you do not want to listen but that it is unnecessary for you to know it all for him to successfully process.

Many clients who come to our doors have told their stories several times to previous clinicians. If you have sufficient information for the assessment phase, you probably have enough detail for the client to bring his traumatic memory to a successful resolution without unnecessary retraumatization. EMDR is the client's internal process. What he wants and needs us to know can only be revealed by him when he is willing, able, and ready.

TARGET ASSESSMENT

Effective EMDR Equals Effective Targeting

The assessment phase begins by confirming the specific target that the clinician and client previously agreed upon as part of an extensive treatment plan. In selecting the target, the clinician considered whether it was the most effective for resolving the client's issue. An effective target leads the way to the dysfunctionally stored *material* and, thus, the dysfunctional memory *networks*. Targets generally emerge during a thorough assessment of the client's presenting problems. From the client's responses to the questions in the history-taking and treatment planning phase, the clinician is able to help identify salient targets for the client. As stated earlier, in your initial interviews with the client, watch and listen for behavioral, emotional, cognitive, and physical cues; the duration of the presenting issue; how the problem manifests in the present; and what the client needs to be more adaptive in the future. In addition, assess whether the client possesses adequate affect tolerance and stability to process the negative states and access anything positive that may arise during the EMDR process.

If a client presents with a single disturbing or traumatic event, target selection is simply a matter of identifying the worst part of the event. The clinician, however, will also assess for present triggers and future template whenever appropriate. With multiple disturbances and traumatic incidents, target identification and selection become more complicated.

Characteristics of Effective Targets

The target is more specific than general and can be an image, picture, complete or partial memory of an event, sight, sound, taste, touch, dream, metaphor, fantasy, or recurring thought or fear that something is going to happen. A target must be concrete rather than abstract. Simply targeting a "fear of flying" is too abstract. However, the specific target of experiencing extreme turbulence in an airplane 33,000 ft above the ground during a violent storm is more concrete and a more appropriate target for EMDR.

How Is the Memory Encoded?

In assessing how a memory is presently encoded in the client's memory network, Dr. Shapiro (2001) suggests asking questions such as, "What picture represents the incident (i.e., representative)?" or "What picture represents the worst part of the incident (i.e., most disturbing)?" or "When you think of the incident, what do you get (i.e., if no picture)?"

CASE EXAMPLE 3A: JENNIFER

Take the example of Jennifer who reported being molested by her English teacher when she was a sophomore in high school. The teacher in question had requested that she stay after school one afternoon to help him prepare some special handouts for his class the next day. While helping him, this teacher came up behind her, nudged his head into her hair, kissed her on the neck, and fondled her. Jennifer let out a faint cry and ran from the room. She ran down the hall and out the side door of the school where she found her brother waiting to give her a ride home. Jennifer never told anyone of her experience outside of therapy. She is a junior now and is encountering difficulties relating to boys her own age and men in authority positions.

Jennifer had never experienced anything like this before. She indicated that her childhood was uneventful. She felt that she had lived a relatively normal life until this point. So, when she asked the client what part of this particular trauma she wanted to work on, the clinician stated it in this way, "What picture represents the entire incident?" Her answer was, "The car ride home. I felt so ashamed." The clinician asked the question in this manner because it was: (a) a one-time event; (b) she had a clear memory associated with the event; and (c) there appeared to be no other parts to the memory that might have been as disturbing.

Appropriateness of the Target

In assessing the appropriateness of the selected target, it may be helpful to ask the following question: Does the image or event identified by the client represent a single incident that will potentially gain access to the dysfunctionally stored information? Refer to Figures 3.1 to 3.6 to see how the individual blocks of the procedural steps build a powerful tool to assist the client in activating his natural healing process. Below is Figure 3.1.

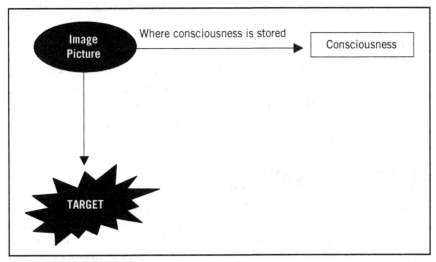

Figure 3.1 Stepping stones to adaptive resolution: Image, picture.

As many clinicians can attest, single-incident trauma is generally not the type of case that they deal with on a day-to-day basis with their clients. Target selection with clients having complex posttraumatic stress disorder (PTSD) or other complex psychological profiles requires a different approach than that described above for single traumatic or disturbing events. In these cases, several clinical aspects may require treatment, and each target needs to be identified and fully processed to obtain positive treatment effects.

A multiple-trauma victim may be asked to cluster his traumatic incidents into groups of like events. He is then asked to choose an incident that is representative of the group to serve as the target. Another means of eliciting targets from this type of client is by asking him to identify his top 10 most disturbing childhood memories. A Subjective Units of Disturbance (SUD) level is assessed on each target, and targets are arranged in order of increasing disturbance. Some clinicians may use historical timelines or genograms to elicit the same type of information from the client. Others may arrange and treat them in chronological order. Some will arrange them in chronological order but treat the most disturbing event first and then proceed chronologically to treat what remains. Dr. Shapiro has developed a comprehensive targeting sequence plan which attempts to identify and address past, present, and future events, incidents, issues, and desired outcomes associated with the presenting problem.

ASSESSMENT OF COGNITIONS

Elements of Negative and Positive Cognitions

It is optimal or suggested to take time assisting clients in the selection of the most appropriate cognitions, particularly the negative, because they focus on a disturbing memory. It is from this selection of cognitions that all else is derived, and the success of the processing is much more likely. The selection of appropriate cognitions ensures greater success in accessing the dysfunctionally stored material surrounding the event as the client's information processing system is activated. When the proper cognitions are identified, "all roads should lead to Rome." That is, all memory networks lead to resolution of the trauma. Accurate cognitions also assist the generalization and resolution of other similarly traumatic memories in the client's system.

The negative and positive cognitions share common components, such as:

- Self-referencing (i.e., typically using an "I" statement)
- Stated in the present because they still exist in the present
- Focusing on the presenting issue
- Generalizable to other related events
- Concrete, rather than abstract

The negative cognition is a self-denigrating or self-limiting, and sometimes an irrational or dysfunctional belief, while the positive cognition represents a shift in self-perception that opens up new possibilities for the client. Negative cognitions aid in eliciting associated affect. When the client focuses on the disturbing event and the words, "I am unsafe," the client can still feel fear, confusion, and shame in the present. Positive cognitions provide marked evidence of the client's desired direction for change, for instance, "I am safe now" or "I am free of fear, confusion, and shame."

Both the negative and positive cognitions are self-referencing and stated in the present tense and therefore are usually, with some exceptions, preceded by an "I" statement. Both are generalizable. That is, they can be related to clusters of similar events or areas of concern. The negative cognition focuses on the client's presenting issue, while the positive cognition focuses on the client's desired direction of change. For example, "I am a bad person" could be a presenting issue, and "I am a good person" might be the desired direction of change. Table 3.1 provides a simple view of the purpose of cognitions in the standard procedural steps.

Table 3.1

PURPOSE OF COGNITIONS

NEGATIVE	POSITIVE
Highlight irrationality (or dysfunctionality) of belief for client	Set a direction for treatment
Stimulate dysfunctional material	Stimulate appropriate alternative memory networks
Establish a baseline from which to measure progress	Establish a baseline from which to measure progress

What Is a Cognition?

It is important to know what cognitions are *not*, as well as what they are. Cognition involves conscious intellectual activity, such as thinking, reasoning, and remembering. For the purposes of EMDR, cognitions are beliefs. They are not feelings, such as "I am scared." They are *not* true statements. In the case of a driver who ran a red light and crashed into another car, the statement, "I was not in control" would be true and an inappropriate negative self-referencing belief if targeting the actual event. Table 3.2 provides a bird's eye view of how not to structure negative and positive cognitions.

Table 3.2

COGNITIONS

| WHAT THEY ARE NOT | |
NEGATIVE	POSITIVE
Statements of simple emotions (e.g., "I am afraid or angry.")	Absolute statements—words like never and always are inappropriate (e.g., "I will always be in control.")
Accurate descriptions of disturbing circumstances, social references, attributes of others or client (e.g., "My father molested me.")	Magical thinking (e.g., "I am a good father" when the father has recently been caught molesting his child) EMDR cannot make a silk purse out of a sow's ear. However, one can say, "I can atone for my behavior." Or "I can learn to be a good father."
Blatant overgeneralizations (e.g., "I am the worst person in the world.")	Negations of negative thinking (e.g.,"I am not guilty.")

Teasing Out Negative and Positive Cognitions

How do you elicit effective negative and positive cognitions without putting words into the client's mouth? When assisting the client in forming her negative and positive cognitions, the clinician might say, "What words go best with that picture that express your *negative belief* about yourself *now*? I am _____." This reminds the client to frame the belief in the present. The clinician is silently saying, "I am what? Please fill in the blank." The client may still attempt to frame her beliefs in different ways, such as "I cannot succeed" for the negative belief or "I can succeed," or "I will succeed" for the positive belief. All are correct.

What if the client says, "I am not successful at my job?" Is this an acceptable negative cognition? This particular cognition only pertains to the client's job. Should the negative cognition (as well as the positive cognition) be generalizable to other areas in the client's life where she might feel she does not succeed? What would be a better cognition, and how would you tease it out? How about, "What does this make you believe about yourself in general?" The statement, "I cannot succeed," has a stronger potential for generalizing to all areas of the client's experience and becoming a more appropriate negative cognition. The corresponding positive cognition may become, "I am a success" or "I can learn to be successful" or even "I can be successful in some ways."

What if a client's response to the clinician's elicitation of a negative cognition is, "I have failed?" In some instances, depending on the client's target, this may be a true statement. The clinician can respond with, "When you think of (repeat description), what negative belief do you have about yourself? What does that say about you as a person?"

If a client responds to the negative cognition question with an emotion (e.g., "I am scared."), the clinician can respond by saying, "What *negative belief* about you goes with that fear?" Or the clinician can reframe the client's response by saying, "In your worst moment, what *negative belief* do you have about yourself *now* when you think of the event?" In either case, the clinician may be able to elicit an appropriate negative cognition.

When a client focuses on the picture/incident being processed and cannot easily provide a negative or positive self-referencing belief, you could hand them the list of cognitions available in your training manual or the laminated SUD or Validity of Cognition (VoC) scale placard sold online and at EMDR trainings by the EMDR Humanitarian Assistance Programs (EMDR-HAP). The front side of the placard illustrates the SUD scale and the VoC scale in more graphic detail as a visual aid for children and adults. The other side provides a sample list of negative and positive cognitions.

The clinician may also offer a list of her own suggestions of possible negative cognitions from which the client can choose. In these cases, it is important for her to verbally and/or nonverbally indicate to the client that he has permisison to choose or reject anything offered by the clinician as an alternative (Shapiro, 2001).

In working with a client setting up the protocol, he may express more than one negative cognition at a time, such as, "I am unlovable and unworthy." When this happens, ask him to "Focus on the picture/incident. Which negative belief resonates the most with the picture or event—worthiness or lovability?"

At other times, the client may provide unparallel negative and positive cognitions, such as, "I am unworthy" (negative cognition) and "I am lovable" (positive cognition). How would you tease out which negative semantic theme the client associates with the picture/incident? You could say one of two things. First, you might say, "If you would like to *believe*, 'I am lovable' as you focus on the picture/event, what does that make you *believe negatively* about yourself *now*? What is the *flip* side of 'I am lovable'?" Or you might say, "What is the *flip* side of 'I am unworthy' for you?"

Some clinicians believe the negative and positive cognitions need to be perfectly parallel to be effective. If the client says his negative cognition is, "I am bad," his positive cognition needs to be, "I am good." Some conclude the cognitions only need to be similar. So what does that mean? Here are some examples:

Picture/Incident	Negative Cognition	Positive Cognition
Rape	I am dirty.	I am okay.
Assault	I am in danger.	I am fine.

Dr. Shapiro (2001) states that the positive cognition is *generally* a 180-degree shift from the negative cognition. In any case, the clinician assures that the positive cognition expresses a positive self-assessment that verbalizes the same thematic schema or issue conveyed in the negative cognition.

Especially under the pressure of processing past trauma, many of our clients are unable to come up with these beliefs. Some cannot distinguish a belief from a feeling. Some just cannot think that quickly on their feet. And some simply go blank. Rather than retraumatize them further by thinking they cannot do EMDR correctly, say, "Here's my 'cheat sheet.' Focus on the trauma and see if any of the beliefs on the left side of the placard resonate." If the client selects more than one negative belief, ask them to pick the one that resonates the most as they focus on the picture/incident. Even with the use of the laminated SUD/VoC scale, allow the client to come up with a corresponding positive cognition. If they cannot, ask them to look at the negative cognition they selected off this placard and ask if the positive cognition horizontal to it fits. If it does, they can go with that.

Can the protocol be continued without assessing for a negative cognition? Dr. Shapiro (2001) states "when the thoughts, emotions, or situation appear to be too confusing or complex, it is appropriate to continue without the negative cognition." In all cases, the clinician attempts to elicit a negative cognition. Information gathered in the assessment phase can assist the clinician in drawing out an appropriate negative cognition from the client that resonates with the targeted memory. The existence of a negative cognition allows for more complete accessing and processing of the dysfunctional information attached to the targeted event.

See Table 3.3 for a more complete listing of negative and positive cognitions. The negative cognitions usually cluster around themes of responsibility (i.e., self-worth/shame or action/guilt), safety, or choices/

Table 3.3

NEGATIVE/POSITIVE COGNITIONS

I am bad/inadequate.	I am okay.
I am a bad person.	I am a good person.
	I am a loving person.
I am a disappointment.	I am okay the way I am.
I am a failure.	I am doing the best I can.
	I am a success.
	I can be a success.
	I can succeed.
	I can learn to succeed.
I am an unloving person.	I am a loving person.
I am crazy.	I am normal.
I am damaged.	I am healthy.
I am permanently damaged.	I can be healthy.
I am helpless.	I now have choices/resources.
I am hopeless.	I am alright.
	I am okay.
I am in danger.	I am safe.
I am unsafe.	I am safe.
I am inadequate/incapable.	I am adequate/capable.
	I am worthwhile.
I am vulnerable.	I am safe.
	I am okay.
I cannot take care of myself.	I can take care of myself.
I am insignificant.	I am significant.
I am not good enough.	I am okay as I am.
	I am fine as I am.
I am not in control.	I am now in control.
	I am comfortably in control.
I am not lovable.	I am lovable.
I am powerless.	I have choices.
	I now have choices.
	I can have choices.
I am shameful.	I am honorable.
I am stupid.	I have intelligence.
I am terrible.	I am fine as I am.
I am ugly.	I am fine.
	I am attractive.
	I am lovable.
	I am okay.
I am unimportant.	I am important.
I am unworthy.	I am worthy.
I am useless.	I am worthwhile.
I am weak.	I am strong.

(continued)

I cannot (fill in the blank).	I can (fill in the blank).
	I can learn to (fill in the blank).
I cannot be trusted.	I can be trusted.
I cannot get what I want.	I can get what I want.
	I can learn to get what I want.
I cannot let it go.	I can choose to let it go.
I cannot let it out.	I can choose to let it out.
I cannot protect myself.	I can protect myself.
	I can learn to protect myself.
I cannot stand it.	I can handle it.
I cannot succeed.	I can succeed.
I cannot take care of myself.	I can take care of myself.
	I can learn to take care of myself.
I cannot trust anyone.	I can choose whom to trust.
I cannot trust my judgment.	I can trust my judgment.
I cannot trust myself.	I can trust myself.
	I can learn to trust myself.
I deserve (fill in the blank).	I deserve (fill in the blank).
I deserve only bad things.	I deserve good things.
I deserve to be miserable.	I deserve to be happy.
I deserve to die.	I deserve to live.
I deserve to suffer.	I deserve to be comfortable.
I cannot do anything right.	I learned from it.
	I can learn from it.
I don't deserve love.	I deserve love.
	I can have love.
I have to be perfect.	I can be myself.
	I can make mistakes.
It is all my fault.	I did the best I could.
I cannot stand up for myself.	I can stand up for myself.
	I can learn to stand up for myself.

control. Some of these negative and positive cognition combinations were cited by Dr. Shapiro (1995, 2001). Additions have been made to provide a more comprehensive listing.

It is not unusual for a client to be unable to come up with a positive cognition. If this happens, do what you can to elicit one from him, but do not belabor your effort. Do everything in your power to facilitate the client having a positive EMDR experience. Remember, he will have another chance to provide a positive cognition in the installation phase, so complete the protocol without a positive cognition, if necessary. It may or may not slow down the processing, but the processing probably will not be halted because of it. EMDR is a forgiving process as long as the clinician stays out of the client's way.

In the case of Jennifer earlier, the negative and positive cognition might be elicited as follows:

Clinician: "Jennifer, what words go best with that picture that express your *negative* belief about yourself now?"

Jennifer: "I did something bad."

Clinician: "What does that make you believe about yourself now?"

Jennifer: "That I am bad."

Clinician: "When you bring up that picture, what would you like to believe about yourself now?"

Jennifer: "Well, I guess, that I am good."

In assisting clients to formulate cognitions that will optimally aid resolution of their trauma, you can use the checklist below to ensure that all components of each cognitive level have been considered (see Table 3.4).

Table 3.4

CRITERIA FOR NEGATIVE AND POSITIVE COGNITIONS

NEGATIVE COGNITION

Self-referential (i.e., usually proceeded by an "I")
Stated in the present
Focuses on the presenting issue
Reflects a belief (i.e., cannot be a simple statement of emotion or a description of circumstances)
Often irrational and/or dysfunctional
Generalizable to related events
Cannot be removed if true or installed if false
Concrete rather than abstract
Interpretive rather than descriptive
Elicits associated affect

POSITIVE COGNITION

Self-referential (i.e., usually proceeded by an "I")
Stated in the present
Focuses on the presenting issue
Ecologically sound (i.e., it is possible under client's circumstances)
Generalizable to related events
The word "not" is not used in the statement
Reflects a positive and desired direction of change
Not clinician-imposed
Does not contain words like "always" or "never"
Concrete rather than abstract
Possesses emotional resonance
Often elicits positive emotion

See Figure 3.2 to identify the completion of the cognitive part of the assessment phase.

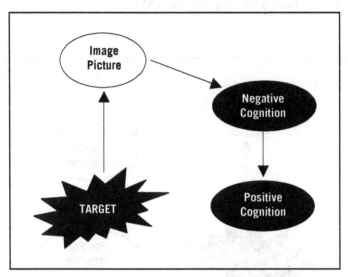

Figure 3.2 Stepping stones to adaptive resolution: Cognitions.

ASSESSMENT OF THE VALIDITY OF COGNITION (VOC)

VoC Scale

The SUD and the VoC are emotional and cognitive rating scales designed and utilized by the clinician to provide a baseline measure for client and clinician alike. The VoC is a 7-point Likert scale which provides a baseline measure for strength of a client's positive cognition. It is assessed at the beginning of the process after the positive cognition is defined and reassessed at the beginning of the installation phase to see if the original cognition is still appropriate.

The VoC usually needs to be at least a "2" for it to be considered a workable cognition because it is very difficult for a client to go from "total disbelief" to "total belief." If a client reports an initial VoC rating of "1" (i.e., completely false), the clinician assesses whether it is unrealistic, improbable, or impossible to achieve. The clinician must evaluate the ecological soundness of the cognition in terms of the client and the event. Therefore, the clinician assesses the suitability and degree of success the client may experience in assimilating a positive cognition with a low VoC level. In some cases, the client's positive cognition may simply be titrated to raise the VoC level. For instance, a "1" rating for, "I am in control," could be changed to "I can learn to have better control," thereby rendering the VoC at least a "2" (see Figure 3.3).

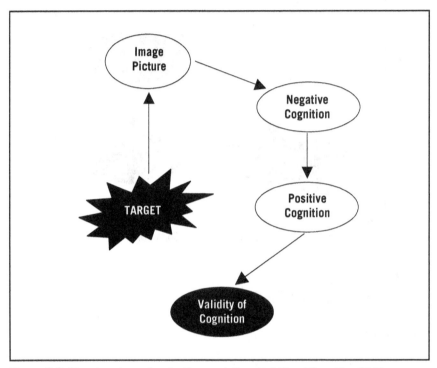

Figure 3.3 Stepping stones to adaptive resolution: Validity of Cognition (VoC).

ASSESSMENT OF EMOTIONS

Emotional Sensations

The next step in the assessment phase is the identification of the negative emotions associated with the event or issue. This is simply where the client identifies the emotion(s) she is currently feeling when thinking about the original event (or incident) and the negative cognition. Let's go back to Jennifer and see what emotions she was able to recognize.

"Jennifer, when you bring up the incident and those words, 'I am bad,' what emotion(s) do you feel now?" "Fear, anger, confusion."

In this case, we want to know what Jennifer feels *now* as she focuses on the incident and her negative cognition, *not when it happened*. She may not be feeling the same emotions that she felt at the time the incident happened; and, in her case, she was able to identify more than one emotion. She was afraid her teacher might approach her again. She was angry at what he did and confused about what to do and how to feel about it (see Figure 3.4).

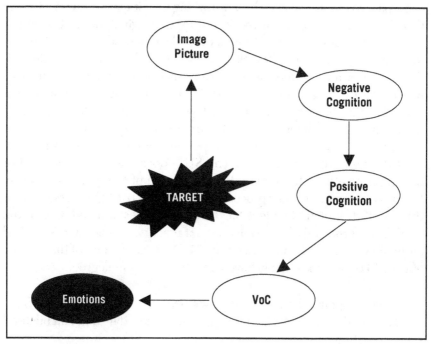

Figure 3.4 Stepping stones to adaptive resolution: Emotions.

ASSESSMENT OF CURRENT LEVEL OF DISTURBANCE

Subjective Units of Disturbance (SUD) Scale

The SUD scale was originally developed by Joseph Wolpe and is an 11-point Likert scale (i.e., a unidimensional scaling method developed by Rensis Likert) utilized in EMDR to measure a client's subjective experience of how distressing an event feels for her at the present moment. It is meant to measure strength of negative feelings identified by the client. The SUD is taken after the client has identified what emotions she is feeling during the assessment phase and at the end of the desensitization phase to indicate whether processing is complete and resolution of the disturbance has been achieved. It can also be used at the end of a channel of association to determine the client's level of progress.

To determine a client's initial SUD level, the clinician simply asks, "From '0,' which is neutral or no disturbance, to '10,' which is the worst disturbance you can imagine, how disturbing does it <u>feel</u> to you <u>now</u>?" Note that the client has not been redirected to the original incident or to her negative cognition. The SUD follows the elicitation of emotion. As such, the clinician is asking how the client feels now with regard to the old incident or "How are you feeling now?" (e.g., fear over initiating the process) or "How disturbed are you <u>now</u>?" The SUD is a baseline measurement that helps the clinician to know the client's level of disturbance. It also provides information to the client as to how the process is progressing.

It is not unusual for clients to experience a range of different emotions during an EMDR session. The SUD does not reflect the level of disturbance with each emotion. It is a measure of the total disturbance. When a client reports after processing a SUD level of "0," we assume that the client's traumatic incident has been totally desensitized. Often, the SUD level at the end of a session does not reach zero. The client's original target may not be fully processed (i.e., SUD = 0) at the end of the session, but the SUD will most likely have decreased to some degree.

What happens when the SUD level becomes stuck at a "1" or "2?"
1. Ask the client, "What is going on in your body?" and add bilateral stimulation.
2. If SUD is still not equal to "0," the clinician may check for blocking beliefs by asking the client, "What prevents it from becoming a zero?" If a blocking belief is identified, the clinician adds bilateral stimulation until the blocking belief has been completely reprocessed.
3. If SUD is still not equal to "0," the clinician may probe for additional blocking beliefs or feeder memories. Note that blocking beliefs may be spontaneously processed (i.e., an EMDR session within an EMDR session) or may be the target in a subsequent EMDR session (i.e., "Where did you learn that belief?") As mentioned previously, additional blocking beliefs may be uncovered using direct questioning, floatback, or affect scan techniques.

4. If SUD is still not equal to "0," the clinician may check for ecological soundness (Shapiro, 2009).

These scales can be confusing to clients, especially since one measures their progress by decreasing in value and the other by increasing in value. If a client questions this, the clinician may provide them with a plausible and simple explanation. "Well, if you think of it in this way, it makes it easier to understand. The EMDR standard procedure is set up in a way so as to decrease the negative emotional charge of your trauma and to increase the charge to your desired direction of change. See Figure 3.5.

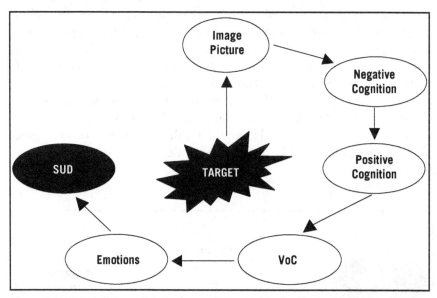

Figure 3.5 Stepping stones to adaptive resolution: Subjective Units of Disturbance (SUD).

ASSESSMENT OF PHYSICAL SENSATIONS

Body Sensations

The final question that you will ask Jennifer is, "And where do you feel it in your body?" She might respond, "In my stomach." The somatic component is an important piece of the client's traumatic jigsaw puzzle. The clinician is asking the client where she is feeling the disturbance when she evokes a disturbing image or picture in her body. Jennifer most likely had a physical reaction while the event was occurring. She might have felt it in her stomach then or maybe not. She might have felt it in her stomach whenever she brought the incident up or maybe not. What is important is where she feels it in her body while she is currently focusing on the event. We do not need or want to know what she was feeling before, during, or after the event in her body. We need to know where she feels it in her body when setting up the last of the EMDR procedural steps.

The significance of body sensations in the assessment phase cannot be overly emphasized. When a client is focusing on a traumatic memory, the emergence of physical sensations may be associated with emotional tension (e.g., tight muscles or rapid breathing), physical sensations stored at the time of a traumatic event (e.g., physically feeling the pain where a perpetrator hit the victim in the jaw), or negative cognitions. As you can see, the body's physical responses to a trauma are an important aspect of the treatment. When the clinician asks the client, "Where do you feel it (the disturbance) in your body (i.e., now)?" there is a clear assumption that there is physical resonance to dysfunctional material (Shapiro, 2001). As long as physical sensations linger, the EMDR process is considered incomplete. Residual tension and atypical physical sensations must be absent for reprocessing to be complete (see Figure 3.6).

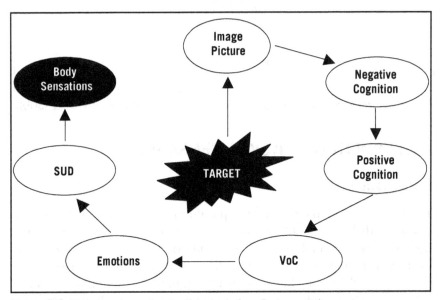

Figure 3.6 Stepping stones to adaptive resolution: Body sensations.

As stated earlier, it is important to mimic Dr. Shapiro's words as closely as possible when assessing the components of the client's targeted memory in preparation for EMDR processing. Her script for the assessment phase procedure is followed precisely in this Primer, as well.

CASE EXAMPLES

The cases below are composites of clients and events. Where appropriate, notes have been inserted to serve as teaching points.

CASE EXAMPLE 3B: TERRY

Terry, a 40-year-old male, suffered from severe anxiety and depression and a phobia of dead animals, especially birds of any kind. When Terry first arrived, he was sluggish and disoriented. His wife joined him in sessions for the first couple of times because she acted as his historian. He had lost track of the last few years in terms of doctors, medications, and episodes. He was scared but knew he needed something more than talk therapy for him to get better. As part of his history, the clinician discovered that his mother had married many times during his childhood and usually to very abusive men. Because of this, Terry had experienced what seemed to him lifetimes of trauma before he graduated from high school.

When Terry arrived to begin EMDR, he was visibly shaken. "I'm scared," he said. "I'm afraid it is not going to work." Because of his discomfort with doing the EMDR, it was decided to start with a less severe memory, that of being chased with a dead bird by his Uncle Roger. Here is how the protocol of Terry's fear of dead birds was set up:

Clinician: Last week, Terry, you stated that you wanted to start with the memory of your uncle chasing you with a dead bird. Can you elaborate *briefly*?

The briefer the better. The clinician does not necessarily need to know the details. It is about the client being able to resolve his trauma as completely as possible. The focus is on the client spending time processing the event rather than describing all the details of it.

Terry: I must have been around 3 years old. I was playing in the yard when I spotted a strange-looking *"thing"* in the yard. It turned out to be a dead bird. I was always a curious kid. Because I wanted to know what it was and what it did, I ran to Uncle Roger and showed him the dead bird. Uncle Roger immediately took the dead bird away from me, thrust it into my face, and began to chase me with it.

Clinician: What picture represents the entire incident?

Once a client has revealed a traumatic memory, we ask him for a single image or picture as the initial focus, an image that represents a link to neurological and dysfunctional material.

Terry: It was his evil laugh. He chased me and laughed hysterically.

The picture that the client has selected is very concrete (e.g., "his evil laugh" rather than "being treated cruelly by my uncle"). This is an important element of an effective target.

Clinician: Terry, what words go best with that picture that express your *negative* belief about yourself now?

Terry: I am in danger.

This is an excellent negative cognition. It is irrational (or dysfunctional), negative, and self-referencing. It is stated in the present and focuses on the client's presenting issue. And it can be generalized to other traumatic events in which the client may feel unsafe. It also reflects the associated affect of fear identified later by the client.

Clinician: When you bring up the picture, what would you like to believe (not what do you believe) about yourself now?

Terry: I am not in danger.

The positive cognition is not acceptable or effective. The way it is stated, it is simply a negation of the negative cognition as it appears above. A negative (i.e., "no," "not") within a positive statement does not bring the client to his desired direction of change. This is when it becomes necessary for the clinician to tease it out without putting words into the client's mouth, if at all possible.

Clinician: How can you phrase that in a more positive direction?

Terry: Oh, I don't know. How about, "I am safe?"

Does this cognition fit the criteria for a positive cognition? Yes, it does. It is a positive, self-referencing belief. It reflects the client's desired direction of change. It is generalizable to other areas of the client's life. And it provides clear indication of a positive associated affect. In addition, the positive cognition in this instance matches the theme in the negative cognition. Both deal with the theme of safety.

Note that the cognitions are not perfectly parallel in this example (i.e., "I am in danger" and "I am safe"). They are comfortably similar, and this is okay. It is important to use the client's words, not what we think the client's words ought to be.

Clinician: Good. Terry, when you think of the event (or incident), how <u>true</u> do those words, "I am safe," <u>feel</u> to you <u>now</u> on a scale from 1 to 7, where "1" *feels* completely false and "7" *feels* completely true?
Terry: Two. It does not feel very true.
Clinician: When you bring up that incident and those words, "I am in danger," what *emotion(s)* do you feel now?
Terry: Fear! Total fear!
Clinician: From "0," which is neutral or no disturbance, to "10," which is the worst disturbance you can imagine, how disturbing does it <u>feel</u> to you <u>now</u>?

Notice that the clinician ends most questions with the word *now*. We are not interested in what the client believed negatively at the time of the event or what physical and emotional sensations he experienced then. We want to know what is happening in the present—in the *now*. This is an important point because some clients will report what they believed, felt, and experienced then. Make sure that the client knows the difference, because it could adversely affect the processing.

Terry: It's an eight.
Clinician: Where do you <u>feel</u> it in your *body*?
Terry: In my gut.

A client's bodily response to trauma is an important aspect of treatment and provides a valuable addition of information apart from the verbalizations provided by the client (Shapiro, 2001). When a client is asked where the body sensation is located in his body, what that clinician is really asking is, "Where does the dysfunctional material physically resonate in your body?"

Sometimes it may be difficult for a client to identify where he feels the disturbance in his body. When this is the case, the clinician can assist the client in assessing body sensations by referring them back to their original SUD level. For example, if the client reported a SUD level of "9," the clinician might say, "You reported a '9' as the level of disturbance. Where do you feel the '9' in your body?" If the client is still having difficulty, say "Close your eyes and notice how your body feels. Now I will ask you to think of something; and, when I do, just notice what changes in your body. Okay, notice your body. Now, think of the memory (or bring up the picture). Tell me what changes. Now add the words, 'I am in danger.' Tell me what changes." See Figure 3.7 for a graphical picture of the EMDR components in the assessment phase for Terry.

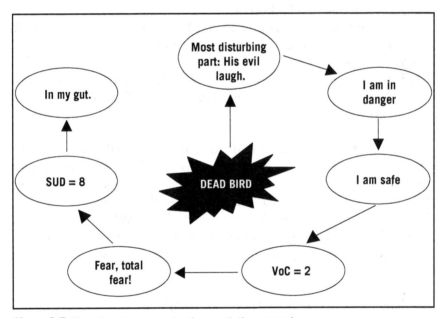

Figure 3.7 Stepping stones to adaptive resolution example.

When you are going through the procedural steps with the client, it is important to write down everything similar to what is done in Tables 3.5 to 3.8. Write down exactly what the client says, not what the clinician thinks the client says, and reflect the words back to him in his exact language when the need arises. If a clinician were to say to Terry, for example, "When you focus on the event and those words, 'I am unsafe' (what Terry did not say) instead of 'I am in danger' (what Terry did say), what emotions come up for you now," the clinician has not allowed the client's process to work for him. The clinician is using his words, not the client's. This format also gives a bird's eye view of the client's responses to the questions in the protocol for the clinician to look at.

This was a straightforward setup. Even though this client had not reprocessed with EMDR before, he was able to understand and provide what was needed without too much effort. This is not always the case. It sometimes will become necessary for the clinician to tease out what is needed to smooth the way for adequate processing of the dysfunctionally stored material around the targeted event. Table 3.5 is a reminder for the clinician to write everything down the client says, especially during the assessment phase.

Table 3.5

PROTOCOL SETUP: TERRY

Target: When he was around 3 years old, Terry found a dead bird in the yard. Peaked by his curiosity and his thirst to know more, he brought the dead bird to show his Uncle Roger. Uncle Roger took the dead bird, immediately thrust it in Terry's face, and chased him with it.
Worst part: It was his evil laugh. He was chasing me and laughing hysterically.
NC: I am in danger.
PC: I am safe.
VoC: 2
Emotion: Fear
SUD: 8
Body: Gut

CASE EXAMPLE 3C: JULIA

Julia suffered severe neck, back, and shoulder injuries during a car accident with a drunk driver 2 years ago. While proceeding north on a divided four-lane highway, Julia told the police officer that she saw a vehicle heading toward her. While she tried to avoid the car, Julia became hemmed in by other moving traffic and was struck by the vehicle driven by a young woman. Julia's car was hit on the passenger side and spun around before it came to rest backwards partially in the highway median. Julia had collided with a 27-year-old woman who was driving in the wrong direction. At the time, the young woman stated that she did not know she was driving the wrong way and was unsure how that happened.

Immediately following the accident, Julia was rushed to a local hospital with significant injuries. She later had to have back surgery as a result. When Julia came to therapy, she stated that she had not been able to drive since the accident. As a single parent, she was the sole provider of income for herself and her two children. Julia realized the importance of getting back behind the wheel of her car as soon as possible. She was mending physically and nearing the time when her long-term disability would expire.

Clinician: Julia, what picture represents the worst part of the incident?

Because there was more than one possible image or picture the client could select that was linked to the event, the clinician asked the client to select the image or picture that held the most disturbance.

Julia: Seeing the car heading toward me and not being able to do anything to get out of the way. There were cars on both sides and behind me. There was just nowhere for me to turn. I had no choice but to get hit by this oncoming car.
Clinician: What words go best with that picture that express your negative <u>belief</u> about yourself <u>now</u>? I am _____ (the client fills in the blank).
Julia: I was afraid.

This is not an appropriate negative cognition. Why? It is self-referencing. Is it a belief? No, it expresses the emotion of fear. The task then is to tease out the negative belief that is associated with this negative emotion.

Clinician: I understand that you were afraid. What belief about you goes with the fear? Or "What does the fear make you <u>believe</u> about yourself <u>now</u>?"
Julia: That I am out of control. I feel so helpless.

Here the client has stated one belief, "I am out of control," and is feeling a sense of helplessness that might be translated into, "I am helpless."

The clinician teases this out further so that he can obtain the belief that goes with the negative emotion the client has already expressed.

Clinician: As you focus on the event, which *belief* resonates the most, as you focus on the event, lack of control or helplessness, <u>now</u>?
Julia: Lack of control.
Clinician: So "I am out of control" is what you <u>believe</u> about yourself as you focus on the event <u>now</u>?

The negative cognition is restated to be certain that this is what the client believes about herself as she focuses on the past event. This cognition meets all the criteria for an appropriate negative cognition. It is self-referencing. It is stated in the present. It is generalizable, and it reflects the negative emotion that the client associates with the accident.

Julia: Yes.
Clinician: When you bring up that picture, what would you <u>like</u> [not what do you believe] to <u>believe</u> about yourself <u>now</u>?
Julia: I can take care of myself.
Clinician: What could be the flip side of "I can take care of myself" for you?

This positive cognition does not match the corresponding negative cognition the client just provided. So, again, it becomes necessary to tease out the negative and positive belief that fit for the client.

Julia: I can't take care of myself.
Clinician: Does this resonate with you as you focus on the incident or does, "I am out of control"?
Julia: I am out of control.
Clinician: What is the reverse of "I am out of control" for you?
Julia: I always have control.

The positive cognition cannot be an absolute statement. Therefore, avoid the use of words such as "always," *and* "never." When this happens, assist the client in reframing her cognition to something more reasonable or realistic.

Clinician: Is it possible to always have control?
Julia: Probably not.
Clinician: What would be a more reasonable version of "I always have control"?

Julia: I have control, I guess.

Clinician: When you bring up that picture, is this what you would <u>like</u> to <u>believe</u> about yourself <u>now</u>?

Julia: Yes.

Clinician: Julia, when you think of the event (or incident), how <u>true</u> do those words, "I have control" <u>feel</u> to you <u>now</u> on a scale from 1 to 7, where "1" *feels* completely false and "7" *feels* completely true?

Julia: It's a one. It's not true at all.

When the client states that the positive belief feels like a "1," it is indicative that this might not actually be a possibility for the client. It may just be part of the client's magical thinking that she can have control over all people, places, and things. So, we need to fine-tune it so that the positive cognition is more realistic and attainable.

Clinician: Is it realistic to state in this situation that you have control?

Julia: No. Probably not.

Clinician: What might a more realistic belief look like for you as you focus on the event?

Julia: I have some control.

Clinician: And how <u>true</u> does, "I have some control" <u>feel</u> on a scale of 1 to 7 <u>now</u>?

Julia: It's not much higher. Let's say a "2."

Clinician: When you bring up that memory and those words, "I am out of control," what emotion(s) do you feel now?

Julia: Fear. I still feel so afraid.

Notice that the negative cognition resonates with the associated affect stated by the client.

Clinician: From "0," which is neutral or no disturbance, to "10," which is the worst disturbance you can imagine, how disturbing does it <u>feel</u> to you <u>now</u>?

Julia: "10." I'm terrified.

Clinician: Where do you <u>feel</u> it in your body?

Julia: In my stomach and in my chest.

Table 3.6 is a reminder for the clinician to write down everything the client says, especially during the assessment phase.

Table 3.6

PROTOCOL SETUP: JULIA

Target: Worst part: Seeing the car heading toward her and not being able to do anything to get out of the way.
NC: I am out of control.
PC: I have some control.
VoC: 2
Emotion: Fear.
SUD: 10
Body: Stomach and chest

CASE EXAMPLE 3D: JERRY

Originally presenting with generalized anxiety, Jerry had successfully reprocessed the death of his younger brother with EMDR. Previously, he had worked through guilt over his brother's death and his wish that he could have done something more to help his brother through his lingering illness. He worried incessantly about the stress of his brother's death on his fragile mother's health but obsessed more about the day when she would pass and the pain he anticipated that he would feel.

Jerry came from a family of one brother and three sisters. Now that his brother was dead, there was no one to carry out the family lineage. Tragically, he discovered at a very young age that he was sterile as a result of an earlier bout with meningitis. He did have three sons whom he and his wife adopted at birth. But he still felt that he had failed in his familial responsibility to carry on the family name. These were the issues that Jerry had previously successfully reprocessed with the aid of EMDR. Yet, there was one final lingering splinter that still seemed to stick out as he focused on his brother's death.

His younger brother's new wife was still in the picture. Prior to his death, his brother apparently was unable to manage his financial matters on his own. He had set up a will in which he named his wife the chief beneficiary but did not name his wife as the executor of the will. He named Jerry instead, which created two problems. Jerry became overwhelmed by the intricacies of the legal matters with which he had to deal. His brother's wife was not happy about the arrangement and caused difficulties within the family.

Most of Jerry's apprehension centered on his feelings of inadequacy involving legal matters of any kind. He was a teacher, not a lawyer.

It was his insecurity regarding the meetings with the lawyer handling his brother's will that bothered him the most.

Clinician: When you think of the situation, what do you get?

Jerry: The last meeting with my brother's lawyer. I felt so inept at legal matters. I don't want to disappoint my brother even in death.

Clinician: What was the worst part?

Jerry: I remember stuttering when the lawyer started asking me questions about what was in the will. I never stutter.

Clinician: What words go best with that picture that express your *negative* belief about yourself now?

Jerry: I am incompetent.

Clinician: When you bring up that picture, what would you *like* to *believe* about yourself *now*?

Jerry: I am competent.

Clinician: Jerry, when you think of that event (or incident), how true do those words, "I am competent" feel to you now on a scale from 1 to 7, where "1" *feels* completely false and "7" *feels* completely true?

Jerry: It feels, well maybe, about a "3."

Clinician: As you bring up the incident and those words, "I am incompetent," what *emotion(s)* come up for you now?

Jerry: I am feeling really apprehensive about these meetings. I possess a lot of self-doubt, too.

Clinician: From "0," which is neutral or no disturbance, to "10," which is the worst disturbance you can imagine, how disturbing does it feel to you now?

Jerry: It's only about a five. I thought it would be higher.

Jerry reported feeling apprehension and doubt. The SUD level measures total disturbance, rather than the level of disturbance on each separate emotion identified.

Clinician: Where do you feel it in your *body*?

Jerry: I don't know.

Some clients are unable to report body sensations, no matter how hard a clinician tries to coach them. When this is the case, the clinician only needs to have the client focus on the identified components of the target and concentrate on assisting in locating the emotions in his body as reprocessing progresses through the immediate or successive sessions. Or, the clinician may utilize the client's calm (or safe) place to elicit body consciousness.

Clinician: Do you remember your calm (or safe) place?

Client: Yes.

Clinician: Please bring it up. (Pause) Notice how that feels to be there *now*. Head to toe . . . how safe, how relaxing? Let me know when you have it by nodding your head. (Pause) Good. Now, bring up the disturbing incident. What changes in your body?

Client: I feel jittery in my stomach.

Table 3.7 is a reminder for the clinician to write down everything the client says, especially during the assessment phase.

Table 3.7

PROTOCOL SETUP: JERRY

Target: Worst part: The upcoming meetings with his brother's lawyer.
NC: I am incompetent.
PC: I am competent.
VoC: 3
Emotion: Apprehension and self-doubt
SUD: 5
Body: Feels jittery in stomach

CASE EXAMPLE 3E: HENRY

Henry and his clinician had been working for weeks, identifying and clearing out old memories that were fueling his current symptoms. He was feeling better and better about how he was handling his relationship with his wife, 15 years his junior.

Despite his successes in therapy, Henry continues to be self-loathing. It was this negative deep-seated feeling about himself that he simply could not lose. "I hate myself," he would say. "I simply do not like myself, and I do not know why." When asked about historic events and memories that may have elicited this feeling, he could identify none.

Clinician: Focus on the words, "I hate myself. "Where do you <u>feel</u> that self-hatred in your *body*?"

Henry: In my gut.

Clinician: "What *emotion* is associated with that *physical sensation* in your gut?"

Henry: "Anxiousness," he said.
Clinician: As you focus on those words, 'I hate myself,' the *physical sensation* in your gut, and the anxiousness that you <u>feel</u>, what words go best that describe your *negative* <u>belief</u> about yourself right <u>now</u>?"
Henry: "I am worthless."

Having identified his negative self-belief, "I am worthless" and the negative emotion associated with this self-belief, the clinician led Henry into the floatback technique (see chapter 4).

Clinician: Henry, bring up that (negative) belief, "I am worthless" and the emotions you are feeling now and let your mind float back to the earliest time when you may have felt this way before and just notice what comes to mind. . . " (Shapiro, 2009).

Henry floated back to when he was 5 years old. He was in the basement playing while his dad was busy cutting on a piece of plywood. The plywood had been placed between two sawhorses. He did not remember what his dad was working on. He just wanted to play and was busy doing so when his dad jerked him up and placed him firmly on the piece of plywood. And then his father continued cutting with his circular saw.

Henry was terrified. All he remembers seeing and hearing from that point on was the buzzing of the saw as it made its way toward him. His father used Henry as an anchor to keep the board from shifting out of place while he made his cuts. Henry said, "I shook. I cried. I was so scared." Aggravated, his father jerked him off the board, threw him angrily on the floor, picked up his 3½-year-old sister, Martha, made her take Henry's place on the plywood, and continued his project.

It was at this point that the clinician set up the EMDR protocol around this event and Henry was able to process to a successful resolution.

Clinician: Henry, what picture represents the incident?
Henry: I can still see myself standing on the board.
Clinician: Henry, what words go best with that picture that express your *negative* <u>belief</u> about yourself <u>now</u>?
Henry: I am weak. Afraid. I can't do it. I am incompetent.

Except for one, the client rattled off several valid statements which could possibly serve as the negative cognition around this event. "I am afraid" is not a valid negative cognition. It is a feeling. Because there were valid cognitions available, the clinician did not say, "Fear is what you feel. What does that make you believe about yourself as you focus on the event?" The clinician believed that it was more important to weed out the best cognition from the three that the client provided. Had the clinician not done this, it is possible that the results would have turned out differently. This was a judgment call on his part. As you will see later, the client did bring this trauma to a successful resolution.

Clinician: Other than feeling afraid, which one of those statements resonates the most when you focus on the event?

Henry: I am incompetent.

Clinician: When you bring up that picture, what would you <u>like</u> to <u>believe</u> about yourself <u>now</u>?

Henry: I am competent.

Clinician: When you think of the event (or incident), how *true* do those words, "I am competent," <u>feel</u> to you <u>now</u> on a scale from 1 to 7, where "1" *feels* completely false and "7" *feels* completely true?

Henry: About halfway. Maybe a "3."

Clinician: When you bring up that memory and those words, "I am incompetent," what emotion(s) do you feel now?

Henry: Anger and fear mostly.

Clinician: When you bring up the *original* event (or incident), on a scale from 0 to 10, where "0" is no disturbance and "10" is the worst disturbance you can imagine, how disturbing does it <u>feel</u> to you <u>now</u>?

Henry: It's pretty high. Let's say an "8."

Clinician: Where do you <u>feel</u> it in your *body*?

Henry: In my chest.

Table 3.8 is a reminder for the clinician to write everything down the client says, especially during the assessment phase.

Table 3.8

PROTOCOL SETUP: JERRY

Target: Worst part: I can still feel myself standing on the board.
NC: I am incompetent.
PC: I am competent.
VoC: 3
Emotion: Anger and fear
SUD: 8
Body: Chest

Once the standard procedural steps have been set up, the desensitization process can begin. If this is the first time a client has experienced EMDR, it is a good practice to introduce the client to the process by saying, "When a disturbing event occurs, it can get locked in the brain with the original picture, sounds, thoughts, feelings, and body sensations. EMDR seems to stimulate the information and allows the brain to reprocess the experience. That may be what is happening in rapid eye movement (REM) or dream sleep—the eye movements (tones, tactile) may help to process the unconscious material. It is your own brain that will be doing the healing, and you are the one in control (Shapiro, 2001)." If the client ends up having multiple sessions of EMDR, you can say, "Just let whatever happens, happen." And you might remind the client to distance himself from the trauma by saying, "To help you 'just notice' the experience, imagine riding on a train or watching a video and the images, feelings, and thoughts, are just going by."

Reprocessing includes the desensitization, installation, and body scan phases. Reprocessing is complete when SUD = 0, VoC = 7, and the body scan is clear.

RECENT TRAUMATIC EVENTS AND SINGLE INCIDENT TRAUMAS

Most clinical problems are treated with the 11-step standard EMDR procedure (i.e., image, negative cognition, positive cognition, VoC, emotion, SUD level, location of body sensation, desensitization, installation, body scan, and closure) and the standard three-pronged approach (i.e., past, present, and future). However, protocols are available for special populations (e.g., children, couples, sexual abuse victims, combat veterans, or clients with dissociative disorders) or special conditions or disorders (e.g., phobias, performance anxieties, substance abuse, pain control). It is important not to overlook the importance and differences in processing these types of events utilizing EMDR. These cases may require special protocols or customized treatment regimens (Shapiro, 2001) and are beyond the scope of this Primer. Explanations and examples of many are available (Luber, 2009a, 2009b) from other sources.

In chapter 1, incidents described as recent and single-incident traumas were identified and discussed. Because references to each type of trauma are interspersed throughout the Primer, the specific protocols outlined by Dr. Shapiro (2001) are presented here as well.

Recent Traumatic Events

Unlike most traumatic events where the client focuses on an older traumatic memory or the most disturbing part of the identified traumatic memory, working with recent events entails asking a client to focus on a "picture" that represents the entire incident or the most disturbing part. What Dr. Shapiro found in working with clients who attempted to process memories that were fairly recent was that the memory had not had enough time to sufficiently "consolidate into an integrated whole" (Shapiro, 2001). As a result, these memories tended to be more disorganized and fragmented. It usually takes 2–3 months for a memory to sufficiently integrate into existing schemas. In the case of a recent event, not enough time has elapsed for it to be generalized to a single image from the entire event. As a result of this observation, Dr. Shapiro developed a more extended recent events protocol, which is described below utilizing an anecdotal illustration (Shapiro, 2001).

CASE EXAMPLE 3F: PATRICK

Approximately 3 months before coming to therapy, Patrick was directly involved in a chemical explosion and fire at a plant where he worked as a maintenance technician. Although many others were taken to the hospital as a result of this explosion, Patrick was the only seriously injured employee and the only one who was in the room where hazardous materials had spilled and caught fire. He had just checked a valve in the vicinity of the explosion and was walking away when the explosion occurred. His shocking comment about himself was, "Thirty more seconds, and I would have been toast." The recent events protocol proceeds as follows:

1   **Obtain a Narrative History**
    Clinician: Patrick, tell me what you remember from beginning to end.

   Utilizing the recent events protocol, the clinician asks the client to relate the details of the event in narrative form.

   Patrick: I had just finished checking a valve on my regular safety rounds and was walking away and, "BOOM!" I didn't know what was happening. I just knew I had to get out of there quickly. I don't even know where I was when the explosion occurred. I just know that I had to get out. I was disoriented.

It was dark and smoky. I didn't know which way to go. I was panicking because I couldn't breathe. I kept thinking, "What happened? What happened?" And, I don't know how, but I reached the door to the outside quickly. The second the light and air hit my eyes, they started burning. I threw myself down in the snow and started rolling around. It was so cold. I threw snow on my face and rubbed my eyes with it. I hadn't been out long when Bill and Pete grabbed me and led me back into another entrance of the building. Bill said, "You know the drill," and threw me into a cold shower, clothes and all. I still couldn't see. I was freezing. It was so cold. Whenever I tried to get out of the shower, one of them would push me back in. Then they made me take all my clothes off and shoved me back in. (This was a documented safety procedure. It was important that Patrick got all the chemicals off his body to ensure that no further complications might arise.) God, it was cold! I was freezing. Next thing I remember is being loaded into the ambulance. I kept thinking, "What happened? Why me? Where's my wife? I can't see. I can't see! Why can't I see?" My wife arrived at the hospital about the same time I did. The doctor told us both that I may need a corneal transplant. "Oh God. Why me?" When I was in the hospital, I kept retracing my steps. "Was it me? Did I do something wrong? Oh, God, I can't see."

2 Target the Most Disturbing Aspect of the Memory

There are several experiences in Patrick's narration that could be treated as separate events (e.g., the explosion, not being able to see or breathe inside the building after the explosion, the air and light hitting his face and eyes and the burning sensation that occurred, the shower experience, the ride to the hospital, and being told by the doctor that he might need a corneal transplant). As the client is providing a narrative, the clinician records these separate events.

Clinician: Patrick, is there a particular part of your story that is more distressing than another?
Patrick: Not being able to see.

Patrick was able to identify the most disturbing part of his memory. Although not shown here, the clinician would set up the EMDR standard procedure specified in the assessment phase by identifying the negative cognition, positive cognition, VoC, emotions, SUD, and physical sensations associated with this particular aspect of Patrick's traumatic memory of the explosion. This memory would then be reprocessed completely, including performing an installation of the positive cognition and a body scan. It would not be surprising if the positive cognition does not reach a "7" or the body scan does not clear out completely. There are other targets relating to this same event that may need to be reprocessed first before this can occur.

3 Target the Remainder of the Narrative in Chronological Order
At this point, the clinician needs to target the chronological events in the client's narrative. If he were to have identified one of the events to be more disturbing than the rest, the clinician would target this one first and then the remainder as they occurred during the telling of his story. Each target is treated separately in terms of the standard EMDR procedure up to the installation phase, being mindful to exclude the body scan for each. The body scan is initiated only after the last target of this traumatic event has been identified and addressed so that all the associated negative physical sensations can be eliminated.

4 Visualize Entire Sequence of the Event With Eyes Closed
Once all the separate events in Patrick's narration have been identified and reprocessed, the client is asked to visualize the entire sequence of the event from start to finish.

> **Clinician:** Patrick, close your eyes and visualize the entire sequence of events of the explosion.
> **Patrick:** Okay.
> **Clinician:** Any time a disturbance arises in any form (i.e., emotional, cognitive, or somatic), stop processing and open your eyes. (Pause)
> **Patrick:** I can't see. Why? Why did it happen to me? The company had just replaced the valve. Didn't anyone check it to see if it was connected correctly?

Something disturbing has arisen. Because it is still disturbing, the clinician would implement the EMDR procedure through the installation phase again with this most recent disturbance. Once this has been processed, he would then ask the client to visualize the entire sequence of the event once again to see if further disturbances arise. If so, he would reprocess each disturbance that surfaces using the standard EMDR procedure.

5   Visualize Entire Sequence of Events With Eyes Open
When the client has run the experience through and no distressing material comes up, have him run the experience coupling it with the positive cognition visualizing the entire sequence of the event one more time with his eyes open. Then initiate a long set of bilateral stimulation. The client is asked to scan the experience mentally and to give the "stop" signal when his processing has been completed.

6   Conclude With Body Scan
Once this open-eyed visualization has been completed, the body scan is done.

7   Process Present Stimuli, if Necessary
When reprocessing a present trigger, the client is instructed to run a movie of the desired response for coping with or encountering it in a similar situation in the future.

Caveats When Using Recent Events Protocol. There are several caveats (Shapiro, 2001) the clinician needs to keep in mind when administering the Recent Traumatic Events Protocol (see Table 3.9).

Table 3.9

CAVEATS ASSOCIATED WITH RECENT EVENTS PROTOCOL

■ The clinician must ensure that the timing for this intervention is adequate. Do not initiate this protocol if the client is still in shock, numb, or in a highly dissociative state.
■ The clinician may need to work on present distressing stimuli (e.g., startle response, reminders of the event, nightmares) that may emerge for a client after reprocessing the entire event.
■ Reprocessing of a recent event may take more than a few sessions. Be patient with the client if it does.
■ Distressing material from unresolved earlier events may surface with the same thematic issues (e.g., safety) as the recent event.

Adapted with permission of Guilford Press from Shapiro, F. (2001). Eye Movement Desensitization and Reprocessing: Basic Principles, Protocols, and Procedures. NY: Guilford Press.

How Do You Know When Its Use Is Appropriate? A common question regarding recent events is: "How recent is recent?" Or "How does a clinician know when a memory has consolidated or is consolidated enough to use the standard three-pronged approach?" There are two possibilities in answering this question. First, if a client is processing the worst part of a traumatic incident and other channels of association open up, the event may have been consolidated. Second, if the first memory reprocessed using the recent events protocol processes down to a "0" SUD, "7" VoC, and a clear body scan, it is likely that the memory has been consolidated. In either case, the past, present, and future prongs need to be processed.

Refer to Figure 3.8 for the illustrative example related to Case Example 3f – Patrick.

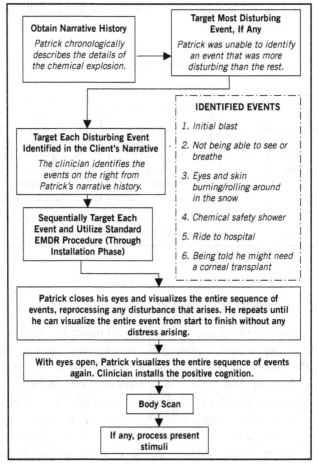

Figure 3.8 Recent traumatic events protocol.

Single-Incident Traumas

A client may present with a single traumatic event. When this occurs, the clinician will want to consider using the standard EMDR procedure and apply it to the following targets identified by Dr. Shapiro (2001) if they are available: (a) the memory (or image) associated with a traumatic event; (b) a flashback scene the client has experienced; (c) a recurring dream or nightmare or the most disturbing or traumatic scene in the dream; and (d) stimuli that trigger the client in the present.

With single-event traumas, there are some targeting possibilities the clinician may want to consider. For instance, are there historical linkages that need to be elicited? Or, are there additional related events associated to the traumatic event (Shapiro, 2009)? If possible, thorough questioning during the intake interview may help to elicit this information. See Figure 3.9 for information that may be needed to fully reprocess a single incident trauma.

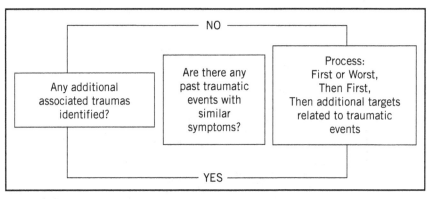

Figure 3.9 Single incident targeting sequence.

Targeting Sequence Plans

Targeting sequence plans may be structured using Dr. Shapiro's (2009) *standard targeting sequence* plan applying the three-pronged approach. However, the plan may also be structured around recent trauma, single-incident trauma, and presenting problems defined by negative and positive cognitions, problem behavior, disturbing affect or body sensation, and external stimuli, such as odor, touch, experience, situation, perpetrator, or anniversary date. A more comprehensive plan may revolve around a complex presentation (e.g., client with an Axis II diagnosis).

Targeting sequence plans may be generated using chronological time lines and genograms or by eliciting the top 10 traumas identified by a client during the history-taking and treatment planning phase. In any case, the incident/event selected for targeting in the assessment phase comes from some version or variety of the targeting sequence plan suggested by Dr. Shapiro.

It is during the initial intake interview that the clinician begins noting and recording the past, present, and future (i.e., anticipated) negative and positive incidents/events reported by the client. It is from this collection of recorded events that the clinician may develop a targeting sequence plan utilizing the three-pronged format. It is here that the clinician can uncover past experiences that resonate with the presenting problem, beginning with the touchstone event (if any), past events, present triggers, and future desired outcomes.

SUMMARY STATEMENTS

1 An assessment for past, present, and future is made with all types of client presentations.
2 Targets are more concrete versus abstract, more specific than general.
3 Negative and positive cognitions do not need to be perfectly parallel. However, they focus on the presenting issue and address the same thematic schema.
4 Write down as much as possible during the assessment phase. It is important to be able to reflect accurately what the client has said.

4 Building Blocks of EMDR

EMDR IS A THREE-PRONGED APPROACH

In the client history-taking phase of Eye Movement Desensitization and Reprocessing (EMDR), the clinician begins the process of identifying past disturbances/traumatic experiences, present triggers, and anticipated future occurrences or situations. These are the true building blocks of EMDR. A client's success with EMDR relies on a balanced focus on all three prongs of the EMDR protocol and the order of processing in which they are accessed and reprocessed. It is on these blocks—past, present, future—that the momentum and treatment effects can build and the healing process can be completed.

When new to EMDR, it is easy to overlook the second two prongs, especially the third. Clinicians may become accustomed to focusing on a client's past for answers to what is happening in the present and what is feared in the present but do not always get an opportunity to process the final prong. For instance, some EMDR clients feel so good after having resolved some of their past issues and present triggers that they terminate therapy prematurely.

As the three prongs of EMDR are reviewed, return the focus to assessing appropriate targets and outcomes in relationship to past, present, and future. An understanding of this relationship is important to the construction of an EMDR treatment planning guide (i.e., assessment sheet, session notes, processing/follow-up notes, reevaluation) suggested by Dr. Shapiro (2006) to ensure the successful accomplishment of overall treatment goals.

Building Blocks of EMDR: Past, Present, and Future

A client who has experienced a single traumatic event can usually be treated by targeting the disturbance/trauma-causing memory and additional incidents related to the primary event (e.g., car accident and related traumas: the car catching on fire while trapped in the car; being told she would never walk again; the long, difficult recovery). Clients who present with multiple issues and/or symptom presentations or with complex presentations of traumatic life events or extreme stress over a prolonged period of time will require a more comprehensive treatment approach. When a client's history is traumatically complex, it is important to identify and treat these three areas of concern: touchstone memories, present triggers, and future alternative behaviors. Whether targeting single or multiple traumatic events, it is necessary to sequentially target the traumatic event(s) and present triggers that have manifested as a result and work on skills a client needs to be more successful or comfortable in the future (see Figure 4.1).

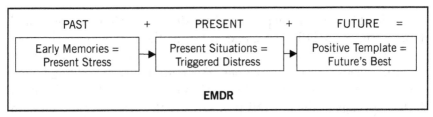

Figure 4.1 Three-stage protocol: Building blocks of EMDR.

In the first prong of EMDR treatment, the clinician and client work together to reprocess incidents associated with the presenting issue and, if present, the early and critical touchstone memories (i.e., crucial memories that set the foundation for a client's current disturbance). The second prong is much like the first in that the clinician and client focus on reprocessing present triggers (e.g., people, circumstances, places, or other forms of stimuli that activate disturbing reactions or responses). The third prong focuses on alternative behaviors to aid the client in meeting his future therapeutic goals. Although past incidents, present triggers, and future outcomes associated with the presenting issue are initially identified in the assessment phase, they may also emerge anywhere throughout the eight phases (e.g., emergence of blocking beliefs or feeder memories, during reprocessing, between sessions). Figure 4.2 identifies the targeting sequence suggested by Dr. Shapiro (2008) and will serve as the targeting model for this Primer.

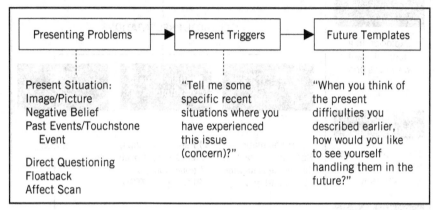

Figure 4.2 Three-stage protocol: Targeting sequence model.

CLINICAL PRESENTATION POSSIBILITIES

Clients initially present to therapy with specific issues, problems, and disturbing events that are accompanied by a constellation of symptoms (i.e., cognitive, affective, somatic, and behavioral). The presenting issue can be driven by associated negative cognitions (NC), such as, "I am unsafe," or "I am different (don't belong)." It may be defined by a problem behavior or a self-destructive pattern, negative affect (e.g., overwhelming sadness), or physical sensation (e.g., unexplained chronic headaches). Or it may be activated by external stimuli, such as touch (e.g., brushing up against something or someone), odors (e.g., the smell of aftershave), a particular experience (e.g., driving past an intersection where a bad accident occurred), or an anniversary date (e.g., the death of a loved one; Shapiro, 2001, 2008).

A pictorial conceptualization of the types of EMDR presenting issues identified by Dr. Shapiro (2001, 2008) and how they fit the three-pronged targeting and reprocessing schema developed as a result can be found in Figure 4.3. As the figure demonstrates, there are several types of traumas with which a client can present. And clients do not always present with a trauma. They more often come in with symptomology, such as depression, anxiety, or panic attacks.

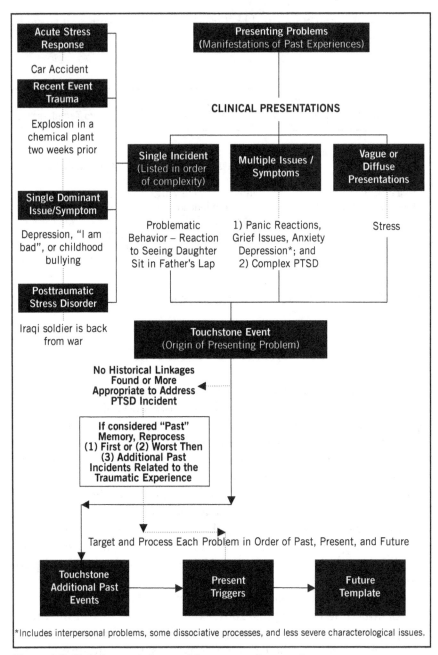

Figure 4.3 Clinical presentations and three-pronged approach.

Here are some types of traumas and other issues with which clients may initially present:

Single-Incident Presentations (Shapiro, 2009)

Acute Stress Response (i.e., "fight or flight"). An acute traumatic event that has happened within the past few days and has caused a set of symptoms directly attributed to the event.

Example: Kelly was working as a cashier at a fast food restaurant when a man wearing a ski mask walked up to the counter, pulled out a revolver, pointed it at her, and shouted angrily, "Give me all the money in the drawers or I will shoot you." Three days after the event, Kelly came to therapy complaining of fatigue, irritability, and sleeplessness. She had frequent nightmares of the event and found it increasingly difficult to concentrate.

Posttraumatic Stress Disorder (PTSD). The client has experienced a life-threatening event or series of events that meet diagnostic criteria for PTSD outlined in the *Diagnostic and Statistical Manual of Mental Disorders (DSM-TR-IV)* and has experienced hyperarousal, intrusions, and/or avoidance of stimuli that trigger negative symptoms with possible origins in early childhood incidents of neglect and/or abuse. Cases of simple PTSD involve single-event traumas or one cluster of similar events. The symptoms of simple PTSD stem from the occurrence of a critical event. The clinician needs to identify the incident, including earlier contributing events, if any, the triggers, including current manifestations (e.g., nightmares, flashbacks, reoccurring dreams), and future templates.

Example: A young woman witnessed a fatal car–pedestrian accident while driving on the interstate on her way to work. The victim was a pedestrian who was killed instantly when the speeding car that hit her did not stop. Nine months later, the woman is still finding it more and more difficult to drive on the interstate. She becomes extremely tense and anxious while driving on more than two-lane highways, has experienced several full-blown panic attacks while driving in high-speed interstate traffic, and has had difficulty getting up on the mornings she has to go to work. With regard to a prior traumatic history, the client's past is unremarkable. In the case of this tragic incident, the accident itself is the touchstone event and was the first to be targeted and reprocessed in the EMDR sessions that followed.

Recent Event Trauma. A recent traumatic event is when "the memory has not had sufficient time to consolidate into an integrated whole" in terms of information processing (Shapiro, 2001). For recent events, the clinician will use the EMDR protocol for recent traumatic events. A recent event is one that has occurred within a 2- to 3-month period.

Example: Within 3 months of his accident, Patrick came to therapy after being seriously injured in an explosion at the chemical plant storage facility where he worked. He continues to experience flashbacks, intrusive thoughts and nightmares, anxiety, sleeplessness, and fatigue. He remains in a constant state of hypervigilance and experiences frequent bouts of anxiety. A complete transcript of Patrick's EMDR recent traumatic event session can be found in chapter 3 under Recent Traumatic Events and Single-Incident Traumas.

Single Dominant Issue/Symptom. An event or series of events may also be categorized as a single incident if there is a dominant theme or issue organized around a single symptom. These types of events may arise as a result of a small "t" event experienced in early childhood.

Example: Jesse was on the swim team at his high school. He had a strong sense of competitiveness and had won major swim competitions in prior years. This year, he was beginning to fall way below the mark in competitions. The clinician learned that Jesse's swim coach was aggressive and often hurled verbal insults (e.g., "You're stupid." "You're fat." "You will never measure up."). Jesse began to exhibit pervasive anxiety and issues of self-doubt. Other possible single presenting symptoms in this case could be a belief of "I am no good," having frequent leg cramps, or perfectionist behavior in all areas of his life.

Multiple Issues/Symptoms Presentations (Shapiro, 2009)

Multiple Issues/Symptoms. It is not uncommon for a client to seek out therapy to overcome more than one presenting problem and/or symptom.

Example: A client presented with both work-related difficulties and grief issues, citing ongoing symptoms of depression, anxiety, and frequent panic reactions. His wife had died 3 years earlier with a brain aneurysm. Because of the stressful nature of his high-profile job and his immediate need to care for his three small children, his focus went straight from the funeral to full speed ahead in getting his life together.

As his children got older and the demands of his job got larger, the client began to experience symptoms of anxiety and depression on a regular basis. His boss put him on notice for his absenteeism, being late for work and leaving early, and missing deadlines and meetings. In this case, numerous incidents have caused his pathology, but he does not meet the full diagnostic criteria for PTSD.

Complex PTSD. Complex PTSD is chacteractized by: (a) a complex presentation of traumatic life events; (b) over an extended period of time; and (c) often presenting with symptoms of a severe personality disorder and/or dissociation.

Example: Sandra's mother died when she was 5. Her abusive father was left to care for their four young children. He sexually abused and beat Sandra if she was not totally submissive and obedient from the time her mother died until she ran away from home at the age of 17. She was used as replacement for his deceased wife and told it was her job because she was the oldest female. She became highly dissociative.

Vague or Diffuse Presentations

A client may present who appears to have a perfect life yet feels joyless and unfulfilled and does not know why. When the clinician asks such a client with this type of traumatic presentation about past traumas, he may answer, "I can't think of anything." This is what is called a vague or diffuse presentation.

In this case, the clinician needs to strategically tease out potential targets. One way to find out the "why" of this kind of client's condition is to use the Socratic method (see chapter 5). "What would you like to be doing in 5 years? What would you like to be doing by the end of the year? What keeps that from happening?" If nothing significant arises out of this line of questioning, the clinician may want to consider a more extensive look into the client's developmental history and/or a deeper exploration of his individual and family belief systems. A thorough accounting of his medical history and a depression screen would also be in order.

The presenting problems in each type of case (single-incident trauma, vague or diffuse, and the comprehensive presentations—single and multiple) need to be processed in order of the past events (touchstone event and all additional past events), present triggers, and future template.

The types of a client's possible presenting issues have been limited in this Primer to those covered in the EMDR Weekend 1 and 2 trainings.

Other possibilities for presentation types may be of a relational nature (e.g., divorce or sibling rivalry), ongoing stressful events, someone who is in imminent danger (e.g., being stalked), or other complex presentations.

FIRST PRONG: EARLIER MEMORIES/ TOUCHSTONE EVENTS

Touchstone Event

A touchstone event is synonymous with the earliest memory the client can remember that created the foundation for a client's present dysfunction or pathology. It usually is identified at the beginning of the assessment phase. In some cases, touchstone events may not be apparent in the assessment phase. They may emerge spontaneously during processing or may be revealed through a clinician's use of strategies for blocked processing or other interventions, such as direct questioning, floatback technique, and affect scan. And, with some cases, there are no touchstone events.

The touchstone event brings home the fact that our presenting problems are often linked to traumatic events in the past (i.e., "the past is present"; Shapiro, 2008). With the exception of clients who present with intense, recent trauma or those who may not be able to tolerate going back to a painful touchstone event (e.g., a police officer losing his partner in the line of duty), the client's touchstone event is generally identified and reprocessed first.

Past events may also be recent events or events that happened in childhood. Note that the symptoms presented by the client are not always precipitated by events in the past. There are cases where the presenting issue is the issue and the target; that is, there is no earlier touchstone event. This may be true in relational issues, ongoing stressful events, or in recent traumatic events.

A simplified example of uncovering the touchstone event in an EMDR-directed session begins with the client presenting a problem (i.e., complaint, issue, or concern) on which he would like to work. Maybe the client is having a difficult time saying "no" or handling stress in the workplace. Perhaps he is experiencing relationship issues or has anxiety attacks in elevators. In an effort to uncover more information about the presenting issue, the clinician either asks the client explicitly if he can relate some specific and recent situations or events where he experienced his particular concern or remembers the first time he encountered the problem. If not forthcoming, the clinician may need to obtain the information implicitly through intensive history taking.

In the case of a client who has difficulty saying "no," the clinician might ask, "Tell me about some recent situations where you have experienced that issue." A summary of the client's possible answers can be found below:

- Volunteering to take on extra work at the office even when she knows she already has more work than she can handle.
- Agreeing to take care of her sister's three dogs for a week when she can't find time to adequately care for her own two dogs.
- Being the only one of five siblings who visits her mother twice a week and does her grocery shopping before she does her own.

The client may have an entire laundry list of events that fits the criteria of the presenting issue. In this case, the clinician needs to sort out which incident is most disturbing and representative of the issue (i.e., "Which is the most disturbing incident that represents your issue?"). "My boss knew I would never say, 'No,' to his personal requests. He never once stopped to think about my feelings and what I thought about what he was asking." This statement exemplified her presenting issue and became the focus of her first target. Other events needed to be targeted; however, this was deemed an effective starting point.

Strategies for Accessing the Touchstone Memory

Direct questioning, the floatback technique, and the affect scan can be utilized to access the touchstone event. As an organizing technique, it is probably most useful for the beginning EMDR clinician to utilize these tools in the order presented here.

Direct Questioning. During the history-taking process, the clinician attempts to identify the last time a client remembers experiencing the current difficulty that represents the presenting issue (e.g., her boss asked her to pick up his laundry yesterday, and she was unable to say "no."). Once a recent incident is identified, the clinician attempts to elicit an image and an associated NC (e.g., "I am insignificant."). Through direct questioning, the clinician assists the client in identifying past events where the client felt or believed something similar. The earlier the event, the better (e.g., somewhere in the formative years of the client's life—from birth to 10 years). Below are some questions clinicians might ask to elicit this information:

- When was the first time you remember feeling (thinking, reacting) that way?
- When was the first time you heard (or learned) "I am insignificant?"
- What incidents come to mind from childhood or adolescence?

Once the earliest event has been identified, the clinician can help the client identify the image and NC that go with it.

Floatback Technique. If the client is unable to identify the touchstone through direct questioning, the clinician's next option is to use the floatback technique developed by William Zangwill (Browning, 1999; Young, Zangwill, & Behary, 2002) to elicit the past event that is responsible for the client's current dysfunction. The floatback is an imagery exercise that acts as a bridge to earlier dysfunctional memories. Use the floatback technique:

- If the NC is clear (i.e., "I am insignificant") and is identified as a relevant and important part of the client's presenting issue (i.e., inability to say "No").
- When the present event is not fully accessible.
- If the NC is unclear or difficult to access. You can still implement the floatback technique to access the touchstone event responsible for the client's current dysfunction by using the client's current emotions or physical sensations as a bridge to the past.

If the NC is clear, the clinician instructs the client to focus on the earliest identified memory up to this point, the NC, and emotions associated with the event by saying, "Float back to the earliest time when you experienced these." Or, if the client cannot easily focus, consider saying, "Now, bring up that negative <u>belief</u> (i.e., 'I am insignificant.') and the <u>emotions</u> you are <u>feeling</u> <u>now</u> and let your mind <u>float</u> <u>back</u> to the earliest time when you may have felt this way and just notice what comes to mind."

Affect Scan. A hypnotherapeutic technique called an affect bridge was developed by Watkins (1971). This is similar to what we use in EMDR when we ask a client, "When was the first time you experienced this emotion?" In either case, the client is asked to focus on the most recent memory of an event as a starting point for floating back into time through similar memories to find the original memory or cause of the client's presenting problem/issue. The affect scan (Shapiro, 1995: independently developed and without the hypnotic/reliving component contained in Watkins & Watkins, 1971) is probably the easiest and quickest way to get to the touchstone event and can be the most powerful. However, it may elicit higher levels of emotion and body sensation that the client may not be prepared to experience. Thus, the floatback technique may be preferred with clients who have a higher level of negative affect.

"Bring up that experience (i.e., the <u>most recent memory</u> identified in the floatback, the <u>emotions</u>, and the <u>sensations</u> that you are having now, and allow yourself to <u>scan</u> <u>back</u> for the earliest time you experienced something similar."

If nothing emerges, the clinician may want to explore family of origin issues with the client by inquiring, "Do you remember feeling like this in your family when you were young?" Or, "As you were growing up in school or in the neighborhood, do you remember similar things happening?" It is important not to limit exploration of the touchstone event to her family of origin. The disturbing event may have happened outside the familial circle (e.g., molestation by a neighbor, bullying on the playground).

It is not unusual for a client to come to therapy to work specifically on an early pivotal experience that happens to be the touchstone event. There are cases in which a client cannot identify an earlier memory and weeks later it may (i.e., most likely, but not always) spontaneously emerge. Touchstone events are usually traumatic events that occur in a client's formative years from birth to age 10. It is best to find the earliest possible memory for reprocessing because it is identified as the event that laid the foundation for the client's current problem. Exceptions to this may be: (a) clients who present with intense, recent trauma (e.g., the client may not be able to tolerate going back to the touchstone event [i.e., fireman losing a friend in a fire]); or (b) returning military personnel involved in combat and survivors of an acute recent trauma, such as first responders and medical emergency personnel (Shapiro, 2008).

These techniques are used with appropriate but not without caution as they have a tendency to increase clients' current levels of distress because they are getting in touch with the emotional and physical sensations associated with the disturbing material. In all cases, it is important to ensure that clients are able to tolerate whatever comes up and also feel that the therapeutic relationship is safe.

In the case below, the client's presenting issue will be used to elicit the touchstone event through use of the direct questioning, floatback, and affect scan techniques.

CASE EXAMPLE 4A: BETTY

Betty, a 55-year-old retiree, had been suffering with depression and low self-esteem after a long, drawn out divorce from her husband of 36 years. She had great success with EMDR in the past, and she was determined to use it again to help with current relationship issues.

Even though she had a rough marriage and an even tougher divorce, Betty wanted to be in a loving relationship. She thought it was a possibility after she had undergone the empowering effects of EMDR. Six months before coming back to therapy, Betty had met Richard, a wonderful man who was warm, compassionate, smart, and independent. She was comfortable with herself in this relationship.

Betty came into the session upset over an incident involving Richard. Both maintained separate residences and spent time away from each other with their own children and other family members. So, Betty had looked forward to spending time with him over the entire Labor Day weekend. When her companion left on Sunday morning instead of that night, she was devastated and could not understand why. She cried the entire day and was upset with herself.

This case will be utilized to demonstrate the use of direct questioning, floatback, and affect scan in identifying Betty's touchstone event.

Target: Richard left rather than spend the day with me.
Negative Cognition (NC): I am unimportant.
Positive Cognition (PC): I am important.
Emotions: Loneliness, sadness
Body: Throat, stomach

Identifying the touchstone through direct questioning. Because of Betty's previous history in therapy, the clinician knew that this was not an isolated event and that there was an inherent relationship pattern that had been with Betty for most of her life. The clinician wanted to identify the earliest event that established the foundation for her current symptoms.

Here is how the *direct questioning* went:

Clinician: Are there earlier times in your life when you thought you were unimportant?

Betty: Yes, I remember in college my dorm mates often excluded me from social events.

Clinician: Can you think of any other times when you thought you were unimportant?

Betty: Yes, my father was rather distant. He never had much to say or do with me. Once he just looked at me and grunted.

Clinician: As you focus on that experience and the negative thoughts, are there any childhood memories that come up?

Betty: I remember waking up from an afternoon nap. I had had a nightmare. I was terribly afraid, so I ran to find my mom. I said, "Mommy, mommy. Hold me. I'm scared." My mother just looked at me and said, "Not now. I don't have time for you right now, little missy."

If a touchstone had not been identified using direct questioning, the clinician may consider using the floatback technique.

Identifying the Touchstone Event Using Floatback. *When implementing the floatback technique, the clinician is asked to repeat the last direct question used above for the direct questioning technique.*

Clinician: As you focus on that experience and the negative thoughts, are there any childhood memories that come up?

Betty: *No, I can't think of anything.*

Clinician: *Okay, Now, bring up that negative belief (i.e., 'I am unimportant') and the emotions you are feeling now and let your mind float back to the earliest time when you may have felt this way and just notice what comes to mind.*

Betty: I remember waking up from an afternoon nap. I had had a nightmare. I was terribly afraid, so I ran to find my mom. I said, "Mommy, mommy. Hold me. I'm scared." My mother just looked at me and said, "Not now. I don't have time for you right now, little missy."

If, again, Betty had been unable to access an earlier or touchstone memory, the clinician could also explore family of origin issues at this point by asking, "Any incidents from your family of origin where the negative thought 'I am unimportant' come to mind?"

If a touchstone had not been identified using the floatback technique, the clinician may consider utilizing the affect scan.

Identifying the Touchstone Event Using Affect Scan. If the client is still unable to identify an earlier memory, utilize the affect scan by incorporating the earliest memory already identified from the floatback technique. The affect scan can be used to access the touchstone event based on her emotional and physical sensations. Be sure to start by using the client's most recent memory identified in the floatback.

Clinician: *Bring up that experience (i.e., the most recent memory identified in the floatback), the emotions, and the sensations that you are having now, and allow yourself to <u>scan back</u> for the earliest time you experienced something similar.*

Betty: I remember waking up from an afternoon nap. I had had a nightmare. I was terribly afraid, so I ran to find my mom. I said, "Mommy, mommy. Hold me. I'm scared." My mother just looked at me and said, "Not now. I don't have time for you right now, little missy."

Note that direct questioning was employed first to see if Betty could recall an earlier time in her life when she experienced similar thoughts of "I am unimportant." It was only after it was determined that she could not that the floatback technique was utilized. Remember, floatback and affect scan may occasionally cause the client to experience high levels of emotions and body sensations that they might not be able to tolerate at the time. Use these two techniques cautiously.

It is unnecessary to have a NC to identify touchstone memories. If it cannot be accessed, you can use the affect scan "to use the sensations as a bridge to the past" (Shapiro, 2006).

If appropriate, identify and reprocess the touchstone memory before continuing on with the processing of present triggers and future situations when using either direct questioning, floatback or the affect scan (Note: There is not always a touchstone memory to reprocess). Once the memory has been accessed, use the procedural steps to complete the assessment using this identified earliest memory for processing (see Figure 4.4).

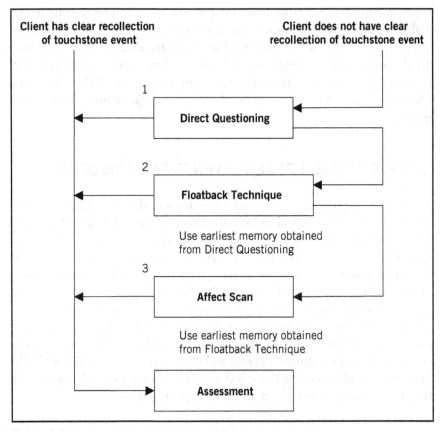

Figure 4.4 Past event: Strategies for identifying touchstone event.

When the touchstone event and all the past events have been identified using the methods described above, they need to be targeted and reprocessed before continuing to the next prong. Once completed, the clinician then progresses to targeting and reprocessing the client's present triggers and future templates.

Touchstone Revisited

A greater emphasis is being placed on identifying and targeting a touchstone event before reprocessing other memories that arise. The discussion above follows this new training evolution. However, the training focus in no way negates the importance of dealing with present issues as they arise. Be cautious about being overzealous in looking for these touchstone events. There may not be one, or it is not significant to utilize effectively. Sometimes, an orange is an orange. The clinician needs to be aware of the clinical choices (or trauma presentations listed above) in order to determine whether a client's current focus needs to be on the present or the past. The appropriateness of the clinician's choice will be apparent in light of the client's presenting issues and history.

SECOND PRONG: PRESENT EVENTS AND TRIGGERS

The second step of the three-pronged protocol is identifying and processing the present events and situations that continue to cause disturbance for the client. In other words, identify all recent events or situations that may have caused the client's current symptomology (i.e., negative emotions, physical sensations, beliefs, or behaviors) that spontaneously emerge. Contributory earlier memories that were processed may be reassessed along with present stimuli. These current situations are generally obtained during the initial or early clinical intake interviews with the client. The clinician will attempt to identify and have the client reprocess conditional responses, events, and other stimuli associated with the presenting problem using the standard EMDR protocol and ensure that they have been processed prior to moving to the third stage.

What to Look Out For

When processing present disturbances, the clinician also attends to the following:

1   *Ecological validity*: Is the level of disturbance appropriate under the client's circumstances? For example, a client states that she cannot reach a "0" or "1" on the Subjective Units of Disturbance (SUD) scale by saying, "I don't ever want to forget that this happened." This could refer to a client who is a recent victim of domestic abuse. She has physically left the marital residence, but her husband currently lives in the community (i.e., she is still in imminent danger and does not ever want to forget and let her guard down). It would not be appropriate for her SUD level to be a "0" because she has to be on her guard and attend to her safety.

2 *Blocking beliefs*: Is there an inappropriate belief existent in the current disturbance? In the example of the domestic violence case above, she is unable to reach a "0" on the SUD scale because of the emerging belief "I can't let this go since I am not worthy enough to feel safe."

3 *Peelback memories*: Did an earlier associated memory emerge? Even when targeting an obvious critical incident in the present, such as a rape, associations to earlier experiences may surface.

4 *Feeder memories*: Is an earlier memory feeding the underlying disturbance identified in a nonchildhood target? For instance, a client is processing his most recent disturbing incident of being stuck in an elevator when a memory of being trapped in a closet that was being held shut by his older brother emerges. This is a memory that was made available during the history-taking phase.

Comprehensive history taking prior to EMDR processing is helpful in identifying these types of beliefs and memories and curtailing stalled processing later on. If they do arise, use of the floatback technique or the affect scan can help identify the earlier memories.

To the benefit of the client, many of the triggers present at the beginning of EMDR will no longer exist once the touchstone events have been thoroughly identified and reprocessed. Current events or situations that previously induced a high level of disturbance will no longer cause the symptoms reported by the client in the past. The negative behaviors, emotions, sensations, and thoughts associated with the earlier events may have been flushed out and no longer accessible. The client's present distress may have been resolved, and trauma can now be considered a learning experience, rather than something to be looked on with dread.

How Can Triggers Remain Active After So Much Processing?

There are at least three reasons why some triggers may be active after all past events have been reprocessed and a complete generalization did not result:

1 *Because of second-order conditioning.* Second-order conditioning refers to a conditioned stress response created as a result of past distress being repeated in the presence of certain situations. In the case of a process phobia called cyberphobia (i.e., fear of computers or working on a computer), for example, there could be additional

stimuli that need to be processed separately because of unrelated circumstances or events that may trigger the fear. In the case of cyberphobia, a client may become frightened upon hearing that his young child is learning to use the computer in school, his wife has signed up for a computer class to learn word processing, or his older daughter is begging for a laptop of her own.

2 *Fed by information left over from earlier events.* This information was not processed because every channel of association may not have opened up.

3 *Recent situations may have occurred where the emotions and perceptions were different than the earlier event.* These triggers are freshly charged by recent events and have been stored in memory along with other emotions and perceptions that are different from what was originally stored.

These triggers will need to be accessed and fully reprocessed before continuing forward with the third stage. The clinician will need to direct the client in assessing recent events that might have caused the distress and evaluate together whether it is still disturbing or not. One of the ways the clinician can accomplish this is by asking the client, "Bring up the last time you remember feeling/behaving (fill in the blank)." "What do you get?"

If the disturbance cannot be eliminated, the clinician will perform a separate assessment and reprocess each event identified. The recent event or trigger will be reprocessed until the SUD = 0 and the Validity of Cognition (VoC) = 7. A future template is then installed for each trigger by imagining an encounter with the situation sometime in the future or reprocessing anticipatory anxieties.

CASE EXAMPLE 4B: PETER

Peter, a proud military person who served his country voluntarily and honorably, was back from his second tour of duty in the war with Iraq. His wife and he presented initially for couples counseling, but it quickly became clear that it was Peter who needed individual work. All efforts at marital counseling were suspended while Peter came to therapy to work on individual issues. Peter worked for weeks on both early childhood and war experiences to the point where he was navigating his civilian world more than just adequately. He was eating and sleeping better, his irritability had almost completely abated, and his marriage was also beginning to flourish again.

Certain things still triggered him, however, such as loud noises, gun shots, flashes of light of any kind, and construction zones. With these in mind, the clinician and Peter set out to settle his startle responses to these external triggers. Below is Peter's session:

Target: Peter lives in hunting country and had been bird hunting many times before the war without much attention to the sounds of guns shooting around him. "Bird shot," he said, "is so heavy that it does not travel far nor can it do much damage at large distances." *While he was in therapy, he happened to go hunting with his friends.* During the hunt, someone fired in his general direction—not an uncommon event—and the shot exploded yards before him. "I hit the ground," he said. "I thought I was going to die." The worst part was the sound of the bird shot coming toward him.

NC: I'm in danger.
PC: It's over. I'm safe now.
VoC: 2
Emotions: Anger, fear, irritation
SUD: 8
Body: Chest

Clinician: Throughout the EMDR process today, I will be asking you to tell me what you are experiencing. Tell me, as clearly as possible, what comes into your mind. Sometimes things will change, and sometimes they won't. There are no "supposed to's." Just let whatever happens, happen. Remember your stop signal and your calm (or safe) place when you need them. (Pause) Focus on the original incident, those words, "I'm in danger" and where you feel it in your body. Just let it go wherever it goes. (Set of eye movements) Let it go. Take a deep breath. (Pause) What comes up for you <u>now</u>?
Peter: I still feel it in my chest.
Clinician: Go with that. (Set of eye movements) Let it go. Take a deep breath. (Pause) What's happening <u>now</u>?
Peter: No change. I feel it in my chest.
Clinician: Go with that. (Set of eye movements) Let it go. Take a deep breath. (Pause) What are you noticing <u>now</u>?
Peter: It has moved to my stomach.
Clinician: Go with that. (Set of eye movements) Let it go. Take a deep breath. (Pause) What are you noticing <u>now</u>?

Peter: It feels like it is moving just above my legs.

Clinician: Go with that. (Set of eye movements) Let it go. Take a deep breath. (Pause) What's happening <u>now</u>?

Peter: I'm feeling pretty good.

Clinician: Go with that. (Set of eye movements) Let it go. Take a deep breath. (Pause) What do you get <u>now</u>?

Peter: It's about the same.

Clinician: Go with that. (Set of eye movements) Let it go. Take a deep breath. (Pause) What are you getting <u>now</u>?

Peter: I'm safe now. It's over.

Clinician: Go with that. (Set of eye movements) Let it go. Take a deep breath. (Pause) What are you noticing <u>now</u>?

Peter: It's the same.

Clinician: When you go back to the <u>original</u> event (or incident), what are you getting <u>now</u>?

(Reminder: Original event [or incident]—the sound of the bird shot coming toward him)

Peter: I'm feeling real relaxed.

Clinician: Go with that. (Set of eye movements) Let it go. Take a deep breath. (Pause) What comes up for you <u>now</u>?

Peter: I'm not feeling anything.

Clinician: What does "I'm not feeling anything" mean?

The clinician is asking this question because she is unclear about what is happening. This could be a sign of dissociation, or it could represent completed reprocessing.

Peter: I feel kind of numb.

Clinician: Go with that. (Set of eye movements) Let it go. Take a deep breath. (Pause) What are you noticing <u>now</u>?

Peter: I am getting tingly all over.

Clinician: Notice that. (Set of eye movements) Let it go. Take a deep breath. (Pause) What are you noticing <u>now</u>?

Peter: There's something in my head. I don't know what it is. It's not a headache. It's numbness. I can't describe it. I don't hurt. I can just feel something going on.

Clinician: Go with that. (Set of eye movements) You're doing fine. Let it go. Take a deep breath. (Pause) What are you getting <u>now</u>?

Peter: Nothing.

Clinician: What does "nothing" mean?

Peter: I feel good. Relaxed. Calm.

Clinician: Go with that. (Set of eye movements) Good. Good. Let it go. Take a deep breath. (Pause) What are you getting <u>now</u>?

Peter: It's the same. I feel good. Still relaxed. Still good.

Clinician: When you go back to the <u>original</u> event (or incident), what are you getting <u>now</u>?

Peter: It's over. I am safe.

Clinician: Go with that. (Set of eye movements) Good. Good. Let it go. Take a deep breath. (Pause) What are you noticing <u>now</u>?

Peter: I feel safe.

Clinician: When you think of the original event (or incident, issue), on a scale from 0 to 10, where "0" is neutral or no disturbance and "10" is the worst disturbance you can imagine, how disturbing is the event (or incident, issue) to you now?

Peter: One.

Clinician: What keeps it from being a zero?

When a blocking belief emerges, it is reprocessed with bilateral stimulation until SUD = 0 or VoC = 7. The clinician also needs to consider any new skills needed by the client and ecological validity when dealing with blocking beliefs.

Peter: My knowing that I'm going to get mad if it happens again. My believing that my body will react.

Clinician: Go with that. (Set of eye movements) Let it go. Take a deep breath. (Pause) What's happening <u>now</u>?

Peter: I'm really relaxed.

Clinician: Go with that. (Set of eye movements) Let it go. Take a deep breath. (Pause) What are you noticing <u>now</u>?

Peter: I am still relaxed.

Remember that one criterion for returning to target is for the client to provide at least two neutral or positive responses.

Clinician: Focus on the <u>original</u> incident and tell me what comes up. What comes up for you <u>now</u>?

(Reminder: Original event [or incident]—the sound of the bird shot coming toward him)

Peter: Nothing.

Clinician: Go with that. (Set of eye movements) Let it go. Take a deep breath. (Pause) What's happening <u>now</u>?

Peter: I am as relaxed as I have ever been.

Clinician: When you think of the <u>original</u> event (or incident, issue), on a scale from 0 to 10, where "0" is neutral or no disturbance and "10" is the worst disturbance you can imagine, how disturbing is the event (or incident, issue) to you <u>now</u>?

Peter: Zero.

Clinician: Go with that. (Set of eye movements) Good. Let it go. Take a deep breath. (Pause) How disturbing does it <u>feel</u> <u>now</u>?

Peter: Zero still.

Clinician: Focus on the <u>original</u> incident. Do those words, "It's over. I'm safe now" still fit, or is there another positive statement you feel would be more suitable?

Peter: Yeah. It's over. I am safe now.

Clinician: When you think of the event (or incident), how <u>true</u> do those words, "It's over. I'm safe now," feel to you <u>now</u> on a scale from 1 to 7, where "1" <u>feels</u> completely false and "7" <u>feels</u> completely true?

Peter: Seven.

Clinician: Think of the event (or incident) and hold it together with the words, "It's over. I'm safe now". (Set of eye movements) Let it go. Take a deep breath. (Pause) On a scale of 1 to 7, how true do those words, "It's over. I'm safe now," feel to you when you think of the <u>original</u> event (or incident)?

Peter: It's still a "7." I feel relieved.

Clinician: Close your eyes and focus on the <u>original</u> incident and those words, "It's over. I'm safe now." Scan your body from head to toe for physical discomfort. If you feel anything, let me know.

(Reminder: Original event [or incident]—the sound of the bird shot coming toward him)

Peter: It's a void. Relief. It's like I kicked something out. There is space for something else now.

Clinician: Go with that. (Set of eye movements) You're doing fine. Let it go. Take a deep breath. (Pause) What are you getting <u>now</u>?

Peter: Nothing.

Clinician: Peter, what does "nothing" mean?

Peter: I'm good. I feel great.

Clinician: Go with that. (Set of eye movements) You're doing fine. Let it go. Take a deep breath. (Pause) What are you noticing <u>now</u>?

Peter: I'm good.

Clinician: The processing we have done today may continue after the session. You may or may not notice new insights, thoughts, memories, or dreams. If so, just notice what you are experiencing. Take a snapshot of what you are seeing, feeling, thinking, and any triggers, and keep a TICES (target = image, cognitions, emotions, and sensations) log. Then do a calm (or safe) place exercise to rid yourself of the disturbance. We can work on this new material next time. If you feel it is necessary, call me.

Peter came back the next week impressed with his progress. He stated that his startle response was "back to normal." He said, "I don't seem to be as jumpy as I was before. I'm home. I am happy, and I just want to get on with my life."

Present Triggers Subsumed by the Reprocessing of the Touchstone Event

As a client reprocesses triggers, other reported triggers may dissipate. There are times when a client's present triggers are cleared by simply reprocessing earlier or touchstone memories. So, when the clinician revisits the presenting problem, the triggers often no longer exist.

An example of this is Andrea, a client who experienced extreme fear whenever her boss asked to see her. "Whenever I stood before him, I felt like a 7-year-old who was in trouble. I never could shake the fear of it. The minute I would get an e-mail or a telephone call requesting my presence, I could immediately feel myself shrinking. By the time I got to his office, I was a mess. I just knew I had done something wrong. I had screwed up."

During the initial history-taking interview, the client shared with the clinician that, whenever she misbehaved at home, her mother always said, "Wait until your father gets home." Her dad never really talked to or played with her so, when he called for her, she knew she was in trouble. This was a global touchstone event. She could not recall one particular incident, because there were so many. They were similar in that she would shrink inside the second her dad called for her. She knew the reason he was summoning her could not be good and that consequences for her ill behavior would be worse.

After the original event (or incident) had been fully processed, the clinician went back to the event that brought her to counseling in the first place so that she could process the present triggers. It turned out to be no longer relevant, as it had been fully resolved by processing the touchstone events. The processing of the earlier events had turned the current difficulty into an important learning experience.

THIRD PRONG: FUTURE EVENTS AND FUTURE TEMPLATES

A future (or positive) template is utilized as a means of addressing avoidance, adaptation, and actualization within the EMDR process (Shapiro, 2001). The third prong of the approach focuses on a client's ability to identify and make choices and utilizes a protocol for developing a future, positive template that will help the client to incorporate appropriate future behaviors.

Goals of the Future Template

The goal of creating a future template is threefold: (a) to provide the client time to practice or rehearse a behavior before going out into the world; (b) to identify and reprocess residual or anticipatory anxiety; and (c) to develop an action plan or skill building for an actual event in the future. There are two types of future templates. The first is a skills building and imaginal rehearsal future template. The second deals with anticipatory anxiety. The ultimate outcome of the third prong is to assure that the client has assimilated new information that can translate to future successes.

Skills Building and Imaginal Rehearsal

For this type of future template, the clinician does not need to implement a full assessment of the target. He can start with simply having the client run an imaginal "movie" of the anticipated event in his mind. For example, if a client reprocessed memories involving a significant person or a significant situation in the past, he would be asked to run a movie of a future meeting with the person or future situations to see if further disturbances arise. If a disturbance does arise, it could be dealt with by several interventions (e.g., education, modeling of appropriate behaviors, assertiveness training, exploration of boundaries, and reprocessing of the disturbing material). If a client's disturbance is inappropriate, clusters of events are evaluated for unresolved issues. See Figure 4.5 for the steps to these two important processes.

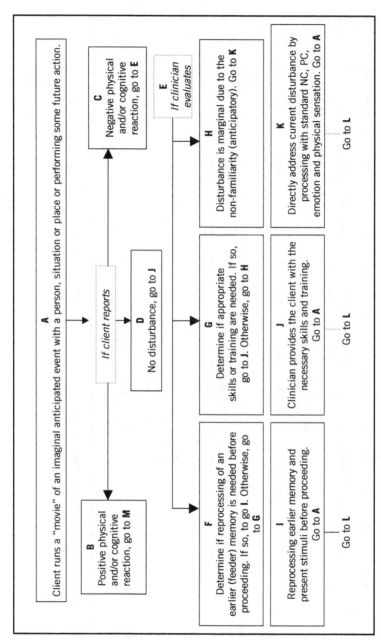

Figure 4.5 Future template flow chart: Skills building and imaginal rehearsal.

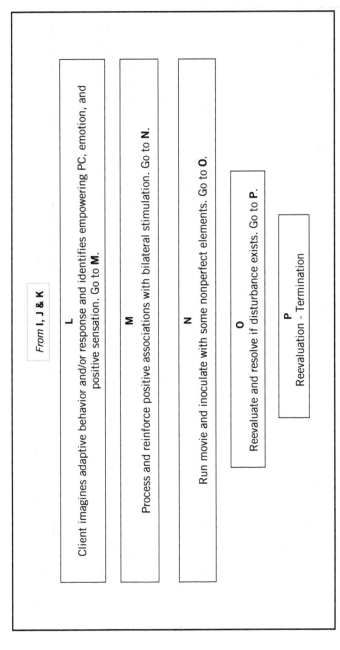

From **I, J & K**

L
Client imagines adaptive behavior and/or response and identifies empowering PC, emotion, and positive sensation. Go to **M**.

M
Process and reinforce positive associations with bilateral stimulation. Go to **N**.

N
Run movie and inoculate with some nonperfect elements. Go to **O**.

O
Reevaluate and resolve if disturbance exists. Go to **P**.

P
Reevaluation - Termination

Figure 4.5 Future template flow chart: Skills building and imaginal rehearsal. *(continued)*

Steps Needed Prior to Creating a Positive Template

Before a future template can be installed, it is necessary that the earlier memories that set the groundwork for a client's presenting problem/issue and present stimuli that elicit dysfunctional material be successfully reprocessed and education and/or skills training (e.g., assertiveness training or social customs and norms awareness) be initiated. In addition, a full exploration is undertaken to explore how a client wishes to perceive, feel, act, or believe in the present and in the future.

Here are the steps that are completed prior to creating a positive template:

1   Resolve earlier memories and present triggers, internal and external.
2   Explore how the client sees himself in the future in terms of thinking, feeling, perceiving, acting, and believing.
3   Teach appropriate skills, such as assertiveness training, social skills, and mindful behavior.
4   Refer for nonpsychological skills (i.e., computer classes, public speaking).
5   Identify anticipated future stressors that emerge during the reprocessing of past and present events.

See Figure 4.6 for the progression of the future template.

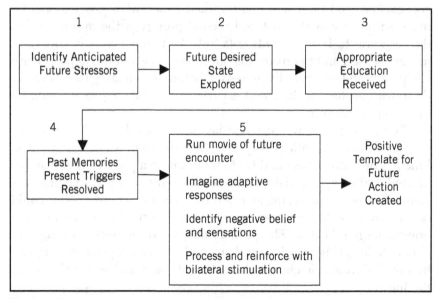

Figure 4.6 Future template: Skills building and imaginal rehearsal.

Once these steps outlined in Figure 4.6 above have been completed, the clinician asks the client to focus on one of the identified anticipated future stressors and imagine his optimal behavioral responses, along with an enhancing PC, if one exists. This information, with successive sets of eye movements facilitated by the clinician, will assist the client in understanding the information and integrating it into a positive template for future action. To accomplish this, the clinician instructs the client to visualize a future adaptive response to one of the identified anticipated future stressors. The client is further instructed to run a mental movie of encountering a previously identified disturbing person, place, thing, or situation in the future, or a disturbing action, and identify negative beliefs or sensations that emerge as a result. As the client once again runs the movie using his newfound skills, the clinician looks for distortions, negative associations, or other bottlenecks that arise in this process. Once the client has identified optimal responses to a future behavior, the clinician reinforces them with bilateral stimulation.

Third Prong: Misunderstood, Disregarded, Forgotten

The third prong of the EMDR approach is probably the most misunderstood and, often, most disregarded or forgotten prong for clinicians who are new to EMDR. One of the reasons may be that the clinician gets excited, and the client is astonished to see what progress can be made so quickly in the first and second prongs of the approach that the response to future events gets lost. As a clinician, it is important to stay focused and to ensure that all three prongs of the approach are adequately and successfully processed before terminating the client. To do so without having the client experience the future prong would be to do so prematurely.

The third prong is processed last and is used specifically: (a) to evaluate future or anticipatory anxieties; (b) to process residual dysfunction or disturbance; and (c) to incorporate a positive template for desired and/or appropriate future action. This prong is imaginal because it requires visualizing an event that has not occurred—but could occur—to look for previously undetected disturbance around the original targeted event. The primary purpose of the future prong is to eliminate lingering anticipatory fears and to create a positive template in order to assure the client's ability to make new and better choices in the future.

If the clinician notices hesitancy on the part of the client in re-processing previously disturbing material, he may find it appropriate to initiate needed skills training. If he discovers a feeder or earlier memory, he may find it necessary to process the contributing event and stimuli before continuing. If either arises, provide needed education and reprocess these memories before the installation of a future template. Remember, the future (or positive) template is a continuation of the installation phase of the EMDR procedural steps. See Table 4.1 below with some instructions and cautions when dealing with issues of anticipatory anxiety.

Table 4.1

FUTURE TEMPLATE

ANTICIPATORY ANXIETY: KEY POINTS

Anticipatory anxiety should be addressed with the standard EMDR protocol identified in the assessment phase.

To proceed with the reprocessing, the SUD level should be no higher than 3–4. If the SUD is higher than 3–4, the clinician will need to retarget feeder memories or present triggers.

In dealing with anticipatory anxiety, the desensitization phase should be brief. If it is not and the SUD level is above 4, then the three-pronged reprocessing approach (past, present, future) will need to be reimplemented.

If a client's presenting issues encompass memories of significant people, places, or situations, the client could be asked to imagine herself with that person, that place, or that situation. Unresolved materials may need to be accessed and resolved, clusters of events reevaluated, residual dysfunctional memories targeted and reprocessed, assertiveness or boundary setting explored and retargeted, or use of a positive template employed to assimilate the newly uncovered information and to help the client identify appropriate adaptive behaviors. The focus on the third prong assures the incorporation of new and appropriate future actions or behaviors and is vital to the client's continued movement toward adaptive resolution.

Each trigger identified in the present prong needs a future template. This process may be part of one session, or it may span many sessions depending on the client's reaction to doing future templates.

There are two basic types of future templates. One addresses anticipatory anxiety, which is reprocessed using the 11-step standard EMDR procedure (i.e., image, NC, PC, VoC, emotion, SUD level, location of body sensation, desensitization, installation, body scan, and closure). The other uses skills building and imaginal rehearsal, which does not require a full assessment.

With skills building and imaginal rehearsal, the client imagines an adaptive response in the future to a previously disturbing person, place, or thing, uncomfortable situation or circumstance, and/or doing a particularly upsetting future action. It is like "running a movie" of a potentially disturbing or upsetting action or event and the optimal behavioral responses to it. Positive beliefs and sensations are identified, and an enhancing PC is incorporated. The clinician leads the client in successive sets of bilateral stimulation as a means of assimilating information and incorporating it into a positive template for future action. During this imaginal rehearsal, residual negative beliefs or sensations are identified and reprocessed as needed.

CASE EXAMPLE 4C: MICHAEL

When leaving work, Michael remembered that he needed to buy a gallon of milk before going home. As he turned a corner to make his way to the grocery store, a young boy ran in front of his car. Michael stomped on his brakes and swerved dramatically to the right, but he could not stop his car before grazing the child. The little boy suffered a broken leg and was taken by ambulance to the hospital. This was a single-event trauma. Nothing in Michael's life compared to the look on the little boy's face just before he was hit. It took several sessions of EMDR to alleviate his suffering.

During previous therapy sessions, the clinician and Michael had successfully processed several current triggers, including his driving anxiety and driving around dusk, the time of day when the accident occurred. Michael also had a dread of encountering the little boy's parents, such as at church or at the mall. The future template script developed by Dr. Shapiro (2009) will be utilized to create a future template for Michael regarding his anxiety around driving at dusk and his dread of unexpectedly encountering the parents. The reader can find the future template script below.

Michael needed to be self-empowered, so the clinician elected to help him develop a positive template around the potential events. Driving was itself a challenging future template, and the session proceeded as follows:

Clinician: I'd like you to imagine yourself coping effectively driving at dusk with your new positive belief of "I am safely in control."

The clinician has identified an area of potential future concern for the client.

"I am safely in control" does not mean that Michael is in control of everything but that he is safely in control of what he can control. This was discussed and agreed upon when the clinician and Michael first targeted the event and that PC.

Michael: It's still difficult

The client reveals his anticipated emotional response to such an occurrence.

Clinician: Notice this event, those words, "I am safely in control," and your sense of control, comfort, and calm. Imagine stepping into that experience and notice what you're thinking, feeling, and experiencing in your body.
Michael: Okay.
Clinician: Are there any blocks, anxieties, or fears that arise as you think about this future scene?
Michael: I can feel myself getting anxious, and my chest feels tight as I visualize myself driving at dusk.

The client reports his doubt and anxiety, so the clinician has him focus on it.

Clinician: Go with that. (Set of eye movements) Take a deep breath. (Pause) What are you noticing now?
Michael: Okay. I am feeling calmer and more relaxed. I can see myself driving at dusk. I am feeling confident.

In this case, the client's block did resolve. If it had not, the clinician might evaluate whether he needed any new information, resources, or skills to enable him to comfortably visualize driving at dusk. If the block continues to be unresolved and the client still could not visualize himself driving at dusk with confidence and calm, the clinician may use direct questioning, the floatback technique, or the affect scan to identify any memories or events related to his fear. These targets would be reprocessed using the standard protocol before proceeding any further with the future template.

Clinician: Focus on the <u>original</u> event, those words, "<u>I am safely in control</u>," and where you feel it in your body. (Set of eye movements) Let it go. Take a deep breath. (Pause) What are you noticing <u>now</u>?

Because the client was able to focus on the future scene with confidence and calm, the clinician asked the client to focus on the image, positive belief, and sensations associated with it.

The clinician implemented several sets of bilateral stimulation until the future template was sufficiently strengthened.

Michael: I feel strong and confident. I have been driving many years without any accidents.

Clinician: Go with that. (Set of eye movements) Let it go. Take a deep breath. (Pause) What are you noticing <u>now</u>?

Michael: I feel good. I can do it.

Clinician: Think about the <u>original</u> event and those words, "<u>I am safely in control</u>." From "1," completely false, to "7," completely true, how <u>true</u> does it feel <u>now</u>?

Michael: Seven.

Clinician: Think of the <u>original</u> event and hold it together with the words, "<u>I am safely in control</u>." (Set of eye movements) Let it go. Take a deep breath. (Pause) How <u>true</u> does it feel to you <u>now</u>?

Michael: It's a seven.

Clinician: Close your eyes and focus on the <u>original</u> event and those words, "I am safely in control." Scan your body from head to toe for physical discomfort. If you feel anything, let me know.

Michael: My body feels calm, relaxed, and confident.

Clinician: Go with that. (Set of eye movements) You're doing fine. Let it go. Take a deep breath. (Pause) What are you getting <u>now</u>?

Michael: Nothing has changed. I feel the same as before.

Clinician: This time, I'd like you to close your eyes and play a movie, imagining yourself coping effectively with <u>driving at dusk in the future</u>. With the new positive belief, "<u>I am safely in control</u>" and your new sense of <u>confidence and calm</u>, imagine stepping into the future. Imagine yourself coping with *any* challenges that come your way. Make sure that this movie has a beginning, a middle, and an end. Notice what you're seeing, thinking, feeling, and experiencing in your body. Let me know if you hit any blocks. If you do, just open your eyes and let me know. If you don't hit any blocks, let me know when you have viewed the whole movie.

The clinician has asked the client to imagine a movie from beginning to end coping in the future.

Michael: Okay, I am finished.

Clinician: What are you noticing <u>now</u>?

Michael: I did feel confident and calm as I ran my movie from beginning to end.

In this case, the client was able to play the movie all the way through with a sense of confidence and calm. He did not hit any blocks along the way. If he had, the clinician could address these blocks with all the resources available, such as bilateral stimulation, cognitive interweaves, introduction of new information, new skills or resources, and the use of direct questioning, floatback technique, and affect scan.

Clinician: Michael, I would like you to play the movie through one more time. (Set of eye movements.)

The end result is that the clinician installed the client's movie as his future template.

In Michael's case, there are other possible triggers (e.g., driving at dusk and having the setting sun in his eyes, at night when everything is harder to see, in a heavy rain storm) previously identified by Michael that may also need to be reprocessed using the future template script. Each trigger would be individually targeted. The future challenges the client may face do not need to reflect what happened at the time of the disturbance or traumatic event. For instance, the clinician could instruct Michael to run a movie of leaving home to run an errand and, as he is nearing his destination, dusk begins to set in and a heavy rain storm occurs. In this case, Michael will decide what he needs to do and whether or not he feels "safely in control."

SUMMARY STATEMENTS

1 There are three prongs to the EMDR approach—past, present, and future.
2 Three primary strategies can be used to access the touchstone event—direct questioning, floatback technique, and affect scan.
3 A touchstone event does not always exist.

5

Abreactions, Blocked Processing, and Cognitive Interweaves

WHEN THE ENGINE HAS STALLED

Stalled Processing

Some clients can be very challenging, even for seasoned Eye Movement Desensitization and Reprocessing (EMDR) clinicians. High levels of abreaction and stalled, disrupted, or stopped processing are the most common challenges that impede a client's reprocessing efforts. Unfortunately, not every client experiences consistent reprocessing effects while focusing on a single targeted event. As previously stated, approximately 40% of EMDR clients reprocess in a straightforward manner with few, if any, direct therapeutic interventions on the part of the clinician. What happens to the other 60%? What does a clinician do if reprocessing does not proceed as anticipated or if its intensity is too high or is blocked in some way? What options does a clinician have that will mimic or restimulate the client's spontaneous movement toward an adaptive resolution?

This chapter explores guidelines for facilitating abreactions, strategies for blocked processing, and applying a more proactive and powerful strategy called the cognitive interweave for achieving full therapeutic treatment effectiveness with challenging and highly disturbed clients. These interventions involve efforts on the part of the clinician to deliberately do what the client usually does but is unable to on her own during an EMDR reprocessing session. Clinicians need to be familiar with the strategies included in this chapter before treating clients who present with high levels of disturbance or with more complex clinical presentations. Clinical supervision and/or consultation in these cases is always recommended.

ABREACTION

What Is It?

For ancient Greek dramatists, the term *abreaction* was used to describe the purging effect that the release of emotion provides. It is a flow of intense emotions with the overall effect of releasing the high levels of affect (Jackson, 1999). The meaning of abreaction has not changed much in the ensuing millennia. In today's world of clinical psychology, it continues to represent a verbal and often emotional and physical expression or discharge of unconscious material. From a psychoanalytic perspective, abreaction involves releasing emotional tension achieved through recalling a repressed traumatic experience.

In EMDR, conscious or unconscious material has been stimulated in the memory network, and the client reexperiences the emotions in the same or reminiscent fashion of how she experienced the original event or incident (i.e., at a high level of disturbance). At other times, a client can experience her reactions to a particular event in a way she was unable to at the time it actually occurred. For example, a client who had been physically restrained, frozen in her response, can experiencefor the first time her reaction to anger and hurt, as well as fear and anxiety that she had to endure in this experience. Conversely, during traditional talk therapy, clinicians will often witness, reassure, express empathy, or hold space for the client as she experiences or reexperiences emotions in the present related to events in the past. In EMDR, the client's own brain, whenever possible, is reprocessing the past experience with all the current information that was unavailable at the time of the event, thereby transmuting the way the memory is actually stored in the brain. The client never has to reexperience the event in the same way because the memory is now stored with all the information that is currently available.

Although abreaction is a critical healing element for most clients, it can also represent a painful, powerful, and difficult process just the same. This is because the client seems to be reexperiencing a trauma as if it were occurring in the present. A client may encounter sights, sounds, and smells that were present in the original trauma or may experience pain in the same part of the body that was hurt at the time of the trauma.

Preparing the Client for Abreactions

During the preparation phase, it is very important that the client be made aware that abreactions or high levels of emotional distress may occur during the session and that: (a) it is a normal phenomenon in EMDR; (b) the clinician will be there to help him through it; and (c) once the client is on the other side of an abreaction, and, assuming there are no undiscovered channels of dissociation, the symptoms are alleviated or disappear altogether. Before any reprocessing is initiated, remind the client that there are ways in which he can distance himself, including: (a) imagining being on a train and allowing the vivid images to be scenery that passes by; (b) imagining he is watching a DVD and has access to use his mental remote control; or (c) placing a thick protective glass between him and the perpetrator. At the beginning of a session, remind him that he has a stop signal he rehearsed during the preparation phase.

What Happens When a Client Abreacts?

There are many ways in which a client can abreact. If a client's original trauma consisted of a near drowning, she may find it difficult to breathe or catch her breath in the present. If he was being chased in the woods by a perpetrator, his breath may rise and fall rapidly and inconsistently. If a client had been grabbed roughly and slapped sharply during the targeted abuse, the actual marks made by the hands of the abuser may appear on her face or arm. If the client is a war veteran, he can mimic the self-protective maneuvers that he used to protect himself when he was attacked. Clients may gasp, scream, shake, sob, choke, or cringe. When this occurs, the clinician provides a safe place for the client to reprocess the experience and then stays out of the way, encouraging the client through the reaction while simultaneously helping her maintain a dual awareness (i.e., that she is in the present, not the past).

From an information processing perspective, when a client experiences strong emotional responses during reprocessing, it is information being released. So, if a client is crying during reprocessing, let him cry. Strong emotions and abreactive processes are part of reprocessing for many clients, particularly clients with a pervasive history of trauma over a prolonged period of time. Successive sets of bilateral stimulation are maintained until the intense reaction dissipates. If a client tends to close or cover her eyes when crying, the clinician may want to consider changing to tactile or auditory stimulation. The clinician can be verbally supportive by saying, "It's in the past," "It's old stuff," "Just notice it" or "It's over. You're safe now," and/or "That's it. Stay with it." This encouragement and assurance helps the client maintain dual awareness so that the brain can reprocess the experience while moving toward a more adaptive resolution. The clinician can also use the tunnel and train metaphors suggested by Dr. Shapiro (2001): "You are in the tunnel, just keep your foot on the pedal and keep moving" and "It's just old information. Watch it like scenery going by" are alternatives to help the client continue processing during an abreaction. All of these strategies may help a client move through his emotional responses. And, if a client asks to stop, it is important to honor his request. Stop immediately and assist the client in determining what he needs in order to be able to resume reprocessing.

Before any reprocessing is initiated, the EMDR clinician is trained to remind the client to maintain her awareness that she is in the present. This is in preparation for the possibility of intense emotional responses that can be experienced as being more about the past, rather than the present. Metaphors, such as imagining herself on a train and allowing the images to be scenery that passes by, or watching it on a movie screen as if in a theater, are used as a framework for the dual awareness. A stop signal is negotiated with the client in advance, signaling to the clinician that it may be "too much" to help prevent retraumatization.

The EMDR clinician is careful to help the client maintain dual awareness by having the client be aware that, while he is reexperiencing events in the past, he is also simultaneously aware of being in the present. Retraumatization can occur when dual awareness is lost and the client is reexperiencing the past event as if it's happening now, without the awareness of the emotional, psychological, and physical resources he has in the present. If the client gives the clinician his stop signal, the clinician is trained to stop the bilateral stimulation immediately. The client, by stopping, has the opportunity to reorient himself to the present. Often, the clinician will then initiate contact with the client to help him reorient, offering reassurance and support. Sometimes, the clinician will initiate a state change intervention, such as the calm (or safe) place or sacred space, until the client is ready to resume reprocessing. The clinician can inquire as to why the client wanted to stop and explore options on how to proceed. It is important for the clinician to negotiate a plan of action based on the client's wishes, as well as the client's capacity to continue. Incorporating the client's feedback into a plan of action is also positive proof that he is the one in control now, contrary to earlier experiences where he often had no choices.

Abreaction Guidelines

Table 5.1 lists guidelines provided by Dr. Shapiro (2001) to aid in dealing effectively with client abreaction during EMDR.

Table 5.1

ABREACTION GUIDELINES

GUIDELINES	WHAT DOES IT MEAN?
EMDR assists in allowing a client to release distress.	EMDR is a catalyst for change. It does not cause high levels of emotional disturbance for the client; it allows the client to access it, reexperience it (if necessary), and eliminate it.
Abreactions have three parts—a beginning, middle, and end.	The abreactions that occur are generally short-lived in nature and can be considered to be nothing more than a "flash-in-the-pan" when compared to the emotional upset that occurred in the original experience.
Information is usually being processed during EMDR.	Although the client can become disturbed during the processing, the disturbing material is transformed and the client is moved to a state of health.
A clinical position of detached compassion is called for during an abreactive demonstration by a client.	The clinician must demonstrate balanced detachment during the client's reprocessing of a traumatic event. (i.e., the clinician should be very empathic without rushing in to "fix" the client).
What a clinician or others might need during an abreactive response is usually what the client needs as well.	The clinician will provide the kind of support that will ensure the client's sense of safety, calm, and support.

(continued)

Table 5.1 *(continued)*

ABREACTION GUIDELINES

GUIDELINES	WHAT DOES IT MEAN?
A sense of safety in the present when processing events in the past is crucial to effective processing.	The clinician reassures the client that it is "old stuff" he is experiencing by providing a metaphor that helps him maintain a sense of control and inform him to keep his eyes open so that the processing can continue. Sometimes the client just needs to hear he is safe at that moment.
Monitor the client's nonverbal responses for indications that a new level of processing has occurred or that the set can be terminated.	Observe minimal cues that often accompany abreaction, such as changes in eye movement, breathing, posture, skin color, or bodily tension. Do not stop eye movements when changes occur to allow client to solidify conscious or cognitive connections.
Monitor a client's nonverbal responses to see if a set needs to be terminated before a new level of processing is achieved.	Should the clinician administer one continuous sequence of eye movements or should he break into sets? Consider these reasons for breaking into sets: (1) to give the client an opportunity to provide feedback; (2) to provide time to integrate new information at a verbal or conscious level; (3) to allow the client to share revelations and receive reaffirmation from the clinician; (4) to provide time to reorient to time and sense of safety; (5) to allow the client rest from the physical stimulation of the abreaction; (6) to let the client realize she is in control of the abreaction; (7) to reassure the client of clinician's continued encouragement; and (8) to allow the clinician to reevaluate need for further clinical interventions.
Constantly reinforce a client's dual sense of awareness.	The clinician reminds the client to simultaneously attend to the information being processed internally and stimuli being presented externally. The clinician can bring the client back to present time by changing the speed and/ or direction of the bilateral stimulation.

(continued)

ABREACTION GUIDELINES

GUIDELINES	WHAT DOES IT MEAN?
In the case of a dissociative response, the clinician does not treat it differently than other layers of emotion that emerge during an abreaction.	If the client reports seeing an event as if she is *"up on the ceiling,"* do not treat the sense of dissociation differently. Do everything possible to ground and keep the client in the present.
Try to use visual manipulation of the target memory to decrease the level of disturbance being experienced by a client.	Have the client employ emotional distancing strategies in the form of visual manipulation, such as changing a memory into a still photo or a black-and-white videotape; having client imagine holding the hand of his adult self; and placing a protective see-through wall between him and the event or perpetrator and the event.
The clinician may need to ensure the emotional stability of the client before leaving the session.	Do whatever is needed to ensure continued emotional stability during EMDR sessions and afterward, including reinstructing use of calm (or safe) place, breathing exercises, and allowing the client to bring in special objects, or arranging for a ride home.
Often, it may be appropriate for the clinician to change to auditory stimuli or hand taps.	If the client is unable to track because she cannot keep her eyes open, an alternative mode of bilateral stimulation needs to be available.
The use of strategies for blocked processing is imperative in the event a client stops processing information during a session.	When looping or other forms of blocking occur, the clinician needs to use the strategies available to restimulate processing (See Table 5.2a and Table 5.2b, Strategies for Maintaining Reprocessing).

Adapted with permission of Guilford Press from Shapiro, F. (2001). Eye Movement Desensitization and Reprocessing: Basic Principles, Protocols, and Procedures. NY: Guilford Press.

STRATEGIES FOR MAINTAINING PROCESSING

Overresponders and Underresponders: Guidelines for Clients Who Display Too Little or Too Much Emotion

It is not unusual for a client to overrespond or underrespond at a higher emotional level than she can comfortably tolerate, and the strategy in these cases is to decelerate in the case of overresponders and accelerate for underresponders. There are three guidelines for clinicians to follow when tracking clients who demonstrate too little or too much emotion or clients with blocked processing, regardless of which strategy is utilized. First, it is not unusual to have clients who overrespond, underrespond, and respond spontaneously and naturally to the basic procedures inherent in EMDR in the same session, or in different sessions, and on the same target or different targets. It is important for the clinician to be aware at all times of the client's present processing modality so that the appropriate strategy chosen will drive the processing forward (i.e., processing will no longer be stalled). Second, any targets that are identified as a result of utilizing these strategies must be reaccessed and reprocessed undistorted by the clinician's interventions. Third, it is suggested that any changes in bilateral stimulation not occur without the knowledge and consent of the client (i.e., communicate clearly with the client what you are going to do; Shapiro, 2001). That being said, what does it mean to decelerate or accelerate (see Figure 5.1)?

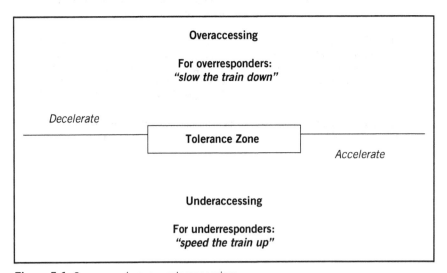

Figure 5.1 Overaccessing vs. underaccessing.

Remember, the goal is not to stop processing; it is to facilitate reprocessing effects. These strategies are designed to slow (or contain) or speed up the processing. This allows the client to be able to continue processing with greater safety and containment and in a more efficient manner.

Tables 5.2a and 5.2b outline Dr. Shapiro's (2001) strategies to open up the processing for underresponders and overresponders.

TICES is an acronym for target = image, cognition, emotion, and sensation. The TICES alternative procedural strategies listed in Table 5.2a and Table 5.2b enable a client to manipulate the memory in a way that provide her with a sense of empowerment (i.e., "I am larger than the disturbance.") and feeling of being in control. They also mimic spontaneously processing (i.e., the clinician asks the client to deliberately do what has not occurred spontaneously on its own).

Table 5.2a

STRATEGIES FOR MAINTAINING REPROCESSING

DECELERATION (FOR OVERRESPONDERS)

Initial Strategies
Increase or decrease speed or length of eye movements (or other forms of bilateral stimulation).
Concentrate only on body sensations: Where do you feel it in your body? Where do you feel it (i.e., emotion) in your body?

Continue bilateral stimulation, but:
Consider changing to tapping or auditory processing.
Change the direction or slow speed of the bilateral movements.
If closed, ask client to open eyes.
Offer verbal support and compassion.

TICES Strategies:
Change color of image to black and white.
Visualize a perpetrator with action.
Instruct client to visualize the disturbing event further away, then seeing it coming closer.
Visualize barrier to obscure part of the memory, then remove.
Provide client with the reality check, "It's in the past."
Instruct client to focus on one sensation at a time.
Instruct client to focus on one emotion at a time.

Table 5.2b

STRATEGIES FOR MAINTAINING REPROCESSING

ACCELERATION (FOR UNDERRESPONDERS)

Initial Strategies
Increase speed, length, direction, and intensity of locations, depending on stimulus used (i.e., eye movement, auditory, tactile).
Concentrate only on body sensations. Where do you feel it in your body? Where do you feel it (i.e., emotion) in your body?
Change mode of bilateral stimulation. Or try a combination of two.
Check for feeder memories (if adolescent or adult memory) that may be influencing reprocessing of current target.

TICES Strategies (in order):

To increase feeling and responsiveness:
Redirect to negative cognition to access more disturbance.
Add color to black-and-white picture.
Visualize an "actionless" perpetrator into action.
Instruct client to imagine getting closer to the event.
Offer client some other behavioral stimulus so the original event can be experienced more actively.
Instruct client to focus on several sensations at once.
Instruct client to focus on several emotions at once.

Cautionary Note

As a cautionary note, while helping a client with an abreaction by using any of the suggestions available in Table 5.2a and Table 5.2b, a position of detached compassion is encouraged on the part of the clinician. This posture allows the clinician to be present to the client, offering containment of the client's experience, as well as being a witness. Newly trained EMDR practitioners who are not experienced at handling abreactive processes are encouraged to consult with a more experienced EMDR practitioner.

Returning to Target Too Soon?

A common error of novice EMDR practitioners is to have the client return to target too soon or too often. This can stunt the client's processing. It prevents the client from completely clearing out the dysfunctional material stored in the channel of association being targeted.

When is it appropriate to return to target? When associations (i.e., changing imagery, sounds, sensations, emotions, tastes, smells) appear to fade in a channel, the client is instructed to return to target. For example if, during the processing of a rape, the client is focusing on the smell of the rapist and she can no longer smell him, it may be time to return to target. Also, a return to target is necessitated in the final stages of reprocessing for the following reasons: (a) to discern if there are additional channels of dysfunctional material; (b) to initiate the installation phase; and (c) to process a body scan to complete the session.

STRATEGIES FOR BLOCKED PROCESSING

Blocked Processing

Have you ever had a client who seemed to stop responding favorably to EMDR? What do you think happened? What was your response? Did you stop the bilateral stimulation? Did you do anything to help restimulate the processing? What are the indications of blocked processing in an EMDR session?

Clinical intervention is needed when the spontaneous linkage between dysfunctional and functional becomes blocked during the reprocessing of a client's traumatic event. Strategies for blocked processing (i.e., a strategy utilized in EMDR to restimulate processing that appears to be "stuck") may vary from: (a) changing the mechanics (i.e., speed, intensity, direction, or modality) of the bilateral stimulation; (b) changing the client's focus (i.e., thought, feeling, physical sensation, sensory—taste, smell) by saying, "Where do you feel it in your body?" or "Is there an emotion that goes with that body sensation?"; to (c) utilizing a strategy for blocked processing or cognitive interweave to help move the client's traumatic memory to adaptive resolution (Shapiro, 2001). Use the order specified above to intervene in the least intrusive way.

Identifying Blocked Processing

Processing can be considered to be blocked during an EMDR session if: (a) the client reports no change in two or more successive sets of reprocessing; (b) the same thoughts, emotions, and bodily sensations occur in successive sets of bilateral stimulation; or (c) the Subjective Units of Disturbance (SUD) scale continues to be the same for two subsequent sets of bilateral stimulation if no change is occurring and the material appears to be stuck. If one of these three situations occurs, the clinician can attempt to change the mechanics of the bilateral stimulation by a different eye movement direction, using tactile or audio stimulators, or changing the client's focus of attention from one aspect of the experience to another (i.e., from affective to physical). If unsuccessful, a mechanical strategy to unblock the processing or a cognitive interweave would be appropriate to stimulate movement or to release the affect that is contributing to the blockage.

There are three primary ways in which a client can potentially respond during the reprocessing of a traumatic event. First, the basic protocol is followed from start to finish without interruption. No special therapeutic interventions are required on the part of the clinician. Second and third, clients may overrespond and underrespond. Some clients may experience all three at one time or even over the course of the EMDR treatment.

The "normal" response to reprocessing is when the memory network is accessed through the target memory experience, activating channels of association related to the original target. As the channels of associations are made, more adaptive networks of memory and experiences are accessed spontaneously which transmute the memory network, resulting in a reprocessing effect. A client with sufficient ego strength or access to positive, adaptive memory networks will largely be able to reprocess with little or no intervention on the part of the clinician. The EMDR protocol is set up; reprocessing begins with the clinician providing bilateral stimulation; the clinician stops between sets of bilateral stimulation to obtain client feedback; the client continues reprocessing spontaneously until no further channels of association are made; and the target memory experience is resolved.

Primary Targets for Blocked Processing

See Table 5.3 for strategies developed by Dr. Shapiro (2001) to be used in clearing debris from a client's "track."

Ancillary Targets for Blocked Processing

Reprocessing does not necessarily resume when a client refocuses attention on another aspect of a target or with a different memory. When processing does not resume after trying the strategies discussed above, the clinician may need to look for the existence of ancillary targets or factors that may be causing the block. These factors include feeder memories, blocking beliefs, and fear (i.e., fear of going crazy, fear of

Table 5.3

STRATEGIES FOR BLOCKED PROCESSING

PRIMARY TARGET

Processing has stopped when a client's response remains unchanged after two consecutive sets of bilateral stimulation.

The clinician can restimulate processing of an immediate target in the following order by:

Changing the direction, length, speed, and height of horizontal movements (if using eye movements) or a combination of these changes.

Focusing on Physical Sensation
a. Focusing only on physical sensations of a client while altering the bilateral stimulation.
b. Focusing only on the most pronounced sensation (if more than one is reported).
c. Verbalizing or giving voice to certain types of body tension (e. g., throat, jaw) and the associated affect (e. g., anger, rage).
d. Acting out movement (e.g., punching, kicking) associated with a particular emotion (e.g., anger).
e. Pressing or focusing attention on a body sensation that will not shift and has no associated images or thoughts.

Scanning for:
a. Something that is more disturbing than the original event being targeted.
b. A sound effect that remains disturbing.
c. A dialogue that occurred during the traumatic event.

Alterations (i.e., in focus of attention or actual target)
a. Ask the client to alter the appearance of the image (e.g., smaller, dimmer, more faded, in black or white, rather than color).
b. Have the client visualize the perpetrator *only*—not what he is doing or what he did do.
c. Alter the target event in terms of time and distance (e.g., have the client imagine the perpetrator in the hallway rather than on top the bed).
d. When different events emerge during processing in a particular channel, one event may appear to have a higher disturbance level. If, in subsequent sets, the client concentrates on the thoughts and feelings of this specific event, allow the client to process this event until the thoughts and feelings begin to possess a milder level of disturbance. Then redirect the client back to the image of the last event with a significant level of disturbance.
e. Reintroduce the original negative cognition, along with the last disturbing image.
f. If processing becomes stuck at a low level of disturbance, processing can be re-stimulated by asking the client to add the statement, "You're safe now. It's over."
g. If, during the installation phase, the client is not processing appropriately, the clinician reassesses the client's positive cognition for appropriateness.

(continued)

Table 5.3 *(continued)*

Return to target for the following reasons:
a. Check for additional channels of association;
b. Implement the installation phase; or
c. Complete the session with a body scan.

Adapted with permission of Guilford Press from Shapiro, F. (2001). Eye Movement Desensitization and Reprocessing: Basic Principles, Protocols, and Procedures. NY: Guilford Press.

losing good memories, fear of change, fear of losing respect or losing contact with the clinician, and wellsprings of disturbance). Review chapter 1 for definitions and examples of these factors. Because resumption of processing does not always occur in blocked processing, Dr. Shapiro (2001) stresses that earlier memories that contribute to present dysfunction are targeted first in order to sidestep this potential outcome. See Table 5.4 for more sophisticated strategies to clear ancillary target blocks from the client's track.

THE ART OF THE COGNITIVE INTERWEAVE

Cognitive interweaves introduce "new information" or "a new perspective" into the processing system when the client gets stuck and the primary methods of jump-starting the process have been unsuccessful. The cognitive interweave can be one of the most challenging EMDR strategies for newly trained and some seasoned clinicians to understand and utilize effectively. Although EMDR is a client-centered psychotherapy approach, the clinician is expected to guide the process to facilitate a successful reprocessing. Thus, the cognitive interweave is subject to underuse, overuse, misuse, and misunderstanding. However, keep in mind that, if used sparingly and cautiously, it is an elegant and artful clinical technique that can greatly enhance EMDR processing. As with any intervention, timing, accuracy, and appropriateness are paramount to positive treatment outcomes.

What Is a Cognitive Interweave?

Initially, the cognitive interweave was used as a proactive strategy for working with challenging or highly disturbed clients. As time and

Table 5.4

STRATEGIES FOR BLOCKED PROCESSING

ANCILLARY TARGETS

Strategies for working with blocks caused by undiscovered channels of association:

Feeder memories
The client focuses on scanning for an earlier memory that incorporates the negative cognition. This strategy is indicative of looking for an earlier dysfunction related to a current experience.

Blocking beliefs
What prevents it (i.e., client's SUD score) from being a "0"?
What prevents it (i.e., client's VoC score) from being a "7"?
If a blocking belief does not emerge, ask the client to close his eyes, focus on the situation, and verbalize anything that comes to mind. The clinician would then scan the client's dialogue for negative blocking beliefs.
Examples: "I don't believe in extremes."
　　　　　 "Nothing is perfect."

Fears (e.g., fear of going crazy, fear of losing good memories, and fear of change).
The client's fears and secondary gain issues must be addressed before targets can be reengaged and processing continued.

Wellsprings of disturbance
The clinician targets the early memories associated with blocking beliefs that hinder a client's ability to feel emotions.

Note: Precise definitions and examples of these ancillary targets can be found in chapter 1.

practice have evolved, clinicians use it more and more with their other clients as well. When utilizing this strategic intervention, the clinician attempts to regalvanize stalled processing by introducing questions, statements, or instructions that can spontaneously "weave" into other, more adaptive memory networks and associations. This equation can help you to remember the basic composition of cognitive interweaves:

**Client-Generated Material + Clinician-Derived/Elicited
Statements (Cognitive Interweave) = Access to Adaptive
Information (hence, reprocessing continues)**

Or, see Figure 5.2 for a more graphic example.

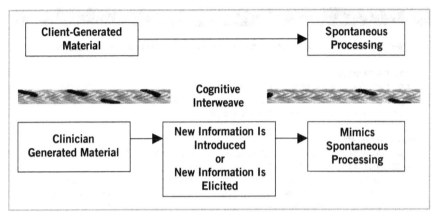

Figure 5.2 Understanding the cognitive interweave.

Cognitive interweaves can also be as simple as changing the speed, direction, and/or modality of the bilateral stimulation. The offering of encouragement with the words "Good," "It's in the past," or "Just ride the wave until you're through it" are also examples of cognitive interweaves. In each case, the clinician is stoking the fire to build more steam in order to get the "train" to its final destination.

Using a Cognitive Interweave Effectively

In order to utilize cognitive interweaves most effectively, it is necessary to begin collecting information from the earliest contact with the client. Zangwill (1997) calls it "a sensuous flowing together of presenting problems, client behavior and clinician skills" and emphasizes the importance of recognizing, collecting, and utilizing a client's vulnerabilities and schemas (i.e., broad organizing principles that help the client make sense of his life experience, such as a "defectiveness" (Young, 2003). Shapiro (2001) states, "clinicians will be able to use the cognitive interweave most beneficially if they are aware of the relevant clinical issues" and "can introduce new adaptive perspectives in a progressive manner that parallels the typical client's natural healing process."

Zangwill (1997) also states that the most important question to ask in terms of effectively utilizing the cognitive interweave is: What are your client's underlying schemas, and how has he coped with them? This entails discovering the client's clinical themes and underlying coping mechanisms and collecting the information to use later in weaving together, which can aid the client in reaching adaptive resolution of his trauma.

When to Use a Cognitive Interweave

Table 5.5 shows the circumstances under which cognitive interweaves can be used (Shapiro, 2001).

Table 5.5

WHEN TO USE A COGNITIVE INTERWEAVE

REASON	WHAT DOES THIS MEAN?
Looping	The clinician has used EMDR variations to unblock processing; and, even after successive sets of eye movements, the client continues to remain at a high level of disturbance with the same negative thoughts, affect, and imagery reoccurring.
Insufficient information	The client is unable to progress cognitively or behaviorally because he did not have the appropriate data.
Lack of generalization	Processing does not generalize to ancillary targets, despite the client's achieved success in reaching a positive emotional plateau with respect to a targeted event.
Time dilemma	Time is running out, and the client erupts into an abreaction or fails to process an abreaction sufficiently. The target may be multifaceted (i.e., more than one negative cognition is associated with it). More time may be needed to reprocess.
Extreme emotional stress	If the client is abreacting to the point of exhaustion, the clinician needs to intercede.

CASE EXAMPLE 5A: RENEE

Renee, age 25, was 10 years old when she was involved in a car accident in which her 34-year-old mother was seriously injured. Renee was strapped in the front seat opposite her mother, who was driving, when a semitruck hit them head on. Her vivid memories include her mother being unconscious and slumped over the steering wheel while Renee crawled out of the window of the car and rushed to the other side to help her mother. The impact of the semi rendered it impossible to budge the bent and crumbled door. No matter how hard she tried, she could not open the door to rescue her mother. The smell of gasoline helped Renee to choke back her tears as she tried to tug the door open. She was near hysteria when the firemen pushed her aside and pulled her mother out of the car just before it exploded into a fiery inferno. She stood and watched as her unconscious and helpless mother was removed from the car with a crowd of strangers looking on in horror. In a matter of minutes, Renee's world became empty and unsafe, and she went on to live a life of anxiousness and uncertainty.

Renee, age 10 at the time of the crash, had experienced fear, terror, disbelief, and helplessness as she viewed her trapped mother, and she continued to experience deep sadness and guilt for her mother's injuries. When Renee presented for therapy 15 years later, she was overweight, struggling with insomnia, and having frequent nightmares and flashbacks of the accident. She also suffered from depression and anxiety.

According to the Adaptive Information Processing model (Shapiro, 2001), Renee's information processing system (i.e., her natural healing mechanism) "stalled on the track" on the day of the accident. The extreme levels of stress that she experienced that tragic day remained in the same emotional and cognitive state until EMDR helped her to clear the debris from the "track" and allowed natural processing to occur. What this means is that the disturbing memories left on the "track" (i.e., the image of her mother slumped helplessly over the steering wheel, the firemen pulling her away from the devastating scene, the fiery explosion, the range of emotions she felt throughout the event, the rise of her adrenaline as she climbed out of the car to rush to her mother's aid) became stuck and isolated in a memory network in the same state-specific form as she had originally experienced it. This dysfunctional material stored in Renee's nervous system subsequently was responsible for the symptoms described above, and she was eventually diagnosed with post-traumatic stress disorder (PTSD).

Even years later, when she passed by an automobile accident or heard about an explosion on the news, Renee experienced the same fear, terror, disbelief, and helplessness, just as if the accident was occurring all over again. The information (i.e., thoughts, images, cognitions, emotions, sensations) from the original accident had been isolated into its own memory network and frozen in time. No new learning appeared to be able to penetrate the steel lining that insulated the information in it. It was only when the memory networks were connected that insight and integration could naturally occur for Renee. With the aid of EMDR, Renee was able to bring up the accident and assimilate the related negative information into its proper perspective (i.e., that it belonged to the past). Renee was able to discharge the dysfunctional affect that caused generalization of the adaptive cognitive content throughout her memory network. The negative material had been isolated since the time of her accident.

During the majority of an EMDR session, adaptive processing spontaneously links dysfunctional or disturbing material to the appropriate memory networks. What would happen if this does not occur? What would have happened during the session if Renee's "train" got stopped by "a fallen timber lying across the track" or if there had been a landslide or an avalanche and "her train could not move further down the track?" What resources are available to help Renee continue her healing journey? The answer is the cognitive interweave.

Choices of Cognitive Interweaves

Dr. Shapiro (2001) identifies and explains several choices of cognitive interweaves. To reiterate, the cognitive interweave is a deliberate effort by the clinician to mimic spontaneous processing by either directly infusing or eliciting information from the client. In doing so, the clinician is attempting to access the more adaptive memory network that contains information that is relevant to the client's present processing. The cognitive interweave may consist of an educational statement, relevant question, or direction in terms of imagery, thought, or movement. It may consist of introducing new information or stimulating presently held information for the client.

Table 5.6 outlines the types and their purposes and offers examples of each with possible responses using Renee's story.

Table 5.6

CHOICES OF COGNITIVE INTERWEAVES

CHOICE	PURPOSE	EXAMPLES
New Information or Perspective	Used when the client lacks the information needed to correct a maladaptive cognition.	Renee: I should have been able to get the car door open. I did not try hard enough. Clinician: Most 10-year-old children do not have the strength to do what you are suggesting, even in the worst of circumstances. Were you stronger than most children your age? Renee: No. Clinician: Go with that.
"I'm confused . . . "	The clinician uses this when it is believed the client already knows the answer to the question.	Clinician: I'm confused. Who was bigger, you or the fireman? Renee: The fireman. Clinician: Just think of that.
"What if it were your child?"	As a variation of the above, this interweave uses the client's children (if any) as a convenient intervention.	Clinician: Do you mean that, if it was your daughter who was trying to get you out of the car, you would want her to stay and save you regardless of the outcome? Renee: No! I would want my daughter safe and out of harm's way. Clinician: Go with that.
Metaphor/Analogy	The clinician uses stories (i.e., fables, fantasies, personal stories) to introduce therapeutic lessons to the client.	Clinician: Recently, I watched a segment on the news about a 10-year-old boy. His father was up in a tree cutting limbs with a chain saw when he cut the limb he was sitting on. He fell 10 ft out of the tree and then the limb dropped on him. Someone videotaped the little boy trying to lift that big limb off his father. He tried really hard, but he was not strong enough. He had to stand back and let his relatives take charge. Renee: Oh, there wasn't anything I could have done either. I was so small. Clinician: Go with that.

(continued)

CHOICE	PURPOSE	EXAMPLES
"Let's Pretend"	To help the client move through issues of inappropriately placed responsibility, the client is asked to visualize a more positive outcome to the issue at hand.	Clinician: Pretend that your mother would say something to you if she were here now. What would she say? Renee: I'm glad you're safe. There was nothing you could have done to get me. You did the right thing. I love you. Clinician: Go with that.
Socratic Method	The clinician leads the client to a logical conclusion by asking questions that are easily answered.	Renee: I feel like I am to blame. Clinician: What could you have done differently? Renee: I could have smashed the window in. Clinician: Did you have anything that you could have used to smash the window in? Renee: No. Clinician: Did the firemen break the window in and save your mother? Renee: Yes. Clinician: Go with that.

Adapted with permission of Guilford Press from Shapiro, F. (2001). Eye Movement Desensitization and Reprocessing: Basic Principles, Protocols, and Procedures. NY: Guilford Press.

CASE EXAMPLE 5A: RENEE CONT'D

It was during an EMDR session where Renee ran into a huge timber lying on her "train track." No matter what strategy was used to unblock processing, nothing seemed to work. When she accessed this particular part of the memory, Renee expressed inappropriate feelings of guilt for failing to be the one who got her mother out of the car. Nothing in Renee's previous learning or education seemed to provide salvation from her guilt. What was needed was a piece of dynamite to obliterate the debris from the blocked "track." During this session, a cognitive interweave was utilized to remove the timber from her "track." It was used to strategically introduce new, but pertinent, information to Renee's system to quick-start her stalled healing process.

Renee: If I only could have jerked the car door open. I could have helped her. I should have done something differently.

The issue of responsibility comes to the foreground.

Clinician: Renee, I'm confused. Are you saying that a 10-year-old should have been strong enough to open a jammed car door and drag an adult to safety?
Renee: Well, I suppose not.
Clinician: Go with that.

From the above examples in Table 5.6, a number of different inter-weaves could have been utilized if continued processing did not cause a spontaneous change in her feelings.

In introducing the information in that manner, Renee was able to get in touch with her more adaptive adult perspective and assist in linking the information that was deliberately inserted to the appropriate memory networks. Remember, Renee's perspective, somatic responses, and personal referents of the accident came from that of a 10-year-old, the age she was at the time of the accident. The cognitive interweave served to link dysfunctional information stored in an isolated memory network to Renee's present-day adult and to activate the adaptive material stored in a healthier network. This provided her with a more realistic adult perspective of the accident.

After eliminating the guilt she had felt for her mother's car accident, Renee realized that she was just a child at the time of the accident. Since the accident, she had difficulty riding in a car for sustained periods of time, and it was a struggle for her to drive. During a subsequent session, she began seeing images of the semitruck hitting them head on and her mother's injured body slumped over the steering wheel. Renee's reprocessing had stalled for the last few sets of bilateral stimulation. The following is how the clinician attempted to unblock her processing and her issue of safety played out during the session:

Renee: I just keep seeing the semi coming at us. It is as if it were yesterday. It came so fast and "bang," it was over. The next thing I noticed was my mother's limp body slumped over the steering wheel. I don't know if she was breathing or not. I didn't take time to think about myself. When I think of it now, I am fearful.
Clinician: Where do you feel the fear in your body?

The clinician used a somatic interweave to help move "the train further down its track."

Renee: In my chest.
Clinician: Go with that.
Renee: I am so vigilant when I drive now. I can never take my eyes off the road. I never feel safe in the car. I'm always too tense in the car.

The issue of safety emerges. The clinician probed further by eliciting information with a pertinent question:

Clinician: Is that what your mother did? She took her eyes off the road?
Renee: Yes. No. For some odd reason, I am seeing my mother slumped over the steering wheel before the semi hit us.
Clinician: Just think of that.
Renee: She was . . . Oh, my God! My mother had a seizure. That's why the semi hit us. I never made that connection before. My mother was an epileptic, and she had a seizure. She hit the truck and not the other way around. She couldn't help it. That's why the truck driver was not charged. I never could figure that one out. It was no one's fault. My mother would have kept me safe if it were in her power.

Renee never made this connection, even though her mother had told her at the time of the accident that she had a seizure.

Clinician: Go with that.
Renee: No wonder I am so tense when driving. I thought that, if I ever took my eyes off the road, I would crash just like my mom. She couldn't help it. It wasn't her fault. She didn't mean to . . .
Clinician: Go with that.

After this session, Renee was able to drive with a higher comfort level. She started to relax more and, as a result, actually became a better driver in her eyes. The resolution of her issue of safety also opened the door to a variety of choices in her life. Previously, Renee had never traveled too far from home. It was beyond her comfort level. Being more comfortable behind the wheel empowered her to drive to different places and try new activities. She actually accepted a teaching position one summer that required her to drive 50 miles round-trip to another city.

After the issues of responsibility, safety, and choice were resolved, Renee was able to complete the session by reaccessing and fully reprocessing the original target. Once the block has dissipated, the client can continue the process of spontaneously resolving associated channels of dysfunctional material that may still exist.

Regardless of how a client moves through these important plateaus, the successful negotiation of one facilitates the possibility of resolution in the next. The client may successfully negotiate these plateaus on her own, or she may be assisted by the use of questioning or educating by the clinician.

Comparison Between Strategies for Blocked Processing and Cognitive Interweaves

Strategies for blocked processing can be described as cognitive (e.g., "What negative thoughts go with that event?"), somatic (e.g., "Where do you feel that in your body?"), affective (e.g., "What are you feeling right now?"), or general (e.g., "What do you need right now?"). Changing the direction, speed, intensity, or location when using or changing alternatives for bilateral stimulation can be effective strategies for blocked processing. These strategies tend to question, inform, and challenge the client's obstacles (i.e., blocked beliefs, secondary gains or losses, feeder memories, ancillary targets, negative abreactions, performance anxiety, and lack of safety) during episodes of blocked processing until they are removed from the "track." They are designed to help the client's processing to move further down the existing "track" by removing the obstacle impeding progress.

See Table 5.7 for an encapsulated view of the differences between the two.

Responsibility, Safety, and Choice

The optimal outcome of an EMDR session entails the client coming to an adaptive resolution. This occurs as appropriate memory networks spontaneously link to each other and move the targeted issue to adaptive resolution. In cases of early trauma, Dr. Shapiro (2001) believes a

Table 5.7

COMPARISON BETWEEN STRATEGIES FOR BLOCKED PROCESSING AND COGNITIVE INTERWEAVES

STRATEGIES FOR BLOCKED PROCESSING:	COGNITIVE INTERWEAVES:
Reactive	Proactive
Uses client's spontaneous processing system.	Mimics client's spontaneously processing.
Concentrates directly on client's emerging material.	Introduces new information or a new perspective.
Helps remove obstacles from the client's "track".	Helps the client lay new "track".
Useful when the "train" has stopped on the "tracks".	Useful when the "train" is still moving, however, slowing down. Accurate timing and sequencing is needed.
Questions, challenges, and informs.	Confronts three major issues: responsibility, safety, choice. Fitted to the client.
Used usually before a cognitive interweave.	Usually used only as a last resort.

client's perspective becomes distorted in terms of responsibility, safety, and choice (See Table 5.8).

Examples of effective cognitive interweaves addressing responsibility, safety, and choice follow:

Responsibility interweaves
■ "Whose responsibility is it?"
■ "Is that about you or them?"
■ "Whose fault is it?"
■ "I'm confused. Who was bigger, you or he?"
■ "Let's pretend. If you could say something to him, what would it be?"

Table 5.8

ISSUES OF RESPONSIBILITY, SAFETY, AND CHOICE

ELEMENTS OF POSITIVE TREATMENT EFFECTS FOR TRAUMA SURVIVORS

PLATEAU	OBJECTIVE	DESIRED COGNITIVE SHIFT	DESIRED EMOTIONAL SHIFT
Responsibility	Recognition and attribution of appropriate responsibility	"It was my fault" to "I did the best I could"	Inappropriate feelings of guilt or self-blame to Disgust or anger
Safety	Awareness of present sense of safety	"I'm in danger" to "It's over. I am safe now"	Feelings of fear or lack of safety to relative sense of present safety
Choice	Confidence in ability to choose alternative actions when necessary	"I have no control" to "I am now in control" or "I have more control now"	Helplessness to empowerment

Safety Interweaves
- "Are you safe now?"
- "Can he (i.e., the perpetrator) hurt you now?"
- "If he (i.e., the perpetrator) tried something now, what would you do?"

Choice Interweaves
- "What happens when you think of the words 'As an adult, I know I have choices' or 'I can now choose' or 'I am now in control?'"

These issues are often processed in this order for processing to be the most effective (see Figure 5.3).

CASE EXAMPLE 5B: SUSIE

When Susie was 10 years old, her uncle took her back behind his house to see the new shed he had built. This was her favorite uncle, so Susie was excited to share this with him. Once in the shed, her uncle grabbed her and pushed her down. Before she could do anything, he was on top of her, his hand clasped over her mouth so that she could not scream.

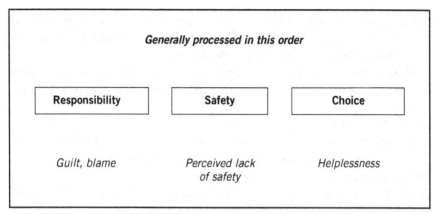

Figure 5.3 Cognitive and emotional plateaus of trauma victims.

The following transcript demonstrates an example of a client moving through these plateaus spontaneously and naturally.

Target: The worst part of the experience for Susie was when her uncle turned around, grabbed her, and roughly pushed her down on the floor of the shed.

Negative Cognition (NC): I am powerless.

Positive Cognition (PC): I have some power.

Validity of Cognition (VoC): 2

Emotions: Fear, shame, disgust, guilt

Subjective Units of Disturbance (SUD): 8

Body: Down there (the client points to her genital area).

Clinician: Throughout the EMDR process today, I will be asking you to tell me what you are experiencing. Tell me, as clearly as possible, what comes into your mind as we go through this process. Sometimes things will change, and sometimes they won't. There are no "supposed to's." Just let whatever happens, happen. Remember your stop signal and your calm (or safe) place when you need them. (Pause) Susie, I want you to focus on the event, those words, "I am powerless" and where you feel it in your body. Just let it go wherever it goes. (Set of eye movements) Okay, blank it out. Take a deep breath. (Pause) What's coming up *now*?

Susie: I see him on top of me, tearing at my clothes. I can hear children in the background playing and giggling. I can feel his weight on me. I tried to fight with him, but I was too weak.

Clinician: Notice that. (Set of eye movements) Good. You're doing fine. Let it go, and take a deep breath. (Pause) What are you getting *now*?

Susie: He kept pushing against me.

Clinician: Notice that. (Set of eye movements) Good. Let it go and take a deep breath. (Pause) What are you noticing *now*?

Susie: I am feeling a sharp pang in my chest.

Clinician: Go with that. (Set of eye movements) Good. Let it go and take a deep breath. (Pause) What are you noticing *now*?

Susie: He touched me. I let him . . . I allowed it . . . He told me he loved me. It was my fault. He asked me to come with him . . . and I did. I am such a bad person.

The client is expressing inappropriate feelings of guilt and is accepting the blame for going with her uncle to his shed.

Clinician: Go with that. (Set of eye movements) Good. Let it go and take a deep breath. (Pause) What are you getting *now*?

Susie: He said what we were doing together was special and our own little secret. He told me that, if I told anyone, he would go to jail. He said if he went to jail it would be my fault. But it wouldn't be. He was bad, not me. It was not my fault. I was so small. I did nothing wrong. I am not a bad person. He is.

The attribution of responsibility belongs solely to the perpetrator, and the client making this emotional connection is tantamount to her reaching the first of three stages of her healing process.

Clinician: Do you mean you are a good person?

Susie: Yes. I am a good person.

The client has spontaneously shifted from "I am a bad person" to "I am a good person." She no longer feels that she is to blame for what happened with her uncle in the shed.

Clinician: Go with that. (Set of eye movements) Good. Good. Let it go and take a deep breath. (Pause) What's happening *now*?

Susie: It's not my fault. No child asks to be treated in this way.

The cognitive and emotional shift continues to materialize in terms of the guilt and blame that she so readily attributed to herself only moments before.

Clinician: Just go with that. (Set of eye movements) You're doing fine. Let it go and take a deep breath. (Pause) What are you noticing *now*?

Susie: I feel dirty. I feel so ashamed. I feel so vulnerable and helpless. I am so scared. I need to get away from him.

Client spontaneously opens another associated channel of her experience. This one involves the issue of *safety*. This cognitive and emotional plateau will need to be resolved as well before proceeding on to the next plateau.

Clinician: Go with that. (Set of eye movements) Good. Good. Let it go and take a deep breath. (Pause) What's happening *now*?

Susie: Every time I saw my uncle after the incident, like at family functions, he would just smirk and wink at me. I was afraid he would try to do it again. I can still feel the fear.

Clinician: Just notice that. (Set of eye movements) Good. Let it go and take a deep breath. (Pause) What are you noticing *now*?

Susie: My uncle died several years ago. He had a heart attack while driving to work. He plowed into a tree. He died instantly. He can never hurt me again. I never have to see him at family events. I never have to feel the revulsion and hatred I felt for him every time I saw him.

The client continues to realize that she is safe from her perpetrator. As an adult, she does not need to fear for her safety.

Clinician: Just notice that. (Set of eye movements) Good. Let it go and take a deep breath. (Pause) What comes up for you *now*?

Susie: I am feeling calmer . . . and safer. I never have to see him again. It's over. I have other family members that care for me and love me.

The client spontaneously separated the past from the present. She is safe now. He is dead, and he cannot hurt her any more.

Clinician: Go with that. (Set of eye movements) Good. Let it go and take a deep breath. (Pause) What's coming up *now*?

Susie: I don't know if I can ever be free of him . . . the tainted feeling still lingers. What he did to me defined me for so many years. How do I get rid of that? How do I move on still knowing what he did to me and the years that he took from me?

Clinician: Just go with that. (Set of eye movements) You're doing fine. Let it go and take a deep breath. (Pause) What are you noticing *now*?

Susie: Maybe I can be free of him. I no longer feel responsible. And I feel safe knowing he is dead. Maybe I can be free of him.

Clinician: Go with that. (Set of eye movements) Good. Good. Let it go and take a deep breath. (Pause) What are getting *now*?

Susie: It's up to me. He's dead and cannot hurt me now. I can choose to live free of him. He can't hurt me anymore. I won't let him. I can take my power back.

The third plateau begins to emerge. The client realizes her ability to *choose* to live free of the effect her uncle has had on her.

Clinician: Just go with that. (Set of eye movements) Good. Let it go and take a deep breath. (Pause) What are you noticing *now*?

Susie: I am feeling strong. I feel like he is gone, and there's nothing he can do now. That's just the way it is.

Dr. Shapiro (2001) believes that processing these issues in order of responsibility, safety, and choice is an integral part of successful treatment for trauma survivors. Susie was able to spontaneously move through these cognitive and emotional plateaus successfully on her own. However, this does not happen with all trauma survivors. In some instances, the clinician may need to introduce or stimulate the issues of responsibility, safety, and choice for the client by strategically utilizing the cognitive interweave.

In an effort to demonstrate how this is done, Susie's transcript will be altered, allowing the clinician to utilize cognitive interweaves to elicit the same information around these three important issues.

Responsibility

Susie: He told me what we were doing together was special and our own little secret. He told me that, if I told anyone, he would go to jail. He said, if he went to jail, it would be my fault.

Clinician: Whose fault is it?

Client: It's his, not mine. He's bad, not me. It's not my fault. I was so small. I did nothing wrong. I am not a bad person. He is.

Clinician: You are a good person.

Susie: I am a good person.

The clinician did for the client what she could not do for herself by weaving together the appropriate memory networks and associations. As a result, the client is able to transmute her belief, "I am a bad person." into "I am a good person."

Clinician: Go with that. (Set of eye movements) Good. Good. Let it go and take a deep breath. (Pause) What's happening *now*?

Safety

Susie: Every time I saw my uncle after the incident, like at family functions, he would just smirk and wink at me. I was afraid he would try to do it again. I can still feel the fear.

Clinician: Where is your uncle now?

Susie: My uncle died several years ago. He had a heart attack while driving to work. He plowed into a tree. He died instantly. He can never hurt me again. I never have to see him at family events. I never have to feel the revulsion and hatred I felt for him every time I saw him.

Using a cognitive interweave to bring the client back into the present where her adult self lives, the clinician is able to demonstrate to the client that her uncle is no longer a danger to her.

Clinician: Just notice that. (Set of eye movements) Good. Let it go and take a deep breath. (Pause) What are you getting *now*?

Choice

Susie: I don't know if I can ever be free of him. What he did to me defined me for so many years. How do I get rid of that? How do I move on still knowing what he did to me and the years that he took from me?

Clinician: What happens when you think of the words, "As an adult, I know I have choices?"

Susie: I never thought of it like that.

Clinician: Go with that. (Set of eye movements) Good. Let it go and take a deep breath. (Pause) What is happening *now*?

Susie: Right! Right! I do have choices now that I did not have then . . . I am feeling calmer . . . and safer. I never have to see him again. I always felt tainted by what he did to me. I choose not to feel that way anymore.

With the assistance of the clinician, the client is able to proceed to the plateau of choice.

Use the Cognitive Interweave With Caution

Cognitive interweave is applied within the overall framework of EMDR's client-centered approach. It is a process that is organized around the client's inherent capacities for healing and striving toward health. As the clinician does not want the client's reprocessing efforts to break down on the "track," caution is suggested with employing the cognitive interweave. Use it selectively and only when other strategies for blocked processing fail to move the client toward full integration of his experience. Cognitive interweaves are delivered within the tenor of the moment and as tentatively as possible. If an interweave does not work, the clinician needs to consider it important feedback about where the client is in his or her process and offer another intervention that is better informed, given the client's response to the interweave. Although spontaneous reprocessing is always preferred, it is not always possible. EMDR is very empowering for the client in that the changes that occur arise out of the client's process and, to the extent that is possible, the client will be able to take ownership of his progress. When a clinician intervenes and knowingly, although skillfully, intertwines pertinent information with material currently being reprocessed by the client, this can unwittingly undermine the client's process and affect the treatment outcome.

The power of intervention on the part of the clinician during a reprocessing session cannot be understated. Therefore, thoughtfulness, as well as caution, is always applied before making an intervention with clients while they are reprocessing. Before implementing its use, the clinician first determines the existence of other conditions (i.e., blocking beliefs, feeder memories, ancillary targets, and secondary gain issues) that could also cause excessive looping. Cognitive interweave can be applied to facilitate an uncovering of these variables, bringing them into consciousness so they can be worked with, either during the reprocessing or at another time. Spontaneous processing is the process of best choice for the client. Once the other techniques have been mastered with some measure of success, it is suggested to reread Dr. Shapiro's chapter 7, "Working with Abreaction and Blocks" and chapter 10," The Cognitive Interweave: A Proactive Strategy for Working with Challenging Clients," in *Eye Movement Desensitization and Reprocessing: Basic Principles, Protocols, and Procedures, Second Edition* (2001) as well as other books and articles by other clinicians on the cognitive interweave before implementing it with a client (Gilson & Kaplan, 2000; Dworkin, 2003).

Laliotis (2000) has categorized levels of cognitive interweave that may be used, from the least to the most intervening on the part of the clinician. Her model supports the notion that clinicians need to be aware of the level of intervention being applied. As a general rule, the more complex the clinical presentation (i.e., clients with multiple presenting problems and issues), the greater the deficits, the greater the need for cognitive interweave. Clients with a history of abuse, neglect, substance abuse, and dissociation have greater fragmentation in their memory networks, making it more difficult to access adaptive memory networks spontaneously. In addition to offering clients information that they don't have, the use of cognitive interweave allows them to stay in their process. The spirit of cognitive interweave is to support the client's process by offering the least amount of intervention with the greatest likelihood of success for an adaptive response.

The following examples of cognitive interweaves in Table 5.9 were adapted from Laliotis (2000):

Table 5.9

TYPES AND EXAMPLES OF COGNITIVE INTERWEAVES

CHOICE	PURPOSE	EXAMPLES
Validating	Validates the client's experience, functioning as a witness. Helps maintain dual awareness. Helps the client feel supported.	That's right. That's good. You're doing fine. That makes sense to me. I can really appreciate how you feel.
Clarifying Mirroring	Helps the client feel understood. Mirroring back to the client what you hear them saying; invoking observing ego function. Could also be in the form of a question when you want to check the client's progress.	Do you mean you're feeling like . . . You mean that . . . Let me make sure I'm understanding what you're saying . . . So, part of you feels _____, and another part of you feels _____, is that right? So, you're thinking about _____, is that right? So, you're feeling _____, is that right? So, you're noticing the _____ in your body?
Focusing	Keeping the client focused on their process. Keeping the client in the moment; expanding his present level of awareness. Deliberately focusing the client's attention away from aspects of his experience or toward an aspect of his experience. In more complex cases, helping the client deconstruct aspects of his experience in order for them to be able to be reprocessed.	Just notice . . . what's it like for you to notice that you're _____ now? What are you experiencing now? What are you feeling right now? Where do you feel it in your body? What are you thinking about? Tell me what you see. What aspect of the memory stands out for you/is bothering you right now? Who is your emotion directed at? What's it like to notice that you're feeling _____ now? What's it like for you to recall this right now?

	What's it like to know that you did the best you could?
	What's it like to name this ____ right now?
	If a client says, "I'm stuck," the clinician may say, "What part are you stuck on?"
	As you're saying ____, notice what it feels like at this moment . . . in your body.
	Just take a few moments to let it sink in.
	Focus on the part of you that ____ and the other part of you that ____ and notice what happens.
Accessing Questioning	Go back to the incident . . . what comes up for you now? Thoughts? Feelings? Body sensations?
Series of questions designed to move the client from the general to the specific, from the present to the past, from the past to the present, from the present to the future.	As you think about this memory/experience, what is the belief you're having about yourself now?
	What does that say about you that you could do that?
	Where does that (feeling, thought, sensation) take you?
Build affect, somatic, and cognitive bridges.	When have you felt this way before?
	Where did you get that message from?
	Whose voice is that?
	What would you like to say to that person/voice now?
	Where/when did you first learn . . . ?
	What are you saying to yourself about this right now?
	What would you like to hear instead?
	What do you need right now?
	What resource do you need in order to ____? (in the context of reprocessing)
	If you could do anything to make it better at this moment, what would it be?
	Is there a part of you that knows exactly what to do?
	Is there a part of you that is unsure about ____?
	Focus on the part of you that ____, and the other part of you that ____, and notice what happens.

(continued)

Table 5.9 (continued)

TYPES AND EXAMPLES OF COGNITIVE INTERWEAVES

CHOICE	PURPOSE	EXAMPLES
Informing Education	Offering the client information that she already has but is not available in the moment.	As a child you were _____. As an adult you are _____.
	Offering information the client may not already have but would be useful in facilitating her process.	What did the doctor tell you?
	Normalizes the client's experience.	Other women/men would have the same reaction in your shoes.
	Corrects misinformation.	I would like you to consider that it does not always have to be this way.
	Gives the client permission when she needs it.	I would like you to consider that it will not always be this way . . . It is okay to _____.
	Uncouples components of the experience that do not belong together.	Using a metaphor or a story to get a point across.
Challenging	Inviting the client to consider another perspective.	So, let me make sure I understand what you are saying . . .
	Challenging the immature logic of the child.	She/he was an adult and you were a child . . . who was responsible?
	Challenging the client when she applies the standards of an adult to a child.	Which of you was bigger?
	Challenging resistance to letting go of the problem or to move toward health.	So, you are saying that it was your job to keep yourself safe as a child?
	Challenging blocking beliefs that are informed by erroneous connections.	If you were to get over this problem, what would it be like? Imagine it . . .
		What would it take to move forward?
		What do you need to hold on to before you can let the rest of it go?
		Is there a part of you that wants to hold on to this problem; is afraid to let go of the problem?
		If there were a good reason to hold on to the (emotion, problem, issue), what would it be?
		What other ways could this need be satisfied?
		What is keeping it from feeling even better than it does at this moment?

| Integrating | Rehearse
Redo
Replace
Future template
Meaning
Past/Present
Present/Future | What positive belief do you have about yourself right now that you were able to _____ (positive thing)?
Imagine how it can be different now and in the future.
Let yourself imagine how you wished it could have been.
If you could do it differently right now, how would you do it?
If you could replace it with _____, what would that be?
What would you like to say to the kid right now that you wished someone had said back then?
What would you like to *do* right now that you wished some-one had done for you back then?
What does the little boy/girl need/want right now? Imagine it.
As you look back on this experience now, how do you make sense of it? |
| Resourcing | Eliciting resources in a specific context during reprocessing.
Helping the client develop resources in a specific context.
Resourcing as a preparation for trauma work.
Resourcing as a container to maintain dual awareness; to resume reprocessing; or to close down an incomplete session.
Bring in a religious figure or archetype as a source of guidance and wisdom or as someone who can help them feel at peace. | What you do need right now to continue?
What would it take to make it feel more tolerable right now?
Just notice that you are an adult looking back on this experience.
I would like to remind you that while you are afraid of what you might feel (or what you might come up with), the worst is already over, and you have all the resources of an adult.
What would feel safe right now?
What do you need in order to feel safer?
What resource do you need in order to _____? (before installing resource)
If you could put this away until our next session, where would you put it or what would you put it in? |

Reprinted from *Advanced Applications of Cognitive Interweave and Resource Development in EMDR* by Deany Laliotis, LCSW-C (2000).

SUMMARY STATEMENTS

1   Blocked processing is addressed first by changing eye movements (i.e., speed, length, direction) or changing the client's focus of attention.

2   When using a strategy to reactivate stalled processing and a shift occurs, allow the reprocessing to resume on its own to the extent possible. It is important to go back to the original target in order to allow the client to reprocess the memory unimpeded by the clinician's interventions.

3   The cognitive interweaves described in this chapter are designed to mimic spontaneous processing and to facilitate change. It is important to remember that it is the client's brain doing the work.

4   The cognitive interweave is a powerful intervention.

5   Spontaneous processing is the most desirable processing as it is determined totally by the client's own brain and Adaptive Information Processing mechanism of the brain.

6 Past, Present, and Future

EMDR CASE EXAMPLES

In this chapter, the clinician will be reintroduced to the basic components of Eye Movement Desensitization and Reprocessing (EMDR) through transcripts of therapy sessions. The EMDR sessions with Jessica, Karen, Delores, Brenda, and Jimmy are introduced in order of past, present, and future. These are simple, uncomplicated EMDR sessions. These cases are being presented in this way to demonstrate to the reader what a successful session looks like when the client is allowed to reprocess disturbing material without any interventions by the clinician. As a newly trained EMDR clinician, it is inadvisable to implement EMDR starting with your most difficult client. Begin using this approach with clients you believe success is possible for them and you. And **practice, practice, practice.** It is wise for any novice EMDR-trained clinician to seek consultation as a strategic course of action with an EMDRIA-Approved Consultant.

The questions below cover some of the basic information needed to complete a successful EMDR session with a client. See how many of them you can answer.

In the following transcripts, it is assumed that the clinician has completed all phases of EMDR up to the assessment phase. The client's

QUESTIONS

After a set of bilateral stimulation, what does the clinician say?

Does EMDR have the ability to change something that is real or factual?

Has adaptive resolution been achieved when the clinician returns the client back to the original target?

How does the clinician know that the client is at the end of a channel of association?

How does the clinician close down the EMDR process?

How fast should the bilateral stimulation be?

How is setting up a future template different from setting up the standard EMDR protocol for a past event or present trigger?

How many times should the clinician reinforce positive treatment effects identified by the client?

How often should the clinician reinforce and encourage the client throughout the EMDR process?

Is a positive cognition (PC) reflective of what the client believes or would like to believe about himself as he focuses on a particular trauma?

Is EMDR focusing on then or now?

Is it ever okay to initiate reprocessing without first establishing a negative cognition (NC) associated with the traumatic event being processed by the client?

Is the issue with which the client presents necessarily the same as the image she eventually reprocesses with EMDR?

Is there any way for the clinician to utilize a negative physical sensation expressed by the client to further his process?

What are the characteristics of an NC and a PC?

What does the clinician do if the client begins to cry or visibly emote in any way?

What does the clinician do if the client only reports physical sensations between sets?

What does the clinician do if the client reports newly emerging memories or changes in what the client originally reported at the beginning of the EMDR?

What does the clinician do if the client states more than one NC or PC related to a specific traumatic memory or event?

What does the clinician do when the client cannot come up with an appropriate NC?

What does the clinician say to the client between sets? What is appropriate? What is not appropriate?

What does the clinician say after each set of bilateral stimulation?

What does the Validity of Cognition (VoC) measure?

What is an option if the client reports an emotion during the feedback process?

What words does the clinician use to initiate processing with the client?

When is it appropriate for the clinician to return the client back to the original target?

When is it appropriate to ask the client what his Subjective Units of Disturbance (SUD) level is?

When is it appropriate to initiate the actual reprocessing of the client's traumatic event?

When should the client proceed with the installation phase?

Why does the clinician redirect the client back to an original target?

Why is it imperative that the clinician does not intrude upon the client's process?

Why is it important for the clinician *to stay out of the client's way?*

Why is it important for the clinician to reinforce any positive shifts by the client?

Why is it important for the clinician to provide encouragement to the client during and between sets of bilateral stimulation?

Should SUD = 0 be reinforced with a set of bilateral stimulation? VoC = 7? Body scan = clear?

Why does the clinician check in with the client between sets of bilateral stimulation? How does the clinician initiate it?

At the beginning of the installation phase, why does the clinician ask the client whether the original PC is appropriate or not?

Can EMDR work successfully with a general target?

What can the clinician do if the client continues to give a narrative report of what happened the day of the trauma?

What does the clinician do if she keeps witnessing movement in the client's process?

What does the clinician do if there is no movement of any kind in the client's reprocessing efforts for two or more sets of bilateral stimulation?

When is it appropriate for the clinician to check the client's current SUD level?

When is it appropriate for the clinician to redirect the client back to the original target?

Why does the clinician check in so frequently with the client?

---

history has been outlined to provide the reader with a clearer understanding of the client's chosen targets. Read the cases below and, when finished, come back and answer the above questions again. Be prepared to write down the components of the target (i.e., NCs and PCs, emotions, and body sensations) and baseline responses (i.e., VoC and SUD) identified by the client.

In each case where the clinician asks the client to focus on the original event (or incident), the client's original target has been placed in brackets with a reminder (e.g., [Reminder: Original incident—when Tom was bitten by a snake when he was in the second grade]) to help the user remember the original target's wording. Do not repeat the target back to the client. The words are placed there only as a reminder to the clinician of the client's original target.

Because of the simplistic nature of a primer, the cases below mirror more what happens in EMDR about 40% of the time – with no or very few interventions. It is important for the clinician to be able to master the basics of EMDR before utilizing it with more complicated cases. The reader is directed to the many EMDR books and articles (see the Francine Shapiro Library) for more sophisticated examples of EMDR sessions).

PAST

CASE EXAMPLE 6A: JESSICA

Situation: At age 20, the client was jammed up against a black-
                         board by several students' desks in the midst of a tor-
                         nado that occurred during one of her college classes.

Type of Presentation: Single incident

Symptoms: Depression, lethargy, poor appetite, joylessness

Issues: Unable to attend classes (eventually flunked out), reacts
                         to extreme weather conditions, multiple failed relation-
                         ships, inability to hold a job

Jessica was looking out of a window daydreaming in one of her classes at a small Midwest college. With little warning, the previously clear sky became immersed with large, rapidly growing clouds until it resembled a grayish black wall. She remembers the clamor of constant thunder in the background and then the torrents of rain that began to descend almost instantly. The day had become night, and the tornado sirens began to roar and signal everyone to head for cover. But it was too late for her to seek cover. Her classmates scrambled for safety in the darkened corridors. The force of the wind popped the windows out of their panes. Desks, papers, and other debris whipped around erratically and dangerously. Within minutes, hail as big as golf balls began to pummel the ground, some flying through into the now glassless windows. Jessica found herself jammed up against the blackboard by two or three of the students' desks. She was quite shaken but appeared to be okay.

This was Jessica's first and only encounter with disaster. Having been brought up in a loving home in what she called a "normal" childhood, she had not experienced any kind of trauma, certainly not one of this magnitude. In her case, this was a one-time event. Even so, she did not fare so well. She found herself isolating in her room, unable to attend classes, especially if the weather was not sunny and clear. She became more and more lethargic and depressed. She had lost her appetite and her joy for living.

By the time Jessica reached the clinician's office, she was 25 years old. She appeared haggard and pale. A year after the tornado, she had flunked out of school, had been involved in multiple failed relationships, and could not hold down a job.

Below is a transcript of Jessica's first EMDR session.

Target

Clinician: Last time we met, you indicated to me what you thought was the worst part of this memory. Could you share that with me now? *What image represents the most traumatic (or most disturbing) part of the incident?*

As a part of an overall treatment plan, this issue was agreed upon by the client and the clinician in the history-taking phase. The issue had been identified, but the image that represents the issue had not. The clinician invited her to select a single image to target in the beginning. She has many potential images, so the clinician asked her for the most disturbing. This is Jessica's first connection to the dysfunctionally stored material that she came to resolve in therapy. By asking this question, the information about the incident becomes stimulated and accessible.

Jessica: It all happened so fast. Within seconds, everything changed. One minute I am daydreaming out the window. The next minute, I find myself flattened like a pancake up against a blackboard with desks piled on top of me. I don't remember anything in between. That's the most disturbing part for me, the time in between sitting quietly in my chair and being flattened against the wall, not exactly knowing how I got there.

Negative Cognition (NC)

Clinician: What words go best with the picture that express your *negative belief* about yourself *now*?

This question can be difficult for some. Jessica could have become confused between a feeling and a belief and blurted out something like "I am scared." Or, perhaps, she might have provided a description of circumstances such as, "I am not in control." In Jessica's case, this is a true statement. She was not in control. EMDR does not have the power to change something that is true or factual. And it does not have the power to change a past thought. If the client does not come up with a belief, try to elicit an appropriate one by asking, "What would that make you believe about yourself *now*?"

Jessica: I am in danger. No, I cannot protect myself.

Jessica's NC is appropriately stated in the present and is a belief about herself, not an emotion or statement of circumstance. It is also self-limiting. In this case, Jessica had quickly decided on an appropriate negative belief. What if she had initially responded with more than one negative cognition, such as, "I am helpless, I am powerless, I cannot protect myself?" These are three separate beliefs. The clinician may help the client elicit the negative cognition that best fits as she thinks about herself with respect to this event. In this case, the clinician might say, "As you think of the incident, which belief resonates the best?" Remember, the clinician is looking for a belief the client has that continues *now* as a result of this experience.

Positive Cognition (PC)

Clinician: When you bring up that picture, what would you *like* to *believe* about yourself *now*?
Jessica: I can learn to protect myself.

Does Jessica's belief as stated meet all the criteria for an appropriate PC? The "I" in the statement is indicative that it is self-referential and it is stated in the present. *Safety* is her desired direction of change; it is future oriented. It is a positive assessment that is generalizable in that it could influence her perception of past events, current assessment, and future expectations.

Validity of Cognition

Clinician: When you think of the event (or incident), how <u>true</u> do those words, "I can learn to protect myself," <u>feel</u> to you <u>now</u> on a scale from 1 to 7, where "1" feels *completely false* and "7" feels completely true?
Jessica: I am not sure what you mean.
Clinician: Remember, sometimes we know something with our head, but it feels differently in our gut. In this case, what is the gut-level feeling of the truth of "I can learn to protect myself," on a scale of 1 to 7, where "1" is completely false and "7" is completely true?

Does this belief reflect wishful thinking or is it an actual possibility for Jessica? The VoC measures the possibility of the PC. If the PC is not possible, the VoC is not valid either.

Jessica: It's about a "2." Maybe a little less than that.

If she were to answer "1," the clinician would have to assess for ecological validity, applicability, and flaws in her logic. Often "1" or *totally false* indicates that the client may have difficulty believing the PC though it is what she would like to believe. Even with her answer of "2," there is a need to assess Jessica's ability to assimilate this PC successfully. The clinician believed she could.

Emotions

Clinician: When you bring up that incident and those words, "I cannot protect myself," what emotions do you <u>feel</u> <u>now</u>?
Jessica: Terror. And I feel helpless.

Subjective Units of Disturbance (SUD)

Clinician: From "0," which is neutral or no disturbance, to "10," which is *the worst disturbance you can imagine*, how disturbing does it <u>feel</u> to you <u>now</u>?
Jessica: Oh, that's easy. It's a "10"!

Body Sensations

Clinician: Where do you <u>feel</u> it in your body?
Jessica: I feel it below my belly button.
Clinician: Throughout the EMDR process today, I will be asking you to tell me what you are experiencing. I will need for you to tell me, as clearly as possible, what comes into your mind. Sometimes things will change, and sometimes they won't. There are no "supposed to's" in this process. Just let whatever happens, happen. Let it go wherever it goes. Remember your stop signal and your calm (or safe) place if you need them.

The clinician usually needs to repeat the complete instructions once to a client, unless the client has difficulty remembering what is expected of her from session to session. What the clinician instructs just before desensitization and reprocessing begins is, "Focus on the event, those words (NC), and where you feel it in your body. Just let whatever happens, happen. Let it go wherever it goes."

Alternatively, the clinician may also say: "Remember, it is your own brain that is doing the healing, and you are the one in control. I will ask you to mentally focus on the target and to follow my fingers with your eyes. Just let whatever happens, happen, and we will talk at the end of the set. Just tell me what comes up, and don't discard anything as unimportant. New information that comes to mind is connected in some way. If you want to stop, just raise your hand" (Shapiro, 2001).

Clinician: (Pause) I would like you to bring up that *picture, those negative words "I cannot protect myself,"* and *notice where you <u>feel</u> it in your body* (and say, "Follow my fingers," if you are using manual eye movements).

If the clinician is using something other than fingers to facilitate the eye movements or some other form of bilateral stimulation, activate it to start and stop the stimulation.

After this initial set of bilateral stimulation, the NC is not referred to again.

Jessica: (Takes a deep breath)

Sometimes, the client will spontaneously take a deep breath. It is up to the clinician whether or not to ask the client to take another one. In either case, the clinician asks the client, "What are you getting *now*?" or "What's coming up <u>now</u>?"

Clinician: What are you getting <u>now</u>?
Jessica: I am resistant to going there.

During the course of the EMDR processing, the clinician checks in frequently to ascertain the client's current condition and to see if new information has emerged. The client reports dominant image, emotional, and/or physical sensations. Based on what the client reports, the clinician will direct the client to, "Go with that," "Notice that," or return to the original target if it is felt a new plateau of processing has been reached.

If using eye movements, the clinician initially uses horizontal movements to ensure for effectiveness.

Clinician: Use your stop signal if you need it.

It is important for the clinician to monitor the client's verbal and nonverbal signals at all times and to check in with the client as needed. In this instance, the client may or may not have wanted to stop processing as indicated by her words, "I am resistant to go there."

Jessica: No, I'm fine. I need to do this.
Clinician: Okay. Just notice that. (Set of eye movements) Good. Let it go. Take a deep breath. (Pause) What's coming up for you <u>now</u>?

Remember to be undemanding when asking the client to report on new information, images, emotions, or when dominant sensations have arisen between sets. The clinician needs only to determine if the actual reprocessing has taken place. Allow the client to report what is most salient to her at the time of the processing. Do not elicit this information by asking the client specifically, "What are you feeling?" or "What is it that you see?"

When pausing between sets of eye movements, it is inappropriate to say "relax" or "close your eyes."

Jessica: I remember how excited I was when I first saw the clouds forming and saying to myself, "I wonder if this is a tornado." I was so excited. I can feel the excitement now. I had never seen one up close before.
Clinician: Go with that. (Set of eye movements) Good. Let it go. Take a deep breath. (Pause) What are you noticing <u>now</u>?
Jessica: The excitement turned to panic when I saw my classmates running toward the door. Before I could react, I could feel myself being lifted from my chair. I was terrified.

It is indicative that information is processing when the client describes a shift in one of the distinct aspects of the memory (i.e., image, sound, cognition, emotion, physical sensation). Another indicator is when a new event arises that is linked associatively (i.e., by an inherent belief, major participant or perpetrator, pronounced stimuli, specific event, dominant emotions, or physical sensations) with the original event (or incident).

Clinician: Notice that. (Set of eye movements) You're doing fine. Let it go. Good. Good. Take a deep breath. (Pause) What comes up for you <u>now</u>?

The clinician is encouraged to make comments like, "Good" or "You're doing fine" to reinforce the client's efforts and reassure her that she is doing EMDR correctly. The clinician may want to be mindful to listen supportively and compassionately. EMDR is a team-driven approach (i.e., clinician and client). As such, the clinician is encouraged to inhale and exhale along with the client. It helps to establish and solidify the bonding that is important to the process (Shapiro, 2001).

Jessica: I can still feel the terror.
Clinician: Notice that. (Set of eye movements) You're doing fine. Let it go. Good. Good. Take a deep breath. (Pause) What are you noticing now?
Jessica: It's the same. It doesn't seem to be going away.
Clinician: Notice that. (Set of eye movements) You're doing fine. Let it go. Good. Good. Take a deep breath. (Pause) What are you getting now?
Jessica: I can still feel the terror.
Clinician: Notice that. (Set of eye movements) You're doing fine. Let it go. Take a deep breath. (Pause) What are you getting now?
Jessica: I'm remembering the tornado siren and how frightening that feels right now.

The new image that the client described now becomes the focus of concentration for the next set of eye movements.

It is also suggested that, if Jessica's shifts in information were primarily cognitive, the clinician may want to increase the number of movements back and forth to 36 or 48 (or, for some clients, a set of less than 24) to see if the client responds better. It is unnecessary to count the exact number of movements. The clinician's attention remains on the client's facial expressions and other body cues, rather than counting the exact number of movements.

Clinician: Notice that. (Set of eye movements) You're doing fine. Let it go. Good. Good. Take a deep breath. (Pause) What are you noticing now?
Jessica: I feel calmer.
Clinician: Go with that. (Set of eye movements) Good. Good. You're safe now. Let it go. Take a deep breath. (Pause) What comes up for you now?

Jessica: It's the same. I just feel calm and relaxed.

Clinician: When you think of the <u>original</u> event (or incident), what do you get <u>now</u>?

(Reminder: Original incident—"The time in between sitting quietly in my chair and being flattened against the wall.")

Notice that the clinician asks the client to focus on the original incident, not specifying "the time in between sitting quietly in my chair and being flattened against the wall." When the clinician asks the client to think of the original incident, he may also use words like incident, memory, or issues where appropriate.

Jessica: I see that the glass has been blown from the windows. My classmates are frantic. There is chaos everywhere.

Just notice as successive channels of association are revealed.

Clinician: Go with that. (Set of eye movements) Good. Let it go. Take a deep breath. (Pause) What are you noticing <u>now</u>?

Jessica: I am looking around, and now I am seeing that the other students appear disheveled. They are dazed and bruised, but they are okay. I am okay. It feels good.

Clinician: When you think of the incident, what are you getting <u>now</u>?

Jessica: Everything happened so fast. One moment there's a classroom and everything is normal. A few minutes later, everything is chaotic and debris is everywhere. I am vulnerable. I was then and I feel so now.

Clinician: Notice that. (Set of eye movements) Good. Good. Let it go. Take a deep breath. (Pause) What are you noticing <u>now</u>?

Again, continue to reinforce the client by saying, "Good," "You're doing fine," or some other words of encouragement during or at the end of a set. It helps keep the client grounded and in the present to hear the clinician's voice. The clinician also needs to remain grounded in the present with his client.

Dr. Shapiro (2001) strongly suggests reassuring the client during processing by gently or unobtrusively saying, "Good." It is a neutral response and is preferred over "excellent" or "great." Those words imply judgment on the client's process and could impede or cloud the client's progress.

Jessica: There's a commercial where the punch line is, "When life comes at you fast." I think it is about insurance or something. I don't remember. That's how I felt, that my life was coming at me fast and that it might be ending fast. In the blink of an eye, everything had changed.

Clinician: Go with that. (Set of eye movements) Good. Take a deep breath. (Pause) What are you getting now?

Do not try to interpret all the details the client provides between sets of bilateral stimulation. By asking questions similar to, *"What are you getting now?"* the clinician tries to determine how the information surrounding the original event (or incident or image) is stored now while the client is reprocessing.

Jessica: I am feeling calmer. I survived with only a few scratches. I am going to be okay. I am okay.

Clinician: Go with that. (Set of eye movements) Good. It's over. It's in the past. Let it go. Take a deep breath. (Pause) What are you noticing now?

Jessica: I am feeling great!

Clinician: When you think of the original event (or incident), what do you get now?

Jessica: I can't seem to retrieve it. It feels far away. It's distant somehow.

Clinician: Go with that. (Set of eye movements) Good. Let it go. Take a deep breath. (Pause) What comes up for you now?

Jessica: It's time to move on with my life.

Clinician: When you think of the original event (or incident), on a scale from 0 to 10, where "0" is neutral or no disturbance and "10" is the worst disturbance you can imagine, how disturbing is the event (or incident) to you now?

Jessica: It is a "0". I just cannot connect with it.

She has reported a "0" level of emotional disturbance. The clinician reinforces it by doing another set of eye movements.

Clinician: Go with that. (Set of eye movements) Good. Let it go. Take a deep breath. (Pause) What are you getting now?

Jessica: It's still a "0".

Once the SUD level is a "0," we can consider the original target to be desensitized. . .then, and only then, the clinician proceeds to the installation phase. At this point, all channels of revealed dysfunctional information have been processed.

Clinician: Do the words, "I can learn to protect myself," *still fit*, or is there another positive statement you feel would be more suitable?
Jessica: Yes, it still fits.
Clinician: Think about the <u>original</u> event (or incident) and those words, "I can learn to protect myself." From "1", which is *completely false*, to "7," which is *completely true*, how <u>true</u> do they <u>feel</u> <u>now</u>?
Jessica: Six point five.

As long as the VoC keeps getting stronger or becomes more adaptive, the clinician continues reprocessing the PC. If the client reports a "6," "7," or, in this case, a "6.5," the clinician will continue with additional sets of bilateral stimulation to strengthen and continue until it can be strengthened no further. Then the clinician can implement the body scan.

If the client reports a VoC of "6" or less, the clinician will need to check the appropriateness and decide whether to address with additional reprocessing of existing blocking beliefs.

Clinician: Think of the event (or incident) and hold it together with the words "I can learn to protect myself." (Set of eye movements) On a scale of 1 to 7, how <u>*true*</u> do those words, "I can learn to protect myself." <u>feel</u> to you <u>now</u> when you think of the <u>original</u> event (or incident)?
Jessica: It's a "7."

Reinforce the PC as well.

Clinician: Go with that. (Set of eye movements) Good. Let it go. Take a deep breath. (Pause) How <u>true</u> does it <u>feel</u> <u>now</u>?
Jessica: It still feels totally true.
Clinician: Close your eyes and keep in mind the <u>original</u> memory and those words, "I can learn to protect myself." Then bring your attention to different parts of your body, starting with your head and working downward. Any place you feel tension, tightness, or unusual sensation, tell me.

Jessica: I feel some tightness in my throat.

The body scan is the last phase of the procedural reprocessing steps, and processing is not considered complete until all residual dysfunctional material associated with the original issue has dissipated.

If the client reports either a negative/uncomfortable or positive/comfortable sensation during the body scan, it will be followed by bilateral stimulation. For the positive or comfortable sensation, it will serve to strengthen it. If a negative or uncomfortable sensation is reported, the reprocessing will continue until it has dissipated.

It is possible that new associations may emerge during the body scan phase and, if they do, they should be completely reprocessed.

With a body scan, the clinician does not have to implement the traditional 24 sets of bilateral stimulation, but it does proceed at the same speed as before. Positive physical sensations may be reinforced in the same way as the negative.

Remember that reprocessing is considered incomplete until the body scan is clear of all negatively associated sensations.

Clinician: Notice that. (Set of eye movements) Good. Let it go. Take a deep breath. (Pause) What are you getting now?

Jessica: The tightness has dissipated, and I am feeling really calm.

The clinician at this point initiates another set of eye movements to reinforce the positive or comfort physical sensations the client is experiencing.

Clinician: Notice that. (Set of eye movements) Good. Let it go. Take a deep breath. (Pause) What is happening now?

Jessica: I am relaxed and calm.

Clinician: The processing we have done today may continue after the session. You may or may not notice new insights, thoughts, memories, or dreams. If so, just notice what you are experiencing. Take a snapshot of what you are seeing, feeling, thinking, and any triggers and keep a log or TICES (target = image, cognitions, emotions, and sensations) grid. Then do a calm (or safe) place exercise to rid yourself of the disturbance. We can work on this new material next time. If you feel it is necessary, call me.

CASE EXAMPLE 6B: KAREN

Situation: *When Karen was about 13 years old, she dropped her pet cat off a second-story balcony.*

Type of presentation: Single-event trauma
Symptoms: Guilt, shame
Issues: Dealing with injustice in her life

Karen was a thirty-five year old who had been seeing the clinician for 3 months. She had completed one or two sessions of EMDR and had been working off a list of top 10 traumas she had prepared. One day she came in and said, "EMDR is good. I can see the effect in all areas of my life. But the list is no longer important. It is a list and I do not feel like I need to keep checking things off." What she had discovered as one of the many insights since beginning EMDR was that a theme of injustice appeared to permeate her life . . . injustices done to her and others, and injustices she had perpetrated onto others. She wanted to start with what she had done to others.

Target: Something "bad" she did to her cat.
NC: I am bad.
PC: I am good.
VoC: 3
Emotion: Guilt, shame
SUD: 10
Body: Chest

Clinician: Throughout the EMDR process today, I will be asking you to tell me what you are experiencing. Tell me, as clearly as possible, what comes into your mind. Sometimes things will change, and sometimes they won't. There are no "supposed to's" in this process. Just let whatever happens, happen. Remember your stop signal and your calm (or safe) place when you need them.
Clinician: Karen, focus on the event, those words, "I am bad," and where you <u>feel</u> it in your body. Just let it go wherever it goes. (Set of eye movements) Let it go. Take a deep breath. (Pause) What's coming up <u>now</u>?

Notice that, when setting up the client to perform the actual processing, the clinician does not recount how the client described her initial target or draw the client's attention back to her reported negative emotions.

Incorrect: "Focus on the image of something 'bad' you did to your cat, those words, 'I am bad,' those feelings of guilt and shame, and where you feel it in your chest." The focus begins to change as the protocol setup emerges. Target, emotions, and physical sensations may begin to shift, even as they are being reported. The clinician does not repeat back to the client her description of the event, her emotions, or the exact place she feels it in her body because the image and where she felt it may already be changing. The clinician does not want to hinder the client's process by asking her to start all over again. Simply focus on the event, the exact words she has chosen as her NC, and where she feels it in her body.

Correct: "Focus on the event (or bring up the picture), those words, 'I am bad' and where you feel it in your body." The clinician, however, repeats the NC just as the client said it. It is a belief that has shaped a lifetime and is deeply engrained in the client's psyche.

After this initial set of bilateral stimulation, the NC is usually not referred to again.

Karen: It makes me want to cry. I feel prickly and sweaty all over.
Clinician: Go with that. (Set of eye movements) Good. Let it go. Take a deep breath. (Pause) What comes up for you <u>now</u>?

After each set of bilateral stimulation, the clinician asks for feedback. And the clinician may ask for it in several different ways, such as "What's coming up <u>now</u>?" "What are you getting <u>now</u>?" "What's happening <u>now</u>?" "What are you noticing <u>now</u>?" These are just variations on asking for this feedback. It is important to include the word <u>now</u> so that the client is reminded to respond with whatever she is dealing with at that particular moment. It is not necessary for her to recount everything that happened to her between sets.

Karen: I am feeling less sweaty and less anxious.
Clinician: Go with that. (Set of eye movements) Good. Let it go. Take a deep breath. (Pause) What are you getting <u>now</u>?

Consistently say words like, "Go with that." "Notice that." or "Think of that." Thoughts, emotions, and physical sensations are meant to flow. One of the aims of EMDR is to get whatever is stuck into a flowing mode. Thoughts, emotions, or physical sensations are not static for very long without changing even slightly from one level to another (e.g., feeling extreme pain in your stomach to feeling less pain) or changing one kind to another (e.g., sadness turning into anger).

Karen: I'm feeling better.

Clinician: Notice that. (Set of eye movements) Good. Let it go. Take a deep breath. (Pause) What are you getting <u>now</u>?

Karen: I feel much better than when we started.

Clinician: Karen, when you think of the <u>original</u> event (or incident), what do you get <u>now</u>?

(Reminder: Original target—Something "bad" she did to her cat)

Note again that, when the clinician took Karen back to the target, she asked her to go back to the original event (or incident) . . . she did not ask her to focus on "something 'bad' you did to your cat." This is an important point. As the clinician, you do not describe the event to the client for several reasons. From the time a client describes her target, the entire memory may begin to change or transform. It begins to lose some of its power over the client. We do not want to interfere with the client getting her power back. And, we may run the risk of tampering with the memory by not describing it fully or accurately.

Karen: I feel some remorse, but I do not feel as guilty as I did.

Clinician: Notice that. (Set of eye movements) Good. Good. Let it go. Take a deep breath. (Pause) What's coming up <u>now</u>?

Try to take a deep breath with the client. It serves to keep you grounded in the present with the client. During sets, it might be easy to drift off and think about other things. It also helps you to sidestep the negativity being dispelled by the client. This is not directly addressed in Dr. Shapiro's works but is something that some clinicians are finding as they experience the process with their clients.

Karen: I was with her when she was put to sleep years later.

Clinician: Notice that. (Set of eye movements) Good. Let it go. Take a deep breath. (Pause) What are you noticing <u>now</u>?

Karen: (Spontaneously blurted out . . .) I just had the strangest thought. I remember where I found her. (Pause) It's gone . . . the guilt and remorse are gone.

Clinician: Notice that. (Set of eye movements) You're doing fine. Let it go. Take a deep breath. (Pause) What are you getting <u>now</u>?

It is important to give the client lots of encouragement throughout the EMDR process, especially during a client's first EMDR session. It is not uncommon for the client to think that she is not doing it correctly but will not ask.

Karen: Nothing.
Clinician: What does "nothing" mean?
Karen: The guilt and remorse are gone.

The client appears to have reached the end of a channel, so the clinician redirected her back to target to see if Karen had other accessible channels in need of processing. She did. Since there was enough time in the session to deal with new material that might have emerged, the clinician asked the client to go back to the original target (i.e., image or memory that was addressed during the initial setup – something "bad" she did to her cat). If there is not enough time to clean out another channel of association, close down and follow the procedure for an incomplete session.

When directing a client back to target, it is unnecessary for the clinician to describe the experience as it may be stored differently now. There are several reasons you might redirect a client back to the original target: (a) when a client's feedback between each set of bilateral stimulation is consistently positive or neutral; (b) to identify and activate another channel of association; (c) to check in on the client's progress; (d) to determine whether or not the end of desensitization has been reached; (e) to refocus on the original target; (f) if you cannot identify changes at the end of processing after one set of bilateral stimulation; and (g) to check in on the presence of ecological soundness. Another reason for taking a client back to target is when a client appears to be distracted. If it feels like a client is running around in circles or losing focus, take her back to target so that she has a starting point from which to begin processing again.

Clinician: Notice that. (Set of eye movements) Good. Let it go. Take a deep breath. (Pause) What comes up for you now?
Karen: I just feel light. It feels so good.
Clinician: Karen, when you think of the original event (or incident), what do you get now?
Karen: I still have a little sadness but not the guilt.
Clinician: Notice that. (Set of eye movements) Let it go. Take a deep breath. (Pause) What are you noticing now?
Karen: It's weird. I went to my safe place, and somebody was there. It was really weird but nice.

Typically, it is important for the client to tell the clinician when she wants to go to her safe place rather than going there spontaneously on her own. However, since this is what occurred naturally during the reprocessing, the clinician just says, "Go with that" or "Notice that."

Clinician: Notice that. (Set of eye movements) Let it go. Take a deep breath. (Pause) What's happening <u>now</u>?

Karen: I feel all right. I don't feel the sadness anymore.

Clinician: Go with that. (Set of eye movements) Good. Let it go. Take a deep breath. (Pause) What comes up for you <u>now</u>?

Karen: Great. I feel wonderful.

Clinician: When you think of the <u>original</u> event (or incident), what do you get <u>now</u>?

Again, the client appeared to be at the end of another channel, so the clinician redirected her back to the original target.

Karen: I can't seem to retrieve the image . . . it's blurred or something.

At this point, the client appears to have exhausted all open channels, so the clinician asked her to again rate her disturbance on a scale of 0 to 10. It is only when you determine or find evidence that a client has cleared out all negative cognitive, emotional, and physical residue from the targeted material that you ask for a new SUD level.

Clinician: When you think of the <u>original</u> event (or incident), on a scale from 0 to 10, where "0" is neutral or no disturbance and "10" is the worst disturbance you can imagine, how disturbing is the event (or incident) to you <u>now</u>?

Karen: It's a "0."

Remember that the goal of EMDR is to process the client's negative experiences toward an adaptive resolution. What this means in terms of the SUD level is that a "0" must be achieved in order for the process to be completed. There are exceptions, such as the ecological soundness.

Clinician: Focus on the <u>original</u> incident. Do those words, "I am bad" <u>still</u> *fit*, or is there another positive statement you feel would be more suitable?

Karen: Yes. I learned from it.

Clinician: Think about the <u>original</u> event (or incident) and those words, "I learned from it." From "1," which is *completely false*, to "7," which is *completely true*, how <u>true</u> do they <u>feel</u> <u>now</u>?

Karen: I feel totally relaxed. It's a "7."

Clinician: Think of the event (or incident), and hold it together with the words, "I learned from it." (Set of eye movements) Let it go. Take a deep breath. (Pause) How <u>true</u> do the words, "I learned from it," feel to you <u>now</u> on a scale of "1" to "7?"

Karen: Still a "7."

Clinician: Notice that. (Set of eye movements) Let it go. Take a deep breath. What's happening <u>now</u>?

Karen: I never thought I could feel this way about the incident.

Clinician: Close your eyes and focus on the <u>original</u> event (or incident) and those words, "I learned from it." Now bring your attention to the different parts of your body, starting with your head and working downward. Any place you find tension, tightness, or unusual sensation, let me know.

Karen: I feel totally relaxed.

The body scan is implemented at this stage of the process to ensure that there are no residual aspects of the target that need reprocessing. If the body sensations change in either direction, the clinician will continue to do additional sets until the change is complete. If discomfort is reported, bilateral stimulation is implemented until it subsides. Then repeat the body scan procedure above. After a neutral body scan, the clinician implements an additional set of bilateral stimulation to set in the neutral or positive change.

Clinician: Just notice that. (Set of eye movements) (Pause) What are you getting now?

Karen: Still relaxed.

Clinician: The processing we have done today may continue after the session. You may or may not notice new insights, thoughts, memories, or dreams. If so, just notice what you are experiencing. Take a snapshot of what you are seeing, feeling, thinking, and any triggers and keep a log or TICES grid. Then do a calm (or safe) place exercise to rid yourself of the disturbance. We can work on this new material next time. If you feel it is necessary, call me.

Direct the client to keep a log of newly emerging after-session insights, dreams, memories, and thoughts. At the next session, ask the client, "What has changed since you did the EMDR? What is different?" Many may say, "Not much" or "Nothing significant." However, as the conversation progresses, the clinician often is able to point out something the client said to her that indicates something has changed.

How about the ambiguity of the target? Was it a problem? What did the client do "bad" to her pet? Originally, the client started to launch into a long dialogue about the pet without actually telling the clinician what she had done. She became emotionally agitated, and the clinician stopped her. The clinician told the client that she did not need to talk about it but could process it instead. It was not revealed what happened to the cat until after the session was completed. Reportedly, Karen was pressured by her friends and dropped her cat off a second-story balcony and into her yard. The cat was not injured.

When Karen said, "I know where I found her," why didn't the clinician ask, "Where did you find her?" Did the cat run away and die somewhere, and she found it later? What happened to the cat? The clinician resisted satisfying her curiosity to ensure the integrity of Karen's process. She did learn later that Karen had rescued her cat Cassie from the side of the road where someone had dumped her. Cassie, a beautiful yellow tabby, lived to be 17. Had the clinician gone along with her assumption that Karen did something to make the cat die, the clinician may have completely derailed or upset her "train" from going down the "track."

When Karen stated that someone was in her calm (or safe) place, one might also be tempted to interrupt her process by asking, "Who was in your safe place?" The clinician did ask after the reprocessing was complete and discovered that the person who showed up was Tim, her brother-in-law. Tim had died 2 years previously. He had a massive heart attack while he was cutting his grass. He came to tell her, "Everything is okay."

PRESENT

CASE EXAMPLE 6C: DELORES

Situation:	*The client had been working in therapy on past issues and was slowly regaining a personal sense of power. She was triggered by an incident involving her husband.*
Type of Presentation:	Present trigger
Symptoms:	Sense of lacking control of her life
Issues:	Husband's job was in jeopardy; his exhibited alcoholic behavior; marital difficulties

The clinician had been working with Delores on issues of self-esteem and self-control over a period of a few months. Delores was gradually reclaiming her power as she discovered that she could exert her influence on the people around her. She had identified and reprocessed the childhood events that had surfaced, which initially ignited the present dysfunction in her life. However, there was a situation in her current life that kept triggering her.

Delores did not feel like an equal in her marriage. "Don is a good father," she would say. "He comes home every night and does anything we need him to do. He brings dinner home sometimes or once in awhile he may even cook. He goes to all the girls' games and is very active in their activities." But, once the girls were put to bed, Don would drive down to the local pub and sit for hours with some old high school buddies and drink beer while they related stories about the "old days." He would come home around 11 or 11:30 p.m.

Don worked as an executive for a retail sales company. Because he did a lot of traveling, he drove a company car. Around the first of the year, Don hit another patron with his company car while trying to leave the parking lot of a bar. He got out of the car to see if the person was okay and then promptly left before the police arrived. Don was eventually apprehended and charged with a hit-and-skip accident, which he did not report to his employer. In June of the same year, the company informed Don that they were in the process of changing insurance companies. As part of the transition, they would be checking current driving records of all employees with company cars. Don feared that his job was now in jeopardy, and Delores' emotional charge surrounding the event had escalated. Delores felt that she was now ready to process the event in therapy.

Target: Hearing from Don that his job was in jeopardy because the company would learn about his hit-and-skip accident charges. Worst part: The blank look on her husband's face when he told her about his company checking employee driving records. "It didn't seem to bother him."

NC: I am out of control.

Check your training manuals. You will find a list of examples of NCs and PCs. If a client is unable to come up with an appropriate cognition, either negative or positive, there is nothing wrong with handing her this list saying, "Here is a list of possible beliefs. Focus on the event (or picture) and tell me if one of them resonates or if it helps you to come up with one of your own."

Again, the EMDR Humanitarian Assistance Programs sells a laminated version of the cognition list, and you may want to purchase it as a donation.

PC: I have some control.

The PC is also a self-referencing belief aimed at the client's *desired direction of change* (i.e., from someone who has no control to someone who has control).

VoC: 3

The VoC scale is measuring on a *gut* level how true or false the PC <u>feels</u>.

Emotions: Desperation, anger, and fear

Again, these are emotions the client *feels* in the present about something that happened in her past.

SUD: 8

The VoC and SUD scales provide a quantitative basis and act as an EMDR report card.

Body: A little in my shoulder. Nothing else.

No matter how slight, the physical sensations reported by the client are targeted. A client's hands or feet may tingle. Respiration or heart beat may accelerate. Anything identified by the client is not to be discounted.

If a client were to state her NC as "I am not good," or her PC as, "I am not bad," the clinician may help the client to frame the cognitions more appropriately by saying, "Do you mean, 'I am bad?' for the negative cognition" or ask the client, "Can you reframe it in a more negative way?" If it is the PC, "Do you mean, 'I am good?'" Or ask the client, "Can you reframe it in a more positive way?" The reframing question is preferable because it allows the client a *choice* of what she would like to believe.

Clinician: Throughout the EMDR process today, I will be asking you to tell me what you are experiencing. Tell me, as clearly as possible, what comes into your mind. Sometimes things will change, and sometimes they won't. There are no "supposed to's." Just let whatever happens, happen. Remember your stop signal and your calm (or safe) place when or if you need them. (Pause) Focus on the event, those words, "I am out of control" and where you <u>feel</u> it in your body. Just let it go wherever it goes. (Set of eye movements) That's it. Good. That's it. Let it go. Take a deep breath. (Pause) What are you getting <u>now</u>?

After each complete set of bilateral stimulation (eye movement or otherwise), the clinician instructs the client to "Let it go (or "Blank it out"). Take a deep breath. What are you getting (or noticing) <u>now</u>?" or something similar. Some clinicians say, "Take a deep breath. Let it go." The original meaning intended for the client was *draw a curtain over the material* (Shapiro, 2001). This gave the client permission to take a break from the intensity of the material being reprocessed, thereby creating space for the client to reorient and to verbalize any new information that has arisen. Regardless of which way the instructions lean, the client will relate to the clinician what she is noticing. Once she is finished, the clinician will say, "Go with that."

When first facilitating the bilateral stimulation, begin slowly and increase the speed as fast or tolerably comfortable for the client. The speed of the bilateral stimulation is adjusted to the client's need.

Delores: I feel like it has extended. It has not left my shoulders. I can feel the tension at the top of my head. It has just extended. It has not moved off me.

Clinician: Go with that. (Set of eye movements) You're doing fine. Good. Let it go. Take a deep breath. (Pause) What's happening <u>now</u>?

The clinician checks in with the client between sets to determine where the client is in the process and what has changed, if anything. The clinician then assesses the information received to determine if the client is moving toward adaptive resolution. Has new information emerged? Sometimes the information will change; sometimes it will not. Sometimes new information will emerge, and sometimes it will not. Regardless, it is important for the clinician to elicit clear feedback from the client. Neither the client nor the clinician is encouraged to judge the efficacy of the newly emerging and changing information. Just let whatever happens, happen and trust the process (Shapiro, 2001, 2008). Whether the client reports something entirely related or unrelated to the original target, the clinician will say, "Go with that" and continues the bilateral stimulation. Reprocessing is in process; and, as a result, associated channels may open up.

Delores: I don't know if it moved down. I am feeling it in my arms, and there is less tension in my head.
Clinician: Go with that. (Set of eye movements) Good. That's it. Let it go. Take a deep breath. (Pause) What's coming up <u>now</u>?

Other than "Good," "Uh-huh," or "You're doing fine," the clinician says little more than "Blank it out." ("Let it go" or "Take a break," however, are less likely to encourage dissociation with clients who have dissociative identity disorder [DID].)

The clinician's best strategy is asking the client to focus only on the new material that emerged during the last set or saying "Go with that."

Delores: There's still tension. Maybe . . . It's still just tense.
Clinician: Go with that. (Set of eye movements) Good. Let it go. Take a deep breath. (Pause) What are you noticing <u>now</u>?
Delores: I feel it in my face . . . frustration, concern, worry.

The client reports the most dominant thought, emotion, sensation, or image. On the basis of what the clinician learns, she will direct the client to the new information or to the original target. In this case, the client reports some new emotions, and the clinician directs the client to focus on the new information.

Clinician: Go with that. (Set of eye movements) Good. Let it go. Take a deep breath. (Pause) What's happening <u>now</u>?
Delores: There is not much change. I feel it maybe less in my face, but I feel more tension or the same here (she points to her forehead).
Clinician: Dolores I am going to switch to the faster speed that we talked about last week. Is that okay?
Delores: Sure.

Clinician: Notice that. (Speed of the bilateral stimulation is increased) (Set of eye movements) That's it. Good. Let it go. Take a deep breath. (Pause) What comes up for you now?

When asking a client what she is experiencing, the clinician uses general statements that allow her to report whatever is dominant in the moment (i.e., a change in thought, feeling, image, physical sensation, new event). The rule of thumb is that, as a significant change occurs with the set, use the same bilateral stimulation (i.e., speed, length, intensity, and direction) as in the previous set. If no change occurs, vary the speed, length, intensity, or direction of the bilateral stimulation. If a change fails to occur after subsequent sets, a more proactive approach may be needed (see chapter 5).

Delores: As I focus on the event then, I feel less stressed. When I focus on the event as it affects me now, it gets worse. I feel it less in my forehead but feeling it more in my neck. I am having a difficult time splitting the two.
Clinician: Go with that. (Set of eye movements) That's it. You're doing fine. Let it go. Take a deep breath. (Pause) What's happening now?

Encouraging the client is important. During each set of bilateral stimulation or at least when a shift is obvious, comment positively to the client by saying at least once, "That's it. Good. That's it" or something similar.

Delores: I am not sure where I should be. I keep things to myself. How can I take control?
Clinician: Notice that. (Set of eye movements) Good. Let it go. Take a deep breath. (Pause) What are you noticing now?
Delores: I believe that I can take control. I can choose to sit back and let the circumstance take control over me, but I can make the decision if I need and want to. I just don't want the circumstance to rule me. When I think about it this way, I don't feel so worried or feel the tension in my head and neck and face.

Movement continues to occur in the client's reprocessing of the event, so the clinician keeps tracking the client's process and progress as it occurs. The biggest responsibility the clinician has during EMDR processing is to stay out of the client's way. As long as movement of any kind is evident, the clinician needs only say, "Go with that."

Clinician: Go with that. (Set of eye movements) Good. That's it. Let it go. Take a deep breath. (Pause) What comes up for you <u>now</u>?

If the client reports newly emerging memories or changes in the client's original image, thoughts, feelings, or sensations, the clinician supports the movement by saying, "Go with that" or "Notice that." What if no movement is reported by the client? In this event, the clinician is instructed to change the direction or speed of the bilateral stimulation. Or the clinician could increase the length of the set.

Delores: I am feeling a bit more relaxed. Still less tension.
Clinician: Notice that. (Set of eye movements) Good. Let it go. Take a deep breath. (Pause) What comes up for you <u>now</u>?
Delores: I am still feeling relaxed.

Delores has not reported anything new or distressing for two consecutive sets of bilateral stimulation. She appears to be at the end of a channel and is unable to make more linkages at this point to the original event (or incident). When a client reaches the end of a channel, the clinician needs to bring the client back to target in order that she may access additional channels, if they exist.

Clinician: When you think of the <u>original</u> event (or incident), what do you get <u>now</u>?

(Reminder: Original incident—The look on her husband's face when he told her about his company checking employee driving records.)

Delores: I am not so much focusing on the event. I find that I am calmer and less stressed in focusing on finding strength within myself. In this situation, where I was stressed because of the jeopardy he put his family in, I feel I can make the decision to stay or go to support my family rather than him supporting the family. It is more calming and more empowering. And, again, there is less tension.
Clinician: Go with that. (Set of eye movements) Good. Let it go. Take a deep breath. (Pause) What's happening <u>now</u>?

Delores: It is an event that had nothing to do with me and, as it impacts our family, I can make a decision as to whether I will let this impact our family or not.

Clinician: Go with that. (Set of eye movements) Good. Let it go. Take a deep breath. (Pause) What comes up for you <u>now</u>?

Delores: My body feels relaxed. I feel more confident. I can handle this.

Clinician: When you think of the <u>original</u> event (or incident), on a scale from 0 to 10, where "0" is neutral or no disturbance and "10" is the worst disturbance you can imagine, how disturbing is the event (or incident) to you <u>now</u>?

Delores: It's a "4." Maybe a "3." It makes me less angry. I still feel some disappointment but less angry.

Did you catch the clinician's omission? She needed to take Delores back to the original event (or incident) by saying, "Focus on the original event (or incident) and tell me what comes up? What are you getting <u>now</u>?" before asking about the SUD level. The clinician made the assumption that the client was down to a "0" and jumped on it. She inadvertently forgot to have her focus on the original event (or incident) to check for other levels of disturbance that may have existed around this event. Fortunately, the next channel of association, the disappointment, became apparent.

Also, the process would have probably been more effective if the clinician had just let her process to see if other insights would emerge.

Clinician: Go with that. (Set of eye movements) That's it. Good.

Delores: I'm not sure if I'm skirting it. If I focus on the disappointment, the tension comes back. If I focus on the strength in me, I feel more relaxed and confident. I don't know if it's right or wrong. It just causes tension.

Clinician: The mind moves faster than spoken word. If you process silently to yourself it will help "speed the train faster down the track."

The client may repeatedly begin speaking before being instructed to do so. When she has finished talking, the clinician may gently remind her to process silently to herself and say, "It will speed the 'train' faster down the 'track.'" And then, "Go with that." Instruct the same way at the next set by saying, "Just go with that silently to yourself" to make sure that she understands.

Clinician: Just go with that silently to yourself. (Set of eye movements) Good. Let it go. Take a deep breath. (Pause) What comes up <u>now</u>?

Delores: I am a little less tense. I still feel it in the same spots, but it is less prevalent . . . which tells me the disappointment is still there.

Clinician: Go with that. (Set of eye movements) Good. Let it go. Take a deep breath. (Pause) What are you noticing <u>now</u>?

Delores: It's a lot less, but it's still there.

Clinician: Go with that. (Set of eye movements) That's it. Good. Let it go. Take a deep breath. (Pause) What are you getting <u>now</u>?

Delores: I tell myself that it happened, but it does not have to affect me. I am my own person, and I control what I do and how I react.

Clinician: Go with that. (Set of eye movements) That's it. Good. Let it go. Take a deep breath. (Pause) What is happening <u>now</u>?

Delores: My body is relaxed again. The confidence is back. It feels permanent. I can handle this in my own way.

Clinician: When you think of the <u>original</u> event (or incident), what do you get <u>now</u>?

The material that the client reports has a neutral feeling, which flags that the client has reached the end of a channel. When this happens, the correct response for the clinician is to bring the client back to target.

Delores: I feel pretty calm. It's difficult to feel much as I focus on it.

No matter what the client reports, the clinician will add a set of bilateral stimulation.

Clinician: Go with that. (Set of eye movements) Good. That's it. Let it go. Take a deep breath. (Pause) What is happening <u>now</u>?

It is only after retargeting the original incident and completing a set of eye movements without the emergence of new associations or new images, emotions, or physical sensations that the clinician goes back and checks the client's current SUD level.

Delores: I feel relaxed and calm.

Clinician: *When you think of the original event (or incident), on a scale from 0 to 10, where "0" is neutral or no disturbance and "10" is the worst disturbance you can imagine, how disturbing is the event (or incident) to you* <u>now</u>?

No change occurred, so the clinician checked the SUD level.

Delores: It's a "2."

Clinician: We have run out of time, and we need to stop. We can take a further look at this next time. Are you okay with stopping right *now*?

Delores: Sure.

Even though they came so far in this session and the client is at a "2" in terms of SUD level, it is still considered an incomplete session.

Since there is obviously more material to be processed, the installation of the client's PC and the body scan are eliminated.

Clinician: You have done some very good work, and I appreciate the effort you have made. How are you feeling?

Even though the session is incomplete, it is important that the clinician provide sincere encouragement and support for the effort the client did make.

Delores: I feel better.

Clinician: Good. What I would like to suggest we do *now* is a relaxation exercise. How would you feel about doing the lightstream technique?

This is an exercise the clinician had previously done with the client. She could have suggested other forms of relaxation, such as imagery or calm (or safe) place. The clinician might ask, "What would you like to do?" Clients often like some forms of relaxation better than others. Other possible alternatives are breathing or container exercises.

Delores: Sure. That would be good.

Clinician leads the client in the lightstream technique.

Clinician: You did a good job. As you review your experience in our session today, what positive statement can you make to express what you have learned or gained today?

While debriefing a client, it is optimal to leave them with a positive statement so that they will not leave dwelling on the negative with the possibility of opening up other negative channels of association.

Delores: I am too dependent on others, especially my husband, and I let them lead my life. I don't like it. I don't need it. I can and will be independent is what I learned today.

When a sessions ends in incomplete reprocessing, the clinician needs to use judgment in terms of the client's ability to manage any emotions that may arise after she leaves the session. The clinician may request that she practice some form of self-control technique between sessions and to keep a log of what emerges during the intervening week.

Clinician: The processing we have done today may continue after the session. You may or may not notice new insights, thoughts, memories, or dreams. If so, just notice what you are experiencing. Take a snapshot of what you are seeing, feeling, thinking, and any triggers and keep a log or TICES grid. Then do a calm (or safe) place exercise to rid yourself of the disturbance. We can work on this new material next time. If you feel it is necessary, call me.

Delores arrived at her session a week later feeling more prepared to handle whatever comes in terms of her husband's work and driving record. She and her husband had talked about how it could affect them financially. She had lost trust in her husband and believed that she needed to begin taking steps toward making herself and her children more independent of him. "I find myself distancing myself from him," she stated, "but also see how dependent I actually am on him. It's scary." Because Delores's SUD level ended up at a "2" at the last session, the clinician takes her back to the original event (or incident) to see what other layers have emerged during the intervening week.

Target: When the clinician asked what image came up as she looked at the overall situation, she said again, "The look on his face when he told me about his company checking his driving record. He didn't seem to care how it affected me or his daughters."
NC: I am out of control.
PC: I am now in control.

VoC: 4
Emotions: Frustration

SUD: 2
Body: Stomach

Clinician: Throughout the EMDR process today, I will be asking you to tell me what you are experiencing. Tell me, as clearly as possible, what comes into your mind. Sometimes things will change, and sometimes they won't. There are no "supposed to's" in this process. Just let whatever happens, happen. Remember your stop signal and your calm (or safe) place when you need them. (Pause) Focus on the event, those words, "I am out in control," and where you <u>feel</u> it in your body. Just let it go wherever it goes. (Set of eye movements) Let it go. Take a deep breath. (Pause) What is happening <u>now</u>?

Delores: I really feel it in my shoulders, eyes, and chest.

Clinician: Go with that. (Set of eye movements) That's it. Good. Let it go. Take a deep breath. (Pause) What are you noticing <u>now</u>?

Delores: I'm trying to think what *being in control looks like.* If I had not been so dependent, would I have reacted earlier to what had been happening all along in our marriage?

Clinician: Go with that. (Set of eye movements) Good. Let it go. Take a deep breath. (Pause) What's coming up <u>now</u>?

Delores: I'm feeling a lot less tension in my shoulders and neck, but I still feel it in my eyes. There's the feeling there that I can be in control.

Clinician: Go with that. (Set of eye movements) You're doing fine. Let it go. Take a deep breath. (Pause) What are you noticing <u>now</u>?

Delores: Again, I'm a lot less tense.

Clinician: Go with that. (Set of eye movements) You're doing fine. Let it go. Take a deep breath. (Pause) What are you getting <u>now</u>?

Delores: I can be in control. I have been—long before I met him. I can be again.

Clinician: Go with that. (Set of eye movements) You're doing fine. Let it go. Take a deep breath. (Pause) What is coming up <u>now</u>?

Delores: I will be in control again.

Clinician: Delores, when you think of the <u>original</u> event (or incident), what do you get <u>now</u>?

[Reminder: Original incident – "The look on his face when he told me about his company checking his driving record. He didn't seem to care how it affected me or his daughters."]

Delores: It's his problem not mine.

Clinician: Go with that. (Set of eye movements) You're doing fine. Let it go. Take a deep breath. (Pause) What are you noticing <u>now</u>?

Delores: I can feel my body letting it go.

Clinician: Go with that. (Set of eye movements) That's it. Good. Let it go. Take a deep breath. (Pause) What are you noticing <u>now</u>?

Delores: Good. It's gone.

Clinician: When you think of the <u>original</u> event (or incident), what do you get <u>now</u>?

Delores: He's the one who is losing, and I can feel more separated from that event.

Clinician: Go with that. (Set of eye movements) That's it. Good. Let it go. Take a deep breath. (Pause) What comes up for you <u>now</u>?

Delores: Before, I was saying, "I can handle this." Now I believe, "I will handle this."

Clinician: Go with that. (Set of eye movements) Good. Let it go. Take a deep breath. (Pause) What are you noticing <u>now</u>?

Delores: Yes, I will handle this.

Clinician: When you bring up the <u>original</u> event (or incident), on a scale from 0 to 10, where "0" is no disturbance and "10" is the worst disturbance you can imagine, how disturbing does it <u>feel</u> to you <u>now</u>?

Delores: It's between a "2" and a "3." There's the reality that I have to make sure I remember that it is his problem. I do not want to be pulled back into it. I want to remain separate from him. I want to decide what to do for me despite the situation. I will have to remind myself of it. I'm afraid prior concerns will come back.

The clinician erroneously believed that the client had opened and challenged all channels of association related to the current trigger. Obviously, she had not. Because EMDR is such a fluid, dynamic process, no harm is done to the client. Simply continue on with the reprocessing.

Clinician: Go with that. (Set of eye movements) Good. Let it go. Take a deep breath. (Pause) What's happening <u>now</u>?

Delores: I am just thinking to myself that I don't want it to come back and interrupt what I believe I need to do. I don't want it to bother me any more. When I continue to do that, it does not have the same impact. I can call it a "2." I feel like I have to keep reminding myself to let it out. Let it go. It's not about me. It's not my problem.

Clinician: Go with that. (Set of eye movements) That's it. Let it go. Take a deep breath. (Pause) What's happening <u>now</u>?

Delores: As long as we continue to have to deal with it and it even involves him, I am connected in some way. It can never be a zero. I can continue to tell myself that it's not my problem. It's not my fault. Anything ahead will affect the family. Today, that's where we are.

Clinician: Go with that. (Set of eye movements) You're doing fine. Let it go. Take a deep breath. (Pause) What are you noticing <u>now</u>?

Delores: The same. I just have to go day by day and regain my control a day at a time. But, I can and will handle it.

Clinician: Go with that. (Set of eye movements) Good. Let it go. Take a deep breath. (Pause) What are you getting <u>now</u>?

Delores: I can have some control, and I can have it now.

Clinician: Delores, when you bring up the <u>original</u> event (or incident), on a scale from 0 to 10, where "0" is no disturbance and "10" is the worst disturbance you can imagine, how disturbing does it <u>feel</u> to you <u>now</u>?

Delores: It's a "0!"

Clinician: Go with that. (Set of eye movements) You're doing fine. Let it go. Take a deep breath. (Pause) What are you getting <u>now</u>?

Delores: I know I can regain control. I know I will.

Clinician: Focus on the <u>original</u> event (or incident). Do those words, "I am now in control" still fit, or is there another positive statement you feel would be more suitable?

Delores: No. I think "I am now in control" rings even truer now.

Clinician: Think about the <u>original</u> event (or incident) and those words, "I am now in control" From "1," which is completely false, to "7," which is completely true, how <u>true</u> do they <u>feel</u> <u>now</u>?

In the installation phase, the VoC is strengthened by linking it to the PC and the original incident.

Delores: "7."

Clinician: Think of the event (or incident) and hold it together with the words, "I am now in control." (Set of eye movements) Let it go. Take a deep breath. (Pause) On a scale of 1 to 7, how <u>true</u> do those words, "I am now in control," <u>feel</u> to you <u>now</u> when you think of the <u>original</u> incident?

Delores: I am really beginning to believe it.

Clinician: Go with that. (Set of eye movements) That's it. Let it go. Take a deep breath. (Pause) How <u>true</u> do those words, "I am now in control" <u>feel</u> to you <u>now</u> when you think of the <u>original</u> incident?

Delores: Still totally true.

Clinician: Close your eyes and focus on the <u>original</u> event (or incident) and those words, "I am now in control" and scan your body from head to toe for physical discomfort. If you feel anything, let me know.

Delores: The pain in my neck is gone.

Clinician: Just notice that. (Set of eye movements) (Pause) What comes up for you <u>now</u>? Scan your body again for discomfort. (Pause) What are you getting <u>now</u>?

Delores: I feel good.

Clinician: What's the difference between how you feel now versus when we started the session?

Delores: I feel more empowered, like I can make it without him if I choose to. He is no longer steering my ship. I am.

Clinician: We need to stop for today. The processing we have done today may continue after the session. You may or may not notice new insights, thoughts, memories, or dreams. If so, just notice what you are experiencing. Take a snapshot of what you are seeing, feeling, thinking, and any triggers and keep a log or TICES grid. Then do a calm (or safe) place exercise to rid yourself of any disturbance. We can work on this new material next time. If you feel it is necessary, call me.

Whether the session is complete or incomplete, Dr. Shapiro recommends that the above closure/debriefing statement be made to the client. A review of stress control skills and strategies can also be considered (see chapter 2).

CASE EXAMPLE 6D: BRENDA

Situation: *Client is triggered by an act of love and tenderness of a mother toward her infant daughter.*

Type of Presentation: Present trigger

Symptoms: Depression, anxiety, anger, rage

Issues: Realization of what she missed as a child.

Brenda grew up in abject poverty in a small coal mining town in West Virginia. Her developmental growth was further hindered by a ruthless, critical father and a mother who had been diagnosed with bipolar disorder years before. She had four older brothers, but they were too busy fending for themselves and offered little support. Because her mother was more absent than present, either from laying in her bed most days or recovering from her mental illness at the nearest psychiatric unit, Brenda became her mother's replacement in most phases of her family's life. At an early age she learned to cook and clean and do whatever else was expected of her.

Because she grew up poor and in the country, Brenda felt awkward around most people. And she felt alone. She never had many friendships as a child, and those she did remember were short lived. Her home was never a safe or appropriate place to bring other children home to play. Playing was really not much of an option most days. Brenda suffered cruelly under the harsh words and frightening looks of her father's obvious disapproval. "He just plain didn't like women." So Brenda grew up "motherless" and rudderless throughout her childhood and adolescence.

Brenda and the clinician worked for months trying to ease the painful fragments of her neglected and lonely past. She would make leaps of progress only to slide downhill into the sadness that kept blocking her way. She had plowed through and dissipated the rage and anger from her past and elevated her self-esteem and self-confidence. She was finally becoming comfortable around others and taking risks to be with people.

One day Brenda walked into the clinician's office and told her how deeply affected she was by watching a mother and child while she was grocery shopping at a local market. "I just welled up with sadness as I watched how gentle and playful this woman was with her child. I finally knew what was triggering me. It is what I missed as a child." She really never had a mother to hold her, comfort her, or protect her. Or a father who would do the same. She had no one.

Brenda was realizing that this trigger plagued her often in many types of ways. So it was decided to process the pain associated with the trigger with EMDR.

Target: The image of how gentle and playful a woman was with her child at the grocery store.

A positive experience for one person can be a negative one for another.

NC: I am unlovable.
PC: I am lovable.
VoC: 2–3
Emotion: Sadness
SUD: 6
Body: Stomach

Clinician: Throughout the EMDR process today, I will be asking you to tell me what you are experiencing. Tell me, as clearly as possible, what comes into your mind. Sometimes things will change, and sometimes they won't. There are no "supposed to's." Just let whatever happens, happen. Remember your stop signal and your calm (or safe) place when you need them. (Pause) I would like you to bring up that picture, those negative words "I am unlovable," and notice where you <u>feel</u> it in your body. (Set of eye movements) Good. Let it go. Take a deep breath. (Pause) What comes up <u>now</u>?
Brenda: I feel sad and lonely.
Clinician: Notice that. (Set of eye movements) Good. Let it go. Take a deep breath. (Pause) What comes up for you <u>now</u>?
Brenda: I wish someone cared about me. I wish my parents cared about me.
Clinician: Notice that. (Set of eye movements) Good. Let it go. Take a deep breath. (Pause) What are you noticing <u>now</u>?
Brenda: I'm a kid. I wish this was not my life or life story. I wish I had parents or someone to help me. I wish I had a happy childhood.
Clinician: Go with that. You're doing fine. (Set of eye movements) Good. Let it go. Take a deep breath. (Pause) What's coming up <u>now</u>?
Brenda: I had an image of that day in the grocery store.
Clinician: Go with that. You're doing fine. (Set of eye movements) (She begins to cry uncontrollably.)

If a client starts to cry during EMDR, it is not beneficial to halt the process. When you think she is at a stopping point, ask her to take a deep breath. If tears or other physical signs of emotion (e.g., reddening of the face, rapid breathing) are present, allow the client to continue processing.

Clinician: (The clinician waits until Brenda has stopped crying.) Let it go. Take a deep breath. (Pause) What's coming up <u>now</u>?

Brenda: It's really hard not to have anyone to help or lean on. I tried to put on a good face.

Clinician: Go with that. (Set of eye movements) Good. Let it go. Take a deep breath. (Pause) What's coming up <u>now</u>?

Brenda: When I was a kid, I tried to be so tough and so strong. I don't feel tough or strong.

Clinician: Go with that. (Set of eye movements) Good. Let it go. Take a deep breath. (Pause) What comes up for you <u>now</u>?

Brenda: I just seem to be bouncing around with childhood memories. I remember Dad when I was in first grade. He scared me. Everyone did. I was 6, and I was afraid of people. I remember in the second grade my teacher took care of me because my mom didn't. When I was in the fourth grade, I won the Spelling Bee. I was so proud of myself, but I did not have anyone to tell. I never had any friends. I was such a weird kid. I was so alone.

Clinician: Go with that. (Set of eye movements) Good. Let it go. Take a deep breath. (Pause) What comes up for you <u>now</u>?

Brenda: I don't think I am a good person.

Clinician: Notice that. (Set of eye movements) Good. Let it go. Take a deep breath. (Pause) What's coming up <u>now</u>?

Brenda: I see myself lashing out a lot. I don't feel like people treat me very well, and I feel like I have to defend myself.

Clinician: Notice that. (Set of eye movements) Good. Let it go. Take a deep breath. (Pause) What's happening <u>now</u>?

Brenda: I feel the same. I didn't know what else to do as a kid. I feel sad. I feel like I have lost so much possibility in life . . . being the weird kid that no one likes. It feels like I am spinning around in a circle, bouncing back from one to the other.

Clinician: Go with that. (Set of eye movements) You're doing fine. Just ride the wave. Let it go. Take a deep breath. (Pause) What's coming up <u>now</u>?

Brenda: I can feel it mostly in my arms. There's a lot of activity.

Clinician: Notice that. (Set of eye movements) Good. Good. Let it go. Take a deep breath. (Pause) What's happening <u>now</u>?

Brenda: I am feeling hot and tingly. I think I am not a good person.

Clinician: Go with that. (Set of eye movements) Good. Let it go. Take a deep breath. (Pause) What comes up for you <u>now</u>?

Brenda: I'm grinding my teeth. It's the same kind of sensation. My chest is tightening up. My throat really hurts.

Clinician: Go with that. (Set of eye movements) Good. Let it go. Take a deep breath. (Pause) What are you noticing <u>now</u>?

Brenda: There's a raw feeling in my throat . . . kind of sweet. I'm really a good person even if I am the only person who knows it. I did a really good job of finding my way in this world. I can let it go, and it's okay. I'm okay.

Clinician: Go with that. (Set of eye movements) Good. Let it go. Take a deep breath. (Pause) What comes up for you <u>now</u>?

Brenda: I am so happy that I tried and tried and tried until I found the help I needed. I am so proud I gave myself a chance. I have nothing but opportunities and possibilities ahead of me by letting this go. It is not who I am. It is what I survived.

Clinician: When you think of the <u>original</u> event (or incident), what do you get <u>now</u>?

(Reminder: Original incident—The image of how gentle and playful a woman was with her child at the grocery store.)

Brenda: I don't get anything. The memory is a blank.

Clinician: Go with that. (Set of eye movements) Good. Let it go. Take a deep breath. (Pause) What are you noticing <u>now</u>?

Brenda: I can be loving and gentle with myself. I never allowed myself to be. I think I want to try to be now.

Clinician: Go with that. (Set of eye movements) Good. Let it go. Take a deep breath. (Pause) What is happening <u>now</u>?

Clinician: When you think of the <u>original</u> event (or incident), what do you get <u>now</u>?

Brenda: I feel like I have just met myself for the first time, and it feels good.

Clinician: Go with that. (Set of eye movements) Good. Let it go. Take a deep breath. (Pause) What comes up for you <u>now</u>?

Brenda: I like myself. No, I love myself. I am a good person.

Clinician: When you think of the <u>original</u> event (or incident), on a scale from 0 to 10, where "0" is no disturbance and "10" is the worst disturbance you can imagine, how disturbing does it <u>feel</u> to you <u>now</u>?

Brenda: It is definitely a "0."

Clinician: Just go with that. (Set of eye movements) Good. You're doing fine. (Pause) How <u>true</u> does it feel to you <u>now</u>?

Brenda: Oh, yes. Zero. Oh, finally, "0."

The clinician facilitates another set of eye movements to see what emerges, if anything.

Clinician: Just notice that. (Set of eye movements) (Pause) What are you getting?

Brenda: Zero! Zero! Zero!

Clinician: Do the words, "I am lovable" still fit, or is there another positive statement you feel would be more suitable?

Brenda: "I am lovable" feels right.

Clinician: Think about the *original* event (or incident) and those words, "I am lovable." From "1," which is completely false, to "7," which is completely true, how <u>true</u> do they <u>feel</u> <u>now</u>?

Brenda: Seven.

Clinician: Think of the event (or incident) and hold it together with the words, "I am lovable." (Set of eye movements) Good. Let it go. Take a deep breath. (Pause) On a scale of 1 to 7, how <u>true</u> do those words, "I am lovable," <u>feel</u> to you now when you think of the *original* incident?

Brenda: It feels totally true. I am lovable.

Clinician: Just notice that. (Set of eye movements) (Pause) What are you getting?

The clinician facilitates another set of eye movements to see what emerges, if anything.

Clinician: Now focus on the <u>original</u> event (or incident_) and those words, "I am lovable" and scan your body from head to toe for physical discomfort. If you feel anything, let me know.

Brenda: I feel good.

Clinician: Just notice that. (Set of eye movements) (Pause) What are you getting?

The clinician facilitates another set of eye movements to see what emerges, if anything.

Brenda: I feel great!

Clinician: You did a great job.

Brenda: I had to say good-bye to the "little me." (She smiled.) That was weird. The images I got were of me as a kid, but I felt so mature. I said, "Good-bye. You can go." "Little me" was smiling and waving and telling me, "Everything is going to be okay." And she faded off into the distance. I felt like I was merging. The last time was weird. I realized that my whole life all I wanted to do was save kittens and people and fix things. I was really here to save myself, and to think the only person I need to save is me.

Clinician: The processing we have done today may continue after the session. You may or may not notice new insights, thoughts, memories, or dreams. If so, just notice what you are experiencing. Take a snapshot of what you are seeing, feeling, thinking, and any triggers and keep a log or TICES grid. Then do a calm (or safe) place exercise to rid yourself of the disturbance. We can work on any new material next time. If you feel it is necessary, call me.

FUTURE

CASE EXAMPLE 6E: JIMMY

Situation: The client saw himself as an ordinary guy married to a beautiful woman. He never felt worthy of her or that he quite measured up.

Type of Presentation: Future template—anticipatory anxiety

Symptoms: Insecurity, chronic worry, lack of confidence in relationship with his spouse

Issues: Fear of wife leaving him

Jimmy and his wife had been in and out of couples counseling for years. His wife, Megan, was a beautiful woman; and Jimmy had always thought he played second fiddle to her. He never felt that he measured up to her romantic notion of the tall and handsome knight in shining armor who could physically and sexually swept her off her feet.

Jimmy was far from ugly, but he wasn't exactly stunning either. He was not an athletic man, so he was not particularly well built. He was short and stocky, had wavy hair, and thin lips. He thought these characteristics made him unattractive, and this is how he labeled himself. Nonetheless, he wooed and won the woman of his dreams in college. They eventually married and had two young children. Despite his obvious conquest, Jimmy was never confident in his ability to keep his wife. He always thought that, despite her obvious love and devotion to him, she would leave him one day.

After years of assuring Jimmy that she loved him and would not leave him, his wife did walk out on him. She left him with the kids and went to her older sister's for 3 days. She had grown weary of his chronic worrying and questioning over something that she had no intention of doing. She left in anger and frustration but came back 3 days later tired and remorseful.

Fear of his wife walking away was Jimmy's original presenting issue, and he and the clinician worked for weeks cleaning out all the touchstone events that set his dysfunction into place and the present triggers which kept it in place. After these successful EMDR sessions, his relationship with his wife became closer, and his confidence in their marriage renewed. Here is the transcript of this session:

Target: Possibility of his wife leaving him.
NC: I don't matter.
PC: I do matter.
VoC: 3
Emotions: Fear
SUD: 7–8
Body: Chest

In chapter 4, another example of reprocessing the future prong is presented with the case of Michael driving at dusk. This case started much differently than Michael's because it deals with anticipatory anxiety and, as a result, needs to be addressed utilizing a full assessment of the future situation. Michael's case is dealt with utilizing skills building and imaginal rehearsal and does not require a full assessment of the target.

Clinician: Throughout the EMDR process today, I will be asking you what you are experiencing. Tell me, as clearly as possible, what comes into your mind. Sometimes things will change, and sometimes they won't. There are no "supposed to's" in this process. Just let whatever happens, happen. Remember your stop signal and your calm (or safe) place when you need them. (Pause) Focus on the incident, those words, "I don't matter" and where you <u>feel</u> it in your body. Just let it go wherever it goes. (Set of eye movements) Let it go. Take a deep breath. (Pause) What's happening <u>now</u>?

With every set of bilateral stimulation, it is the intention to bring the client to a new plateau of processing. The clinician needs to stay alert to the emergence of this new information during each and every set. Watch the client's face, especially his eyes and skin color. This is where it may show up first, even before the client realizes a shift has occurred, such as a lessening of disturbance.

Jimmy: I am feeling very alone. I am thinking about how hurt I would feel on my own. It's like this has all been a big farce.

Clinician: Go with that. (Set of eye movements) Let it go. Take a deep breath. (Pause) What are you noticing <u>now</u>?

Jimmy: I would feel embarrassed if she left. What do I tell people, and what a fool I would look like.

Clinician: Notice that. (Set of eye movements) Let it go. Take a deep breath. (Pause) What comes up for you <u>now</u>?

Jimmy: Having to tell everyone. Telling my kids and my mom would be the hardest part. (Jimmy begins to cry.)

Clinician: Go with that. (Set of eye movements) Let it go. Take a deep breath. (Pause) What's happening <u>now</u>?

Jimmy: And then the kids would be devastated, especially my five-year-old son, Jason.

Clinician: Go with that. (Set of eye movements) Let it go. Take a deep breath. (Pause) What are you noticing <u>now</u>?

Jimmy: I am thinking about telling my friends, other siblings, and family. It just would be so hard, so hard to do. And where would I be after that? It just didn't work out, and she doesn't love me. I feel like a failure.

Clinician: Notice that. (Set of eye movements) Let it go. Take a deep breath. (Pause) What's coming up <u>now</u>?

Jimmy: How do I recover from that? Would I feel like I could recover from that?

Clinician: Go with that. (Set of eye movements) Let it go. Take a deep breath. (Pause) What are you getting <u>now</u>?

Jimmy: I am feeling like I would make it, and I would be all right. I don't feel it in my chest as much. I feel like I would be okay. It's more about the mechanics of splitting assets and all the other complications.

Clinician: Go with that. (Set of eye movements) Let it go. Take a deep breath. (Pause) What are you noticing <u>now</u>?

Jimmy: My chest does not hurt nearly as bad.

Clinician: Go with that. (Set of eye movements) Let it go. Take a deep breath. (Pause) What comes up for you <u>now</u>?

Jimmy: I feel okay. I feel like I would be all right. I can get through it. No mental pictures.

Clinician: Go with that. (Set of eye movements) Let it go. Take a deep breath. (Pause) What are you noticing <u>now</u>?

Jimmy: I'm having a difficult time concentrating on it. I can see my wife's face, and she is walking away from me. That would be rough. Moving out. (At this point, the client placed his hand over his heart.)

Clinician: Go with that. (Set of eye movements) Let it go. Take a deep breath. (Pause) What are you getting <u>now</u>?

Jimmy: It just feels manageable . . . that's kind of weird. It comes and goes. I guess I would feel embarrassed. I'm tired. I can't see anything happening. I'm not having the emotion I had before. I keep seeing that I am going to be okay. That's alright. That's what keeps coming up. I'm going to be alright. I am worthy of being loved. I see that. My chest feels weird. It's a little tight, and I am a little sick to my stomach but not much.

Clinician: Go with that. (Set of eye movements) Let it go. Take a deep breath. (Pause) What are you getting <u>now</u>?

Jimmy: I can see myself with my wife.

Clinician: Go with that. (Set of eye movements) Let it go. Take a deep breath. (Pause) What's happening <u>now</u>?

Jimmy: Not a lot. My chest does not hurt.

Clinician: Go with that. (Set of eye movements) Let it go. Take a deep breath. (Pause) What comes up for you <u>now</u>?

Jimmy: I can see her face to the side. She is just standing there. She looks like she feels disappointed. My chest feels a little weird.

Clinician: Go with that. (Set of eye movements) Let it go. Take a deep breath. (Pause) What comes up for you <u>now</u>?

Jimmy: I think she is trying to deal with something. That's what I get. That's what it is. I'm at my mom's house for Christmas. I can see my wife. I see all the presents.

Clinician: Notice that. (Set of eye movements) Let it go. Take a deep breath. (Pause) What's happening <u>now</u>?

Jimmy: I'm sitting in my living room now. Everyone is excited about the presents. Everyone is there.

Clinician: Notice that. (Set of eye movements) Let it go. Take a deep breath. (Pause) What are you noticing <u>now</u>?

Jimmy: I guess I feel like she is not going to leave. That's what I feel.

Clinician: Go with that. (Set of eye movements) Let it go. Take a deep breath. (Pause) What are you getting <u>now</u>?

Jimmy: I guess I believe she won't leave.

Clinician: When you think of the <u>original</u> event (or incident), what do you get <u>now</u>?

(Reminder: Original incident—Possibility of his wife leaving him.)

Jimmy: I can't see. I'm having a hard time concentrating on it. I can see her face. She has a smile on her face. She's not saying anything.

It is not always as "cut and dry" deciding when to go back to target or when to check on the SUD scale. The rule of thumb is that a return to target occurs in the final stages of reprocessing if a client's associations seem to have stopped in a certain channel. A return to target is necessitated to discern additional channels of disturbing information or to ascertain the progression to the installation phase and body scan. When we return to target, we are essentially checking to see how the incident or event is currently stored. However, going back does not necessarily mean that adaptive resolution has occurred.

When a client appears to be distracted, the clinician may ask the client to refocus on the original event (or incident). Any time it appears that a client is running around in circles or losing focus, the clinician has the option of taking the client back to the original target so that they have a starting point from which to begin processing again.

Note that, when the clinician takes the client back to the target, she is asking him to go back to the original event (or incident) . . . she does not ask him to focus on the possibility of his wife leaving him. The clinician does not describe the event for the client for several reasons. From the time a client describes his target in any way, the entire memory may begin to change or transform. It begins to lose some of its power over the client. The clinician does not want to interfere with the client getting his power back or run the risk of tampering with the memory by not describing it fully or accurately.

Clinician: Go with that. (Set of eye movements) Let it go. Take a deep breath. (Pause) What are you noticing <u>now</u>?

Jimmy: She really does love me. I know that now.

Clinician: When you bring up the <u>original</u> event (or incident), on a scale from 0 to 10, where "0" is no disturbance and "10" is the worst disturbance you can imagine, how disturbing does it feel to you <u>now</u>?

Jimmy: Let's say a "3." There is some doubt that she will stay in the marriage. Anything is possible.

Clinician: Go with that. (Set of eye movements) Let it go. Take a deep breath. (Pause) What's coming up <u>now</u>?

Jimmy: I keep saying, "I'm okay" in my mind. I'm not sure my chest believes it, but it keeps coming up. I see that I'm a good person. I'm worthy. I'm lovable. I see that. I'm liked.

Clinician: Go with that. (Set of eye movements) Let it go. Take a deep breath. (Pause) What are you getting <u>now</u>?

Jimmy: I am okay. I really am okay.

Clinician: When you think of the <u>original</u> event (or incident), what do you get <u>now</u>?

Jimmy: I see her face. I feel a little twinge in my chest.

Clinician: Go with that. (Set of eye movements) Good. Let it go. Take a deep breath. (Pause) What are you noticing <u>now</u>?

Jimmy: I see her walking away from me, except she is not moving. She is turning around and walking back toward me. She is hugging me. She says she loves me.

Clinician: Go with that. (Set of eye movements) Let it go. Take a deep breath. (Pause) What is happening <u>now</u>?

Jimmy: She's holding me.

Clinician: When you think of the <u>original</u> event (or incident), what do you get <u>now</u>?

Jimmy: I can see her face. She's smiling . . . or kind of a half-smile.

Clinician: Go with that. (Set of eye movements) Let it go. Take a deep breath. (Pause) What are you noticing <u>now</u>?

Jimmy: We are both smiling. And we're holding each other . . . tightly.

Clinician: When you bring up the <u>original</u> event (or incident), on a scale from 0 to 10, where "0" is no disturbance and "10" is the worst disturbance you can imagine, how disturbing does it <u>feel</u> to you <u>now</u>?

Jimmy: It's a "0." I don't feel like she is leaving me.

The equivalent of a change of at least one SUD point (on a scale of "0" to "10") needs to be evident in the responses before requesting a SUD level reading from a client. The clinician will be evaluating the degree of change from set to set by monitoring the client's responses between sets and client-reported changes in emotions and physical sensations. It is unnecessary to take a reading after each set. Remember that increases as well as decreases in a client's stress responses can indicate that processing is occurring.

Clinician: Go with that. (Set of eye movements) Let it go. Take a deep breath. (Pause) What are you noticing now?

Jimmy: I feel good. I can see her grinning now and walking toward me. She loves me and is going to stay with me. I'm confident of that now.

Clinician: Focus on the <u>original</u> event (or incident). Do those words, "I do matter" *still fit*, or is there another positive statement you feel would be more suitable?

There are two reasons for asking this question: (a) The PC may have evolved to a more adaptive one since it was first asked during the assessment phase; and (b) sometimes, during the assessment phase, the client is unable to come up with an adequate PC. Rather than causing him further discomfort by insisting he verbalize one, the clinician knows there is another opportunity for the client to voice what he would like to believe about himself as he focuses on the original event (or incident).

Jimmy: It feels totally appropriate.

Clinician: Think about the <u>original</u> event (or incident) and those words, "I do matter." From "1," which is completely false, to "7," which is completely true, how <u>true</u> do they <u>feel</u> <u>now</u>?"

Jimmy: Six point five.

Clinician: Think of the event (or incident) and hold it together with the words "I do matter." (Set of eye movements) (Pause) On a scale of 1 to 7, how <u>true</u> do those words "I do matter" <u>feel</u> to you <u>now</u> when you think of the <u>original</u> incident?

Jimmy: Now it's a "7."

Clinician: Go with that. (Set of eye movements) Let it go. Take a deep breath. (Pause) How <u>true</u> do they <u>feel</u> <u>now</u>?

Jimmy: Seven!

Clinician: Close your eyes and focus on the <u>original</u> incident with those words, "I do matter," and scan your body from head to toe for physical discomfort. If you feel anything, let me know.

The body scan is implemented at this stage of the process to ensure that there are no residual aspects of the target still in need of reprocessing.

Jimmy: There is nothing.

Clinician: What does "nothing" mean?

Jimmy: There is no discomfort. I feel calm and relaxed.

Clinician: Go with that. (Set of eye movements) Let it go. Take a deep breath. What are you noticing <u>now</u>?

After a neutral body scan, the clinician implements an additional set of bilateral stimulation to insure a neutral or positive change. If the body sensations change in either direction, the clinician will continue to do additional sets until the change is complete.

Jimmy: There is no change.

Clinician: The processing we have done today may continue after the session. You may or may not notice new insights, thoughts, memories, or dreams. If so, just notice what you are experiencing. Take a snapshot of what you are seeing, feeling, thinking, and any triggers and keep a log or TICES grid. Then do a calm (or safe) place exercise to rid yourself of the disturbance. We can work on this new material next time. If you feel it is necessary, call me.

In chapter 4, the future template was illustrated using an example of skills building and imaginal rehearsal. After the session above, the clinician helped target a positive template that incorporated appropriate future behaviors for Jimmy. A subsequent session followed that included appropriate education, modeling, and imagining, along with EMDR targeting to help Jimmy respond differently in the future.

SUMMARY

The understanding and self-efficacy achieved at the end of a session by each of the clients described in this chapter are *the hallmark of a successful EMDR session* (Shapiro, 2001). Remember that typically less than half of a clinician's EMDR sessions occur without having to implement some type of clinical guidance or strategies to unblock stalled reprocessing. In either case, the result is the same . . . a client's previously reported negative images, affect, cognitions, and physical sensation related to a stated trauma become weaker or nonexistent, less colorful, less intense, or however the client happens to describe them. The validity of the client's negative overall response to the trauma becomes absorbed and replaced by the vividness of his present positive images, affect, cognitions, and physical sensations of the same event. The client becomes more empowered, stable, secure, and has a stronger sense of self.

CONCLUSION

Since its introduction in 1989, the treatment effects of EMDR continue to be experienced throughout the world by clients who have suffered from anxiety, depression, obsessions, phobias and panic, stress, relationship conflicts, addictions, chronic and phantom limb pain, grief, and more. Thousands of clinicians have been trained worldwide in this efficacious method since its inception, but many practitioners have chosen to lay EMDR aside and continue using only traditional treatment methods. Some may have deemed EMDR to not be a good fit with their current therapeutic model, work setting, or clinical population. Or, perhaps, managed care or limited sessions appeared to render EMDR impractical or impossible. Whatever the reason, the desire in writing this Primer is to help newly trained EMDR practitioners keep on track and to provide a refresher for those who have not consistently used EMDR in their practices.

The intent of the Primer is to provide a learning tool to assist newly trained and previously EMDR-trained clinicians to better understand the basic principles, protocols, and procedures of EMDR. This Primer is neither a substitute for formal EMDR training nor for Dr. Shapiro's basic text, *Eye Movement Desensitization and Reprocessing: Basic Principles, Protocols and Procedures, Second Edition* (2001).

Now that you have reached the end of the Primer, you are encouraged to go back and reread Dr. Shapiro's basic text again to see what kernels of information leap off the page at you. Read other texts written and/or edited by Dr. Shapiro (1997, 2002, 2007) as you continue to enrich your understanding of EMDR. Over the past 20 years, numerous skilled clinicians, researchers, and students have also written books, articles, and dissertations and have presented papers on EMDR at major trauma conferences worldwide.

Hopefully, your understanding of EMDR has been enriched and deepened and your excitement and commitment to use it more successfully with your clients have increased. If it has been many years since you were trained in EMDR and you are reading the Primer because EMDR is something you are considering initiating with your clients in the future, it would be advisable to seek the training again and seek consultation from an EMDRIA-Approved Consultant. Whatever the case, it is hoped that your interest in and enthusiasm for EMDR have been rekindled and that you have learned something along the way and had fun while doing it.

Appendices

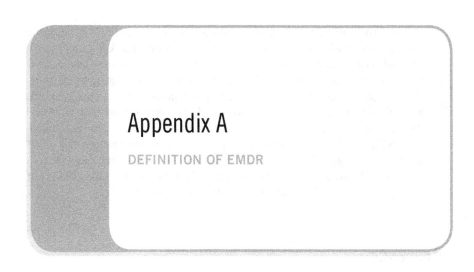

Appendix A

DEFINITION OF EMDR

It is crucial that clinicians trained in Eye Movement Desensitization and Reprocessing (EMDR) be familiar with the definitions of EMDR formulated by the EMDR Institute and the EMDR International Association (EMDRIA). These definitions can facilitate finding your own words for explaining EMDR to your clients.

The following description of EMDR comes from the EMDR Institute's Web site (see www.emdr.org):

> Eye Movement Desensitization and Reprocessing (EMDR) is a psychotherapy treatment that was originally designed to alleviate the distress associated with traumatic memories (Shapiro, 1989a, 1989b). Shapiro's (2001) Adaptive Information Processing Model posits that EMDR facilitates the accessing and processing of traumatic memories to bring these to an adaptive resolution. After successful treatment with EMDR, affective distress is relieved, negative beliefs are reformulated, and physiological arousal is reduced. During EMDR the client attends to emotionally disturbing material in brief sequential doses while simultaneously focusing on an external stimulus. Clinician directed lateral eye movements are the most commonly used external stimulus but a variety of other stimuli including hand-tapping and audio stimulation are often used (Shapiro, 1991). Shapiro (1995) hypothesizes that EMDR facilitates the

accessing of the traumatic memory network, so that information processing is enhanced, with new associations forged between the traumatic memory and more adaptive memories or information. These new associations are thought to result in complete information processing, new learning, elimination of emotional distress, and development of cognitive insights. EMDR uses a three pronged protocol: (1) the past events that have laid the groundwork for dysfunction are processed, forging new associative links with adaptive information; (2) the current circumstances that elicit distress are targeted, and internal and external triggers are desensitized; (3) imaginal templates of future events are incorporated to assist the client in acquiring the skills needed for adaptive functioning.

REFERENCES

Shapiro, F. (1989a). Efficacy of the eye movement desensitization procedure in the treatment of traumatic memories. *Journal of Traumatic Stress, 2*(2), 199–223.

Shapiro, F. (1989b). Eye movement desensitization: A new treatment for posttraumatic stress disorder. *Journal of Behavior Therapy and Experimental Psychiatry, 20*(3), 211–217.

Shapiro, F. (2001). *Eye movement desensitization and reprocessing: Basic principles, protocols and procedures.* (2nd ed.). New York: The Guilford Press.

Shapiro, F. (1991). Eye movement desensitization & reprocessing procedure: From EMD to EMDR/R-a new treatment model for anxiety and related traumata. *Behavior Therapist, 14,* 133–135.

The EMDR International Association (EMDRIA) provides two definitions for EMDR. The following definition was designed specifically for clients (see www.emdria.org):

Eye Movement Desensitization and Reprocessing (EMDR) is a method of psychotherapy that has been extensively researched and proven effective for the treatment of trauma. EMDR is a set of standardized protocols that incorporates elements from many different treatment approaches. To date, EMDR has helped an estimated two million people of all ages relieve many types of psychological stress.

A more elaborate and descriptive definition for clinicians provides information on the goals of EMDR in a psychotherapeutic framework. It includes explanation of the Adaptive Information Processing Model, which serves as the theoretical foundation for the EMDR approach, the specifics of the methodology, and the fidelity of EMDR (see www.emdria.org):

I.   *Purpose of Definition*

The purpose of this definition is to serve as the foundation for the development and implementation of policies in all EMDRIA's programs in the service of its mission. This definition is intended to support consistency in EMDR training, standards, credentialing, continuing education, and clinical application while fostering the further evolution of EMDR through a judicious balance of innovation and research. This definition also provides a clear and common frame of reference for EMDR clinicians, consumers, researchers, the media and the general public.

II.   *Foundational Sources and Principles for Evolution*

Francine Shapiro, Ph.D., developed EMDR based on clinical observation, controlled research, feedback from clinicians whom she had trained, and previous scholarly and scientific studies of information processing. The original source of EMDR is derived from the work of Shapiro as it is described in her writings (Shapiro, 2001). Shapiro made clear that she is committed to the development of EMDR in a way that balances clinical observations and proposed innovations with independent empirical validation in well designed and executed scientific studies. Previously held and newly proposed elements of EMDR procedure or theory that cannot be validated must give way to those that can.

III.   *Aim of EMDR*

In the broadest sense, EMDR is intended to alleviate human suffering and assist individuals and human society to fulfill their potential for development while minimizing risks of harm in its application. For the client, the aim of EMDR treatment is to achieve the most profound and comprehensive treatment effects in the shortest period of time, while maintaining client stability within a balanced family and social system.

IV.   *Framework*

EMDR is an approach to psychotherapy that is comprised of principles, procedures and protocols. It is not a simple technique characterized primarily by the use of eye movements. EMDR is founded on the premise that each person has both an innate tendency to move toward health and wholeness, and the inner capacity to achieve it. EMDR is grounded in psychological science and is informed by both psychological theory and research on the brain.

EMDR integrates elements from both psychological theories (e.g., affect, attachment, behavior, bio-informational processing, cognitive, humanistic, family systems, psychodynamic and somatic) and psychotherapies (e.g., body-based, cognitive-behavioral, interpersonal, person-centered, and psychodynamic) into a standardized set of procedures and clinical protocols. Research on how the brain processes information and generates consciousness also informs the evolution of EMDR theory and procedure.

V. *Hypotheses of the EMDR Model*

The Adaptive Information Processing Model is the theoretical foundation of the EMDR approach. It is based on the following hypotheses:

1. Within each person is a physiological information processing system through which new experiences and information are normally processed to an adaptive state.

2. Information is stored in memory networks that contain related thoughts, images, audio or olfactory memories, emotions, and bodily sensations.

3. Memory networks are organized around the earliest related event.

4. Traumatic experiences and persistent unmet interpersonal needs during crucial periods in development can produce blockages in the capacity of the adaptive information processing system to resolve distressing or traumatic events.

5. When information stored in memory networks related to a distressing or traumatic experience is not fully processed, it gives rise to dysfunctional reactions.

6. The result of adaptive processing is learning, relief of emotional and somatic distress, and the availability of adaptive responses and understanding.

7. Information processing is facilitated by specific types of bilateral sensory stimulation. Based on observational and experimental

data, Shapiro has referred to this stimulation as bilateral stimulation (Shapiro, 1995) and dual attention stimulation (Shapiro, 2001).

8. Alternating, left-right, visual, audio and tactile stimulation when combined with the other specific procedural steps used in EMDR enhance information processing.

9. Specific, focused strategies for sufficiently stimulating access to dysfunctionally stored information (and, in some cases, adaptive information) generally need to be combined with bilateral stimulation in order to produce adaptive information processing.

10. EMDR procedures foster a state of balanced or dual attention between internally accessed information and external bilateral stimulation. In this state the client experiences simultaneously the distressing memory and the present context.

11. The combination of EMDR procedures and bilateral stimulation results in decreasing the vividness of disturbing memory images and related affect, facilitating access to more adaptive information and forging new associations within and between memory networks.

VI. *Method*

EMDR uses specific psychotherapeutic procedures to: 1) access existing information; 2) introduce new information; 3) facilitate information processing; and 4) inhibit accessing of information (Lipke, 1999). Unique to EMDR are both the specific procedural steps used to access and process information, and the ways in which sensory stimulation is incorporated into well-defined treatment procedures and protocols, which are intended to create states of balanced or dual attention to facilitate information processing.

EMDR is used within an 8-phase approach to trauma treatment (Shapiro, 1995, 2001) in order to ensure sufficient client stabilization and reevaluation before, during and after the processing of distressing and traumatic memories and associated stimuli. In Phases 3–6, standardized steps must be followed to achieve fidelity to the method. In the other 4 phases there is more than one way to achieve the objectives of each phase. However, as it is a process, not a technique, it unfolds according to the needs and resources of the individual client in the context of the therapeutic relationship. Therefore, different elements may be emphasized or utilized differently depending on the unique needs of the particular client.

To achieve comprehensive treatment effects, a three-pronged basic treatment protocol is used to first address past events. After adaptive resolution of past events, current stimuli still capable of evoking distress are processed. Finally, future situations are processed to prepare for possible or likely circumstances.

VII. Fidelity in Application through Training and Observation

It is central to EMDR that positive results from its application derive from the interaction between clinician, method and client. Therefore graduate education in a mental health field (e.g., clinical psychology, psychiatry, social work, counseling, or marriage and family therapy) leading to eligibility for licensure, certification or registration, along with supervised training, are considered essential to achieve optimal results. Meta-analytic research (Maxfield & Hyer, 2002) indicates that degree of fidelity to the published EMDR procedures is highly correlated with the outcome of EMDR procedures. Evidence of fidelity in procedure and appropriateness of protocol is considered central to both research and clinical application of EMDR.

REFERENCES

Lipke, H. (1999). *EMDR and psychotherapy integration: theoretical and clinical suggestions with focus on traumatic stress*. Boca Raton: CRC Press.

Maxfield, L., & Hyer, L. (2002, January). The relationship between efficacy and methodology in studies investigating EMDR treatment of PTSD. *Journal of Clinical Psychology, 58*(1), 23–41

Shapiro, F. (1995). *Eye movement desensitization and reprocessing: Basic principles, protocols and procedures* (1st ed.). New York: The Guilford Press.

Shapiro, F. (2001). *Eye movement desensitization and reprocessing: Basic principles, protocols and procedures.* (2nd ed.). New York: The Guilford Press.

Appendix B

EXERCISES

GROUNDING

When an individual is grounded, it says three things. An individual who is grounded is in his body, is present, and is available to experience anything that happens.

Being grounded means "being in your feet." It means being rooted to the ground. It means being solid, stable, and empowered. An individual has the ability to ground himself anywhere. He can ground himself in nature by gardening, for instance, or with anything that anchors or connects him to the earth. Being with animals is grounding. Walking, hiking, running, or just stomping or wiggling your feet on the floor is grounding. Being grounded gives us an energetic connection to the earth that feeds us in powerful ways. Anything that gives us a sense of the earth beneath our feet is grounding.

During the preparation phase, along with a brief introduction to Eye Movement Desensitization and Reprocessing (EMDR), try teaching the client to ground and breathe correctly before leading him into the calm (or safe) place or sacred space exercises. The exercise that follows is one of the easiest and quickest ways to teach clients how to ground.

Grounding Exercise

> Close your eyes. Try to relax and imagine thick tree roots growing out of the soles of your feet and growing down into the ground as deeply as you can possibly imagine. Take them to the earth's core. At the core of the earth is a thick bar. Allow the roots to wrap around it to help draw you taut against the earth. The earth has an energy field just like you and I. As you inhale into your diaphragm (see Diaphragmatic Breathing), *draw the earth's energy up through these roots and into your body through the soles of your feet. You may actually feel it. It may feel cool, tingly, or warm. Do this until you can feel the earth's energy.*

When the client is ready, ask, "How does it feel? What is the difference between now and before you began this exercise?"

Ask the client to ground daily.

DIAPHRAGMATIC BREATHING

Diaphragmatic breathing is the way that we breathe when we are born. It is the manner in which we need to breathe in order to maintain a balance of oxygen and carbon dioxide. This assists the body in maintaining a relaxed state and staving off perpetual anxiety. Diaphragmatic breathing is effective with clients in reducing stress-related symptoms, anxiety, depression, and fatigue. Along with the grounding exercise, breathing from the diaphragm can give the client a big boost in terms of overall health, elevated self-esteem, and a sense of well-being.

Not surprisingly, many clients are shallow or chest breathers. They breathe into and through their chests rather than their diaphragms. Many may present stressed out and anxious or report mind chatter. In an effort to help alleviate these symptoms, retraining clients to breathe diaphragmatically can be effective.

When we are in danger, our first reaction is a primal one. Our autonomic, automatic response is to inhale quickly into our chest as a signal to all our senses to go on hyperalert. This is a startle response. We become more alert, tense, and hypervigilant until the danger is over. The body's response is to then return to breathing from the diaphragm and into a state of relaxation.

Clients who present as chest breathers are often in a hypervigilant state and will need to retrain themselves to breathe into their diaphragm as a way of lessening the stress, anxiety, tightness, and tenseness with which they present.

Breathing Exercise

(The client is sitting comfortably in a chair. His knees are bent, and his feet are flat on the floor.)

Try to relax your shoulders, head, and neck as much as possible. Now place your right hand on your diaphragm and your left hand on your upper chest. This will allow you to better feel your diaphragm move as you breathe. Your diaphragm is just below your rib cage and above the stomach. It will rise as you inhale and fall as you exhale. Breathe in through your nose and out through your mouth. Inhale and hold your breath for a slow count of five, and exhale on another slow count of five. Repeat two or more times. There is to be no movement in your chest or lower abdomen. The key is motionlessness in these two areas. Breathe smoothly, slowly, and evenly.

Note: When clients are first introduced to this exercise, they may have a tendency to breathe too deeply and get light-headed. At first, the diaphragmatic breathing may not feel automatic. Clients may also experience tiredness after only a few minutes of breathing in this way. Although the benefits of this type of breathing are immediate, it needs to be practiced. It is suggested that clients practice this exercise three to four times daily for 5 to 10 minutes.

ANCHORING IN THE PRESENT

This exercise can be conducted routinely with clients. Make sure the client is sitting comfortably and erect in a chair with her feet firmly planted on the ground and then instruct her to do the following:

Close your eyes and become aware of what is going on around you. Feel your feet. Move them. The best way to ground yourself quickly is to feel your feet. Can you feel your socks? (Pause) Can you feel the soles of your shoes? (Pause) Can you feel the rug under your feet? (Pause) Can you feel the concrete under the rug? (Pause) Can you feel the hardness under your feet? (Pause) How about what is under the concrete? (Pause) Can you feel the coldness of the damp earth beneath the concrete? (Pause)

Now feel the texture of the upholstery of the chair on which you are sitting. (Pause) Feel it. Take it in. (Pause) Can you feel the foam under the fabric? (Pause) Can you feel the wood structure that supports the chair? (Pause)

Listen to the sound of my voice as I talk. Listen to what other sounds you can hear. Can you hear the sound of the overhead fan? (Pause) Can you hear the traffic outside? (Pause) Can you hear the sound of voices in the hall outside? (Pause) What else can you hear? (Pause)

Please open your eyes now and look around. What shapes do you see? (Pause) Look at the colors and textures of everything in the room. (Pause) Count 10 things in the room that are blue. (Pause) Now count 10 things that are red. (Pause)

How are you feeling? Are you feeling differently than before we started this exercise?

Seeing or, in this case, feeling is believing. An important offshoot of this exercise is that the client has an opportunity to feel the difference between living in the present versus living in the past or future. Once the client appears to be fully present, ask her to notice how it feels and report her experience of being here. Then ask her to focus on a disturbing event in her past. "How does that feel?" Have her come back to the present. Then ask her to focus on something disturbing that may be happening in the future. "How does that feel?" Often the client is able to experience what it is truly like to be "in the present."

CALM (OR SAFE) PLACE

(Shapiro, 2001, pp. 125–126; 2006, pp. 45, 2009, pp. 29–31)

Dr. Shapiro (2001) prescribes the use of the calm (or safe) place exercise throughout the EMDR process. It assists in preparing a client to process traumatic events, to close an incomplete session, and to help equalize or stabilize a client's distress in session if the information that emerges is too emotionally disruptive. It is called a calm (or safe) place because some clients have been traumatized to such a high degree that it is not ecologically possible for them to even imagine that a "safe" place could exist. This process, if successful and set in by bilateral stimulation (BLS), also serves to introduce the client to BLS in a comfortable way before the BLS is used on disturbing material.

It is important to instruct clients extensively on the correct use of the calm (or safe) place and its potential effects. For instance, if disturbing events arise during the calm (or safe) place exercise, they may halt processing and cause the client to shift cognitively, emotionally, or physiologically. Or, they may increase the current distress level in some clients. And, when a disturbing event is paired with BLS, there is the potential for intensifying negative affect with which the client presents or activate the processing of the client's presenting issue (Shapiro, 2001). As with any technique utilized with a client, use caution. A scripted version of the calm (or safe) place exercise follows:

Identify the Image

Clinician: Bring up a place, some place, real or imagined, that feels calm (or safe). Can you think of such a place? A mountain top or beside a babbling stream, perhaps? Or on a beach? Where would it be?
Client: Oh, that's easy. When I was looking over the Urubamba Valley in Peru from Machu Picchu.

The client is asked to visualize or create a place where he can find calm and safety.

Identify the Associated Emotions and Sensations

Clinician: Good. Focus on this calm (or safe) place—everything in it. What sights, sounds, and smells, if any, come up for you? What are you noticing?
Client: It is so calm and peaceful up there. I could stay there forever.

The client focuses on the image, the feelings evoked by the image, and where he feels it in his body.

Enhancing the Sensations

Clinician: Good. Concentrate on this image and where you feel the pleasant sensations in your body. Allow yourself to connect to and enjoy them. As you are concentrating on these images, follow my fingers. (Pause) How do you feel now?
Client: I am feeling calm and peaceful and safe as well.

The clinician uses guided imagery to enhance the calm (or safe) place by stressing the positive feelings and sensations being experienced by the client.

The BLS utilized with the calm (or safe) place is slow and consists of 4 to 6 passes.

Clinician: Good. Focus on that and follow my fingers once more. (Pause) What do you notice now?

Client: The sensations have strengthened and deepened.

If positive feelings come up, continue with soothing guided imagery and the positive feelings and sensations expressed by the client, along with additional sets of BLS (4–6 passes). Keep repeating as long as the client's sensations continue to be enhanced (i.e., "Bring up your calm (or safe) place and those pleasant sensations.").

Establishing a Cue Word

Clinician: Good. Is there a word or phrase that might represent your calm (or safe) place?

The client is asked to identify a single word or phrase that best represents his calm (or safe) place.

Client: "Sacred."

Clinician: Focus on the word "sacred" and notice positive feelings that arise when you do. Focus on those sensations and the word "sacred" and follow my fingers. (Pause) What do you notice now?

The clinician verbally enhances the positive feelings and sensations identified by the client with slow short sets of BLS (4–6 passes).

Client: I feel like I am in a sacred cocoon.

Repeat the instruction above, along with short sets of BLS (4–6 passes) in an attempt to further enhance the positive feelings experienced by the client. Continue as long as the positive feelings keep being enhanced.

Self-Cuing Instruction

Clinician: Now do the same thing on your own. Say the word "sacred" and notice what you feel and follow my fingers.

Cuing With Disturbance

Clinician: Think of a *minor* disturbance. (This disturbance is about a 1 or 2 on a 10-point scale where 10 = the worst and 0 = calm or neutral. Higher levels of disturbance may cause the client to be unable to successfully use the calm [or safe] place.) Perhaps something that happened this week. Now go to your calm (or safe) place and notice how it feels. Bring up the word "sacred" and notice if there are changes in your body sensations. What did you notice?

If positive feelings arise, the clinician will enhance the calm (or safe) place as above with several short sets of BLS. If a negative shift occurs, the clinician will attempt to guide the client through the process until a shift to positive emotions and sensation occurs.

Client: I felt my whole body kind of sink when I focused on a conflict I had with my boss earlier in the week. When I repeated the word "sacred" to myself, I felt uplifted and strong.

Self-Cuing With Disturbance

Clinician: Good. Now bring up another mildly disturbing event. Bring up the word "sacred" on your own and notice changes in your body as you do.
Client: Same thing happened as before. I just feel so strong and impenetrable.

Again, if a positive shift emerges, enhance as before with passes of BLS a few times (4–6 *slow* passes are recommended by most clinicians who use EMDR).

At the end of the exercise, instruct the client to use his cue word and calm (or safe) place every time he feels even a little annoyed between sessions. The client can keep track of this by keeping what is called a TICES Log (Shapiro, 2001, 2009). Clients are also alerted that attempts to use their calm (or safe) place when they are experiencing high levels of disturbance may not work, especially when they are learning this process. The process will work better as they gain more skill with practice.

Note: See Appendix C for an explanation of the TICES Log.

There are some cautionary elements for the clinician:

1. The initial development of a calm (or safe) place may be disturbing to the client and increase his levels of distress. If this does occur, reassure the client that it is not unusual for this to happen.

Then immediately assist the client in developing another calm (or safe) place or initiate another self-regulating exercise.

2. Pairing the BLS with the development of the calm (or safe) place has the ability to bring some clients to high levels of negative affect very quickly. For example, the client may be in the process of developing a calm (or safe) place in a meadow, and suddenly the image of the rapist appears as a dark figure overshadowing it. In cases like this, try to develop a place that continues to be safe and/or calm to her, probably a different place, as the current place has been "intruded" upon by distressing material.

3. Negative associations may also emerge when the calm (or safe) place is developed and the BLS is introduced. For example, a client who happens to be a policeman is preparing to reprocess a memory of seeing his partner shot in a shoot-out with a gang member. Upon introducing BLS to his newly developed calm (or safe) place, a memory of exchanging gun fire with a group of marauding student protesters emerges. When this happens, the clinician can assist the client in developing another calm (or safe) place.

SACRED SPACE

Grounding the Client in the Moment

Place your feet flat on the floor and keep your eyes closed throughout the duration of this exercise. Become aware of your surroundings and your sense of self in them. Pay attention to your breathing. Imagine that you have big, thick tree roots growing out of the arches of your feet. Let them go down as deep into the earth as you can possibly imagine. Let them go to the earth's core. Imagine that there is a huge metal bar at the core of the earth. Wrap these roots around the bar so that they are taut and tight. Let them anchor you to the earth. Like ourselves, the earth possesses an energetic field and, as you inhale, draw the earth's energy up the roots, on up through the soles of your feet, and on up into the rest of your body. With each breath, this energy can travel further and further up your body until you can feel it at the top of your head. You may actually feel the energy. It may feel cool, warm, tingling, or you may not feel it at all. It does not matter. Breathe like this until you can feel your breath tingle in your torso and upper extremities. Breathe evenly and consistently.

Count your breaths, such as "1" as you inhale, "2" as you exhale, "3" as you inhale, "4" as you exhale, and then start again with "1". (Breathe with the client.) The counting becomes your mantra and helps you to become more centered and grounded. Do this for a couple of minutes. Remember, breath is life.

As you exhale, breathe out any negative or toxic energy. Just feel yourself relax.

Finding the Sacred Space

Take the essence of who you are right now and go inside your body in search of what I call your sacred space. What I mean by sacred space is a special place that I will help you to create where you can go in search of comfort or calm, solace or solitude, safety or support, or anything else that you seek. Start at the top of your head and go to the tips of your toes in search of this space. This is your space, and it belongs to you solely and no one else. You do not need to tell me where it is. It's your special place. No one ever has to know, unless you want them to, where your sacred space is located. If you cannot find a sacred space, just pick a space that you feel might be appropriate. When you are finished, let me know. Try not to forget to breathe.

Preparing the Sacred Space

Wait patiently and silently until the client indicates to you in some way that he has located an appropriate spot in his body for a sacred space. When he has done so, instruct the client as follows:

Now prepare your sacred space. What I mean by this is to bring into your sacred space anything and everything that you might need to help resolve the issues that brought you here today. If you need courage, bring courage. If you need faith, bring faith. You may bring your best friend, your pet, or your favorite item or object. Anything and everything. The sky is your limit. Paint it, texture it, design it, and furnish it. Make this sacred space as comfortable as you can possibly make it. Take your time. When you are finished, let me know.

Getting Comfortable in Your Sacred Space

Once the client has indicated that he has finished preparing his sacred space, invite him to go there.

Now go to your sacred space. Nestle down among the things you have placed there. This is your sacred space and it is important for you to be comfortable in it. When you are comfortable, please let me know.

Imagine that there is a bright light coming through your forehead creating a channel to your sacred space. It is through this channel that you can graciously and respectfully invite wisdom (or guidance) into your sacred space. Wisdom (or guidance) may come in any form. It may come in the form of a book, a picture, an object, a symbol, a person, or a group of persons. When wisdom (or guidance) is there, let me know.

Listening for Wisdom's (or Guidance's) Message

Wisdom (or guidance) has brought you a very special message today. Graciously and respectfully ask wisdom (or guidance) for that message. When you have it, please let me know. (Pause) [Note: If the client does not answer, prompt him by saying, "Just say the first thing that comes to your mind".]

When the client indicates that he has the message, say, "What is the message?"

Make sure you write it down and say, "Now graciously and respectfully thank wisdom (or guidance) for the message, and remember that wisdom (or guidance) can come any time it is called into your sacred space."

Remarkably, most clients do hear messages, such as "I can make it," "I can do this," "I know what I have to do now," or "I am in the right place."

Closing the Sacred Space

Close your sacred space and know that, as you leave here today, you take this space with you. No one knows where it is but you. This is your special place. Go there often. Go there when you are in need of comfort or calm, solace or solitude, safety or support. When you are ready, you may open your eyes.

This sacred space exercise can be a very empowering experience.

Note: Use BLS throughout the entire exercise. The BLS is slow and consistent. During the actual EMDR session, the client can be instructed to go to his sacred space in the same way that others use the calm (or safe) place.

Appendix C

EMDR SCRIPTS

BREATHING SHIFT

(Shapiro, 2006, pp. 46; 2009, pp. 82)

Here is a scripted version of the breathing shift:

Clinician: Bring up a positive memory . . . a memory that is a good or happy memory.
Client: Okay.
Clinician: Just notice where your breath starts and then place your hands over it.
Client: Okay.
Clinician: (Pause) Just notice how it feels. Good. (Pause) Bring up a memory with a low level of disturbance. (Pause) Notice how your breath changes. (Pause) Place your hand over the location where you feel the change. (Pause) Now place your hand where you had it before and deliberately change your breathing pattern accordingly.

If this technique does not cause the disturbance to dissipate, try something else (e.g., spiral technique).

SPIRAL TECHNIQUE

(Shapiro, 2006, pp. 46; 2009, pp. 81–82)

A scripted version of the spiral technique follows:

Clinician: Bring up a disturbing memory and concentrate on body sensations that emerge. This is an imaginal exercise, so there are no right or wrong responses.
Client: Okay.
Clinician: When you think of the *original* event (or incident), on a scale from 0 to 10, where "0" is neutral or no disturbance and "10" is the worst disturbance you can imagine, how disturbing is the event (or incident) to you *now*?
Client: Nine.
Clinician: Where do you feel it in your body?
Client: In my stomach.
Clinician: Concentrate on what you are feeling in your body. Imagine that the feelings are energy. If the energy is going in a spiral, what direction is it going? Clockwise? Or counterclockwise?
Client: Clockwise.
Clinician: Good. Focus on the feelings and change the direction of the spiral to counterclockwise. Just notice what happens as you do.
Client: Okay.
Clinician: What happens?
Client: The sensations seem to be lessening.

If this technique is working, the client's sensations may dissipate and the SUD level may drop. If it does not work, try something else (e.g., breathing shift).

FUTURE TEMPLATE SCRIPT

(Shapiro, 2009, pp. 210–214; 2006, pp. 52–53; 2009, pp. 78)

"I'd like you to imagine yourself coping effectively with/in _____ in the future. With the new positive belief _____ and your new sense of _____ (i.e., strength, clarity, confidence, calm), imagine stepping into this scene. Notice what you see and how you're handling the situation. Notice what you're thinking, feeling, and experiencing in your body. Are there any blocks, anxieties, or fears that arise as you think about this future scene?"

If yes, ask the client to focus on these blocks and introduce several sets of bilateral stimulation (BLS). If the blocks do not resolve quickly, evaluate if the client needs any new information, resources, or skills to be able to comfortably visualize the future coping scene. Introduce needed information or skills. If the block still does not resolve and the client is unable to visualize the future scene with confidence and clarity, use direct questions, the affect scan, or the floatback technique to identify old targets related to blocks, anxieties, or fears. Use the standard protocol to address these targets before proceeding with the future template.

If there are no apparent blocks and the client is able to visualize the future scene with confidence and clarity, ask the client to focus on the image, positive belief, and sensations associated with this future scene and introduce sets of BLS. Do several sets until the future template is sufficiently strengthened. Check with body scan and the VoC scale.

Next, ask the client to move from imagining this one scene or snapshot to imagining a movie about coping in the future, with a beginning, middle, and end. Encourage him to imagine himself coping effectively in the face of specific challenges, triggers, or snafus. Make some suggestions of things to help inoculate him for future problems.

"This time, I'd like you to close your eyes and play a movie, imagining yourself coping effectively with/in _____ in the future. With the new positive belief _____ and your new sense of _____ (strength, clarity, confidence, calm), imagine stepping into the future. Imagine yourself coping with *any* challenges that come your way. Make sure that this movie has a beginning, a middle, and an end. Notice what you're seeing, thinking, feeling, and experiencing in your body. Let me know if you hit any blocks. If you do, just open your eyes and let me know. If you don't hit any blocks, let me know when you have viewed the whole movie."

If the client hits blocks, address as above (BLS, interweaves, new skills/information/resources/direct questions/affect scan/floatback). If the client is able to play the movie from start to finish with a sense of confidence and satisfaction, ask him to play the movie one more time from beginning to end and introduce BLS. In a sense, you are installing this movie as a future template.

TICES LOG

(Shapiro, 2001, pp. 429)

The TICES log (i.e., target = image, cognitions, emotions, and sensations) is a log the client is asked to keep between sessions to record disturbing experiences. The log provides a means of informing the clinician what occurred with the client after the EMDR session. What got activated? What, if anything, was disturbing? What did the client notice when he got triggered? What changed? What is unresolved? The client is instructed at the end of each session to record his experiences in this log. Once this is done, the client is instructed to use one of the self-control techniques learned in his therapy to dissipate the remaining disturbance.

At the end of each session, the clinician may remind and instruct the client to utilize the TICES log in the following manner: "The processing we have done today may continue after the session. You may or may not notice new insights, thoughts, memories, or dreams. If so, notice what you are experiencing and record it in your TICES log. Use the calm (or safe) place exercise to rid yourself of disturbance. Remember to use a relaxation technique daily. We can work on this new material next time. If you feel it is necessary, call me" (Shapiro, 2001).

The recommended format for the client's weekly log report is demonstrated in Table C.1, TICES Log (Shapiro, 2001).

Table C.1

TICES LOG

DATE	TARGET	IMAGE	COGNITION	EMOTION	SENSATION AND SUD

As the titles of the columns indicate, the client is asked for only brief descriptions of any disturbing experiences encountered between sessions. Note that the order of the titles in the columns mirror the information needed to target an event in a subsequent session in the assessment phase of EMDR. Thus, the TICES log acts as a clinical aid for both the clinician and the client. It also trains the client to break the disturbance down into its attendant parts and provides brief descriptors to remember and relate to the clinician the details of the experience in the event future processing is needed.

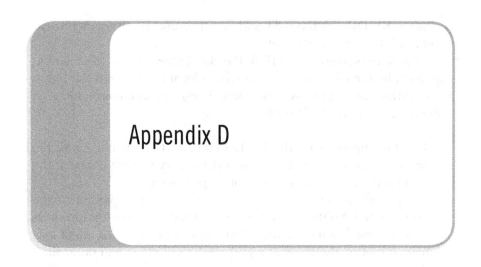

Appendix D

INFORMED CONSENT AND EMDR

Informed consent, like Eye Movement Desensitization and Reprocessing (EMDR), is a process, not an event. It is a two-way communication process whereby the clinician provides information and encourages the client to ask questions or make comments. It is important that the clinician create an environment in which the client can make informed choices as to the types of treatments—medical, psychological or otherwise—in which she chooses to engage.

The criteria for informed consent have been defined over the years by such organizations as the American Medical Association and the American Psychological Association. It is a process of communication that serves as an ethical obligation and a legal requirement. An informed choice is a voluntary decision based on information provided by the clinician, understanding by the client, and a discussion of available options. Informed consent is introduced in the preparation phase of EMDR.

In terms of EMDR and informed consent, Dr. Shapiro (2001) strongly recommends that the following criteria be explained thoroughly and in a way that the client can understand: (a) EMDR and how it works; (b) the nature and purpose of EMDR and its procedural steps; (c) treatment effects; (d) the possibility of emotional disturbance before, during, and after EMDR; (e) the risks and benefits; and (f) alternative treatments and their risks and benefits.

Prior to implementing EMDR, the client agrees to the treatment as explained by the clinician. In cases where legal proceedings are imminent, further caution needs to be taken. If legal proceedings may be an option, Dr. Shapiro (2001) further suggests:

1. It is important for the EMDR clinician to be familiar with the nature of memory and be aware that memory records not what the client remembers but what the client perceives.
2. The client may not be able to access a vivid picture of the event after EMDR. Memories tend to fade or even disappear as they become less intense after EMDR. For example, the client may have forgotten the color of a perpetrator's clothing and other finer details of the traumatic event. If court proceedings are a possibility, the client's legal counsel is contacted prior to EMDR because the quality of the client's memories can be further degraded by the reprocessing of the traumatic event.
3. The client may not be able to access the event again with extreme emotion (i.e., EMDR can take away the intense negative emotional charge associated with the event).
4. The client may also be able to access more information than he had previous to EMDR. The images that were originally remembered may be more vivid and contain more detail. In addition, a heightened level of emotion may occur when the client is reprocessing highly charged information associated with the event. What is remembered is not necessarily factual as the legal system would define it. It is valid to the client and reflects what was stored in the client's memory at the time of the event. However, it may be what was perceived, not necessarily what is factual.
5. The process may tend to be compared to hypnosis by the court.
6. In the case of a client in recovery from substance abuse, relapse may be a possibility when he accesses information from highly charged memories or other reprocessing information that arises from the targeted traumatic events.

The client has the right and the clinician has an ethical obligation to ensure that she is fully informed as to what EMDR is. This includes information on what the client may or may not expect if it is used as part of her treatment, what are possible responses and additional information that paints a picture of why EMDR is used, how it works, and what the treatment effects may be.

Informed consent allows the client to make an informed decision based on the facts that are presented to her before agreeing to EMDR. This also includes relating the legal ramifications if there is a pending lawsuit. In this instance, it is important to discuss court involvement in terms of how memory works with EMDR and other forensic issues (i.e., fading or disappearing memories, lack of intense emotional affect when discussing the events, and the emergence of more information surrounding the event and the accuracy of it) that can emerge as a result of EMDR processing. In all cases, the clinician or the client needs to consult with the client's legal counsel to ensure that all the necessary details of the event have been fully investigated and all notes and depositions have been completed pre-EMDR. It is unwise to initiate EMDR prior to consultation with the client's attorney.

The client is also informed of the high levels of emotion that may occur during this process, as well as the possible emergence of new or unexpected memories. In addition, the client will need to be aware of the potential processing difficulties or benefits encountered if she also presents with a history of substance abuse. In some cases, an addiction can be reactivated by EMDR. In others, it may decrease, especially if the trauma identified and processed is a contributing factor to the client's past substance abuse or relapses.

Appendix E

EMDR AND TRAUMA-RELATED RESOURCES

EMDRIA, EMDRIA Foundation, EMDR-HAP, and the EMDR Institute: What's the Difference?

Understanding the ownership and relationship between the original organizations that arose in the 1990s and 2000s to oversee Eye Movement Desensitization and Reprocessing's (EMDR's) functioning across all boundaries is of importance to all EMDR clinicians. Figure E.1 graphically defines the important differences between EMDRIA, the EMDR Institute, and EMDR-HAP.

EMDR International Association (EMDRIA)

EMDRIA is a 501(c)6 nonprofit membership association founded in 1995 to establish, maintain, and safeguard standards of training, research, and practice for EMDR. EMDRIA is comparable to the American Psychiatric Association, American Psychological Association, or American Counseling Association. This association's mission is to be "a membership organization of mental health professionals dedicated to the highest standards of excellence and integrity in EMDR." EMDRIA's Web site can be found at http://www.emdria.org.

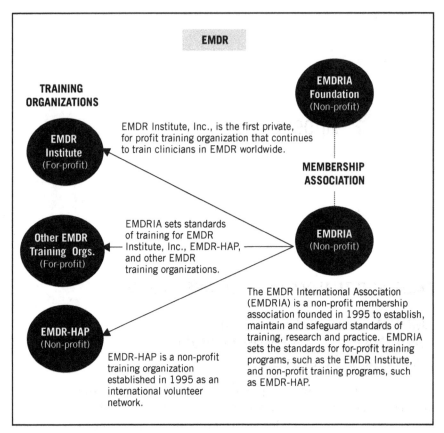

Figure E.1 EMDR and Associated Organizations

EMDRIA Foundation

The EMDRIA Foundation is a 501(c)3 nonprofit association founded in 2006 to help fund and promote the future development of EMDR through research and education. The Foundation is funded by voluntary contributions. Information about the Foundation can be found on EMDRIA's Web site.

EMDR Humanitarian Assistance Programs (EMDR-HAP)

EMDR-HAP was the brainchild of Dr. Francine Shapiro. It is also a 501(c)3 nonprofit organization that offers mental health professionals in Third World countries, as well as domestic community mental health agencies, EMDR training for free or for a reduced fee. EMDR-HAP is an international volunteer network of mental health providers dedicated to alleviate human suffering resulting from man-made and natural disasters. It is funded by private donations. The Web site for EMDR-HAP is located at http://www.emdrhap.org.

EMDR Institute, Inc.

The EMDR Institute, Inc., is the first "for profit" EMDR training organization incorporated in the early 1990s by Dr. Francine Shapiro to meet the increasing demands of EMDR training. Other than university-approved training programs, the EMDR Institute remained the sole deliverer of EMDR training for many years. After the publication of her first book, *Eye Movement Desensitization and Reprocessing: Basic Principles, Protocols, and Procedures* (1995), the number of EMDR training programs proliferated rapidly around the world. The Institute continues to be the longest running and best known of all the training programs.

Institute training schedules can be found at http://www.emdr.com.

FRANCINE SHAPIRO LIBRARY

Created and developed by Barbara J. Hensley, EdD, the Francine Shapiro Library was presented to the EMDR community at the 12th annual EMDRIA Conference in Phoenix, Arizona in September, 2008. Named after the originator and developer of the Adaptive Information Processing (AIP) model and EMDR, the library is the world's premier electronic repository and largest assemblage of EMDR citations. The library is hosted by Northern Kentucky University as a service to EMDRIA. The link for the Francine Shapiro Library is as follows:

http://library.nku.edu/emdr/emdr.data.php.

Thanks go to the following individuals for helping this library become a virtual reality: Irene Giessl, EdD, cofounder of the Cincinnati Trauma Connection; Marilyn Schleyer, PhD, assistant professor, Northern Kentucky University; Scott Blech, executive director, EMDRIA; and Philip Yannarella, documents librarian, and Sheri Myers, systems librarian, Steely Library, Northern Kentucky University.

RESOURCE DEVELOPMENT AND INSTALLATION (RDI)

Although not covered at length in this Primer, stabilization and ego strengthening are not to be overlooked. They are an inherent and important part of the preparation phase of EMDR, especially for difficult and challenging clients, dissociative clients, and clients with low affect tolerance. These topics deserve separate focus and intense study by the clinician.

There are no published, controlled studies of RDI currently available, but there are articles on RDI that discuss it as an effective intervention for stabilization. Clinicians trained in EMDR are encouraged to reference the following resources for RDI:

Leeds, A. M. (1998). Lifting the burden of shame: Using EMDR resource installation to resolve a therapeutic impasse. In P. Manfield (Ed.), *Extending EMDR: A casebook of innovative applications,* (1st ed., pp. 256–281). New York: W. W. Norton.

Korn, D., & Leeds, A. (2002). Preliminary evidence of efficacy for EMDR resource development and installation in the stabilization phase of treatment of complex posttraumatic stress disorder. *Journal of Clinical Psychology,* 58(12), 1465–1487.

Leeds, A. M., & Shapiro, F. (2000). EMDR and resource installation: Principles and procedures for enhancing current functioning and resolving traumatic experiences. In J. Carlson, & L. Sperry (Eds.), *Brief therapy with individuals and couples* (pp. 469–534). Phoenix, Arizona: Zeig, Tucker & Theisen, Inc.

Leeds, A. M. (2001, Dec). Principals and procedures for enhancing current functioning in complex posttraumatic stress disorder with EMDR resource development and installation. EMDRIA *Newsletter,* Special Edition, 4–11.

As a precursor to RDI, see:

Lendl, J., & Foster, S. (1997). Brief intervention focusing protocol for performance enhancement. In J. Lendl & S. Foster (1997), *EMDR and performance enhancement for the workplace: A practitioners' manual.* (2nd ed., p. 97). *EMDR Humanitarian Assistance Programs.*

DISSOCIATIVE DISORDERS

Clinical Signs and Symptoms of Dissociative Disorders

Refer to the following references for clinical signs and symptoms of dissociative disorders:

Dell, P. F., & O'Neil, J. A. (2009). *Dissociation and the dissociative disorders.* New York, NY: Routledge.

Kluft, R. P. (1987). First-rank symptoms as a diagnostic clue to multiple personality disorder. *American Journal of Psychiatry, 144,* 293–298.

Kluft, R. P. (1985). The natural history of multiple personality disorder. In Kluft, R. P. (Ed.), *The childhood antecedents of multiple personality.* Washington, DC: American Psychiatric Press.

Loewenstein, R. J. (1991). An office mental status examination for complex, chronic dissociative symptoms and multiple personality disorder. *Psychiatric Clinics of North America, 14,* 567–604.

Putnam, F. W. (1989). *Diagnosis and treatment of multiple personality disorder.* New York: Guilford Press.

Putnam, F. W., Guroff, J. J., Silberman, E., K., Barban, L., & Post, R. M. (1986). The clinical phenomenology of multiple personality disorder. *Journal of Clinical Psychiatry, 47,* 285–293.

Ross, C. A., Miller, S. D., Reagor, P., Bjornson, L., Fraser, G. A., & Anderson, G. (1990). Schneiderian symptoms in multiple personality disorder and schizophrenia. *Comprehensive Psychiatry, 31,* 111–118.

Spiegel, D. (1993). Multiple posttraumatic personality disorder. In Kluft, R. P. & Fine, C. G. (Eds.), *Clinical Perspectives on Multiple Personality Disorder.* Washington, DC: American Psychiatric Press.

In addition, there are resources available that deal with dissociation and EMDR by Catherine Fine, PhD, Carol Forgash, LCSW, Gerald Puk, PhD, and others. Search the Francine Shapiro Library for these valuable resources.

Dissociative Experience Scale (DES)

Both authorized versions of the DES described below are self-report measures that assess the degree and types of dissociative experiences. Depending on when and by whom the clinician was trained, some EMDR training manuals contain copies of the DES. If not, the clinician may refer to the following resources for an explanation and/or copies of the DES for use with their clients:

- The Colin A. Ross Institute for Psychological Trauma provides an excellent description of the DES at http://www.rossinst.com/dissociative experiences scale.html.
- For further reading, refer to the following citations:
  Dissociative Experiences Scale (DES). Bernstein, C., & Putnam, F. (1986). Development, reliability, and validity of a dissociation scale. *Journal of Nervous and Mental Diseases, 174,* 727–735.
  Dissociative Experiences Scale - II (DES-II). Carlson, E. B., & Putnam, F. W. (1993). An update on the dissociative experiences scale.

Dissociation, 6, 16–27. There is a reproducible copy of the DES-II in this article. Serving as a manual for the DES II, this article summarizes data on psychiatrically healthy and clinical samples.

■ Copies of both versions of the DES can be purchased online from the Sidran Foundation at http://www.sidran.org/store or by contacting the Foundation at the following address:

Sidran Foundation
200 East Joppa Road, Suite 207
Baltimore, MD 21286-3107

The DES is available in several different languages.

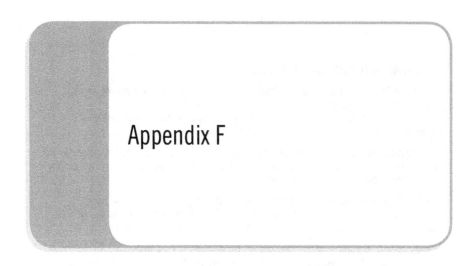

Appendix F

EFFICACY OF EMDR

The research so heavily emphasized and encouraged by Dr. Shapiro since her famous walk in the park in the late 1980s has repeatedly proven the efficacy of Eye Movement Desensitization and Reprocessing (EMDR). It has become the treatment of choice for various trauma centers and mental health groups around the world. It may be helpful for clinicians to have familiarity with the growing number of endorsements given to EMDR by the leading international health associations. Table F.1 describes the organizations to date that have included EMDR in their International Treatment Guidelines for Trauma, particularly posttraumatic stress disorder.

A wide variety of research studies have been implemented using various treatment aspects and protocols as their focus since its initial development. Many of these studies support EMDR as an empirically validated treatment of trauma. Several types of research models are utilized. Among these are meta-analyses (see Table F.2), randomized clinical trials (see Table F.3), and nonrandomized studies (see Table F.4).

Table F.1

INTERNATIONAL CLINICAL GUIDELINES

American Psychiatric Association. (2004). *Practice Guideline for the Treatment of Patients with Acute Stress Disorder and Posttraumatic Stress Disorder.* Arlington, VA: American Psychiatric Association Practice Guidelines. (see http://www.psych .org/psych_pract/treatg/pg/prac_guide.cfm)

Australian Centre for Posttraumatic Mental Health. (2007). *Australian Guidelines for PTSD.* Melbourne, Australia: University of Melbourne. (see http://www.nhmrc.gov .au/publications/synopses/_files/mh14.pdf)

Bleich, A., Kotler, M., Kutz, E., & Shale, A. (2002). A position paper of the (Israeli) National Council for Mental Health: Guidelines for the assessment and professional intervention with terror victims in the hospital and in the community.

Chambless, D. L., Baker, M. J., Baucom, D. H., Beutler, L. E., Calhoun, K. S., Crits-Christoph, P., Daiuto, A., DeRubeis, R., Detweiler, J., Haaga, D. A. F., Bennett Johnson, S., McCurry, S., Mueser, K. T., Pope, K. S., Sanderson, W. C., Shoham, V., Stickle, T., Williams, D. A., & Woody, S. R. (1998). Update of empirically validated therapies, II. *The Clinical Psychologist, 51, 3–16.* (see http://www.apa.org/ divisions/div12/est/newrpt.pdf)

Bisson, J., & Andrew, M. (2005). Psychological treatment of posttraumatic stress disorder (PTSD). *Cochrane Database of Systematic Reviews, 3,* Art. No. CD003388. (see http://www.cochrane.org/reviews/en/ab003388.html)

CREST (Clinical Resource Efficiency Support Team). (2003). *The management of post traumatic stress disorder in adults.* Belfast: Clinical Resource Efficiency Support Team of the Northern Ireland Department of Health, Social Services and Public Safety. (see http://www.gain-ni.org/Guidelines/post_traumatic_stress_disorder.pdf)

Department of Veterans Affairs & Department of Defense (2004) VA/DoD Clinical *Practice Guideline for the Management of Posttraumatic Stress.* Washington, DC. (see **http://www.oqp.med.va.gov/cpg/PTSD/PTSD_cpg/frameset.htm**)

Foa, E.B., Keane, T.M., & Friedman, M.J. (2000). Effective treatments for PTSD: *Practice Guidelines of the International Society for Traumatic Stress Studies.* New York: Guilford Press.

National Institute for Clinical Excellence. (2005). *Posttraumatic stress disorder (PTSD): The management of adults and children in primary and secondary care.* London: NICE Guidelines. (see http://www.emdria.org/associations/5581/files/ NICEguidelinePTSD.pdf)

United Kingdom Department of Health. (2001). *Treatment choice in psychological therapies and counseling evidence based clinical practice guidelines.* London, England. (see **http://www.doh.gov.uk/mentalhealth/treatmentguideline/**)

Table F.2

META-ANALYSES

Davidson, P. R., & Parker, K. C. H. (2001). Eye movement desensitization and reprocessing (EMDR): A meta-analysis. *Journal of Consulting and Clinical Psychology, 69*, 305–316.

Maxfield, L., & Hyer, L. A. (2002). The relationship between efficacy and methodology in studies investigating EMDR treatment of PTSD. *Journal of Clinical Psychology, 58*, 23–41.

van Etten, M., & Taylor, S. (1998). Comparative efficacy of treatments for post-traumatic stress disorder: A meta-analysis. *Clinical Psychology and Psychotherapy, 5*, 126–144.

Table F.3

RANDOMIZED CLINICAL TRIALS

Carlson, J., Chemtob, C. M., Rusnak, K., Hedlund, N. L., & Muraoka, M. Y. (1998). Eye movement desensitization and reprocessing (EMDR): Treatment for combat-related posttraumatic stress disorder. *Journal of Traumatic Stress, 11*, 3–24.

Chemtob, C. M., Nakashima, J., & Carlson, J. G. (2002). Brief-treatment for elementary school children with disaster-related PTSD: A field study. *Journal of Clinical Psychology, 58*, 99–112.

Edmond, T., Rubin, A., & Wambach, K. (1999). The effectiveness of EMDR with adult female survivors of childhood sexual abuse. *Social Work Research, 23*, 103–116.

Edmond, T., Sloan, L., & McCarty, D. (2004). Sexual abuse survivors' perceptions of the effectiveness of EMDR and eclectic therapy: A mixed-methods study. *Research on Social Work Practice, 14*, 259–272.

Ironson, G. I., Freund, B., Strauss, J. L., & Williams, J. (2002). Comparison of two treatments for traumatic stress: A community-based study of EMDR and prolonged exposure. *Journal of Clinical Psychology, 58*, 113–128.

Jaberghaderi, N., Greenwald, R., Rubin, A., Zand, S. O., & Dolatabadim, S. (2004). A comparison of CBT and EMDR for sexually abused Iranian girls. *Clinical Psychology and Psychotherapy, 11*, 358–368.

Lee, C., Gavriel, H., Drummond, P., Richards, J., & Greenwald, R. (2002). Treatment of posttraumatic stress disorder: A comparison of stress inoculation training with prolonged exposure and eye movement desensitization and reprocessing. *Journal of Clinical Psychology, 58*, 1071–1089.

Marcus, S., Marquis, P., & Sakai, C. (1997). Controlled study of treatment of PTSD using EMDR in an HMO setting. *Psychotherapy, 34*, 307–315.

(continued)

Table F.3 (continued)

Marcus, S., Marquis, P., & Sakai, C. (2004). Three- and six-month follow-up of EMDR treatment of PTSD in an HMO setting. *International Journal of Stress Management, 11,* 195–208.

Power, K., McGoldrick, T., Brown, K., Buchanan, R., Sharp, D., Swanson, V., & Karatzias, A. (2002). A controlled comparison of eye movement desensitization and reprocessing versus exposure plus cognitive restructuring, versus waiting list in the treatment of post-traumatic stress disorder. *Journal of Clinical Psychology and Psychotherapy, 9,* 299–318.

Rothbaum, B. (1997). A controlled study of eye movement desensitization and reprocessing in the treatment of post-traumatic stress disordered sexual assault victims. *Bulletin of the Menninger Clinic, 61,* 317–334.

Rothbaum, B. O., Astin, M. C., & Marsteller, F. (2005). Prolonged exposure versus eye movement desensitization (EMDR) for PTSD rape victims. Journal of Traumatic Stress, 18, 607–616.

Scheck, M., Schaeffer, J.A., & Gillette, C. (1998). Brief psychological intervention with traumatized young women: The efficacy of eye movement desensitization and reprocessing. *Journal of Traumatic Stress, 11,* 25–44.

Shapiro, F. (1989). Efficacy of the eye movement desensitization procedure in the treatment of traumatic memories. *Journal of Traumatic Stress Studies, 2,* 199–223.

Soberman, G. B., Greenwald, R., & Rule, D. L. (2002). A controlled study of eye movement desensitization and reprocessing (EMDR) for boys with conduct problems. *Journal of Aggression, Maltreatment, and Trauma, 6,* 217–236.

Taylor, S., Thordarson, D., Maxfield, L., Fedoroff, I., Lovell, K., & Ogrodniczuk, J. (2003). Comparative efficacy, speed, and adverse effects of three PTSD treatments: Exposure therapy, EMDR, and relaxation training. *Journal of Consulting and Clinical Psychology, 71,* 330–338.

Vaughan, K., Armstrong, M. F., Gold, R., O'Connor, N., Jenneke, W., & Tarrier, N. (1994). A trial of eye movement desensitization compared to image habituation training and applied muscle relaxation in post-traumatic stress disorder. *Journal of Behavior Therapy & Experimental Psychiatry, 25,* 283–291.

van der Kolk, B. A., Spinazzola, J., Blaustein, M. E., Hopper, J. W., Hopper, E. K., Korn, D. L., & Simpson, W. B. (2007). A randomized clinical trial of EMDR, fluoxetine and pill placebo in the treatment of PTSD: Treatment effects and long-term maintenance. *Journal of Clinical Psychiatry,* 68(1), 37-46.

Wilson, S., Becker, L. A., & Tinker, R. H. (1995). Eye movement desensitization and reprocessing (EMDR): Treatment for psychologically traumatized individuals. *Journal of Consulting and Clinical Psychology, 63,* 928–937.

Wilson, S., Becker, L. A., & Tinker, R. H. (1997). Fifteen-month follow-up of eye movement desensitization and reprocessing (EMDR) treatment of post-traumatic stress disorder and psychological trauma. *Journal of Consulting and Clinical Psychology, 65,* 1047–1056.

NONRANDOMIZED STUDIES

Devilly, G.J., & Spence, S.H. (1999). The relative efficacy and treatment distress of EMDR and a cognitive behavioral trauma treatment protocol in the amelioration of post-traumatic stress disorder. *Journal of Anxiety Disorders, 13*, 131–157.

Fernandez, I., Gallinari, E., & Lorenzetti, A. (2004). A school-based EMDR intervention for children who witnessed the Pirelli Building airplane crash in Milan, Italy. *Journal of Brief Therapy, 2*, 129–136.

Grainger, R. D., Levin, C., Allen-Byrd, L., Doctor, R. M., & Lee, H. (1997). An empirical evaluation of eye movement desensitization and reprocessing (EMDR) with survivors of a natural catastrophe. *Journal of Traumatic Stress, 10*, 665–671.

Puffer, M., Greenwald, R., & Elrod, D. (1997). A single session EMDR study with twenty traumatized children and adolescents. *Traumatology-e, 3*(2), Article 6.

Silver, S. M., Brooks, A., & Obenchain, J. (1995). Eye movement desensitization and reprocessing treatment of Vietnam war veterans with PTSD: Comparative effects with biofeedback and relaxation training. *Journal of Traumatic Stress, 8*, 337–342.

Solomon, R. M., & Kaufman, T. E. (2002). A peer support workshop for the treatment of traumatic stress of railroad personnel: Contributions of eye movement desensitization and reprocessing (EMDR). *Journal of Brief Therapy, 2*, 27–33.

Sprang, G. (2001). The use of eye movement desensitization and reprocessing (EMDR) in the treatment of traumatic stress and complicated mourning: Psychological and behavioral outcomes. *Research on Social Work Practice, 11*, 300–320.

References

Acierno, R., Tremont, G., Last, C., & Montgomery, D. (1994). Tripartite assessment of the efficacy of eye-movement desensitization in a multiphobic patient. *Journal of Anxiety Disorders, 8*, 259–276.

American Psychiatric Association. (2000). *Diagnostic and statistical manual of mental disorders* (4th ed., text revision). Washington, DC: Author.

American Psychiatric Association (2004). *Practice guideline for the treatment of patients with acute stress disorder and posttraumatic stress disorder.* Arlington, VA: American Psychiatric Association Practice Guidelines.

Andrade, J., Kavanagh, D., & Baddeley, A. (1997). Eye-movements and visual imagery: A working memory approach to the treatment of posttraumatic stress disorder. *British Journal of Clinical Psychology, 36*, 209–223.

Artigas, L., & Jarero, I. (2005). El abrazo de la mariposa [The butterfly's embrace]. *Revista de Psicotrauma para Iberoamérica, 4*(1), 30–31.

Artigas, L. A., Jarero, I., Mauer, M., Lopez Cano, T., & Alcala, N. (2000). *EMDR and traumatic stress after natural disasters: Integrative treatment protocol and the butterfly hug.* Poster session presented at the annual meeting of the EMDR International Association, Toronto, Ontario, Canada.

Australian Centre for Posttraumatic Mental Health. (2007). *Australian guideline for PTSD*. Melbourne, Australia: University of Melbourne.

Barrowcliff, A., Gray, N., MacCulloch, S., Freeman, T., & MacCulloch, M. (2003), September). Horizontal rhythmical eye movements consistently diminish the arousal provoked by auditory stimuli. *British Journal of Clinical Psychology, 42*(Pt 3), 289–302.

Bernstein, C., & Putnam, F. (1986). Development, reliability, and validity of a dissociation scale. *Journal of Nervous and Mental Diseases, 174*, 727–735.

Boël, J. (1999). Child & adolescent issue: A closer look—The butterfly hug: Some history and updates in its use with children. *EMDRIA Newsletter, Special Edition,4*(4), 11–13.

Boël, J. (2000). *The butterfly hug plus drawings: Clinical and self-care applications.* EMDRIA Conference, Toronto, Ontario Canada.

Boudewyns, P. A., & Hyer, L. A. (1996). Eye movement desensitization and reprocessing (EMDR) as treatment for posttraumatic stress disorder (PTSD). *Clinical Psychology and Psychotherapy, 3*, 185–195.

Browning, C. (1999). Floatback and float forward: Techniques for linking past, present, and future. *EMDRIA Newsletter, 4*(3), 12, 34.

Carlson, E. B., & Putnam, F. W. (1993). An update on the dissociative experiences scale. *Dissociation, 6*, 16–27.

Carlson, J. G., Chemtob, C. M., Rusnak, K., Hedlund, N. L., & Muraoka, M. Y. (1998). Eye movement desensitization and reprocessing treatment for combat-related post-traumatic stress disorder. *Journal of Traumatic Stress, 11*, 3–24.

Carrigan, M. H., & Levis, D. J. (1999). The contributions of eye movements to the efficacy of brief exposure treatment for reducing fear of public speaking. *Journal of Anxiety Disorders, 13*, 101–118.

Chambless, D. L., Baker, M. J., Baucom, D. H., Beutler, L. E., Calhoun, K. S., Crits-Christoph, P., Daiuto, A., DeRubeis, R., Detweiler, J., Haaga, D. A. F., Bennett Johnson, S., McCurry, S., Mueser, K. T., Pope, K. S., Sanderson, W. C., Shoham, V., Stickle, T., Williams, D. A., & Woody, S. R. (1998). Update of empirically validated therapies, II. *The Clinical Psychologist, 51*, 3–16.

Chemtob, C. M., Nakashima, J., Hamada, R. S., & Carlson, J. G. (2002). Brief-treatment for elementary school children with disaster-related posttraumatic stress disorder: A field study. *Journal of Clinical Psychology, 58*, 99–112.

Christman, S. D., Garvey, K. J., Propper, R. E., & Phaneuf, K. A. (2003). Bilateral eye movements enhance the retrieval of episodic memories. *Neuropsychology. 17*, 221–229.

CREST. (2003). *The management of post traumatic stress disorder in adults.* A publication of the Clinical Resource Efficiency Support Team of the Northern Ireland Department of Health, Social Services and Public Safety, Belfast.

Csikszentmihalyi, M. (1997). *Creativity: Flow and the psychology of discovery and invention.* New York, NY: HarperCollins Publishers, Inc.

Davidson, P. R., & Parker, K. C. H. (2001). Eye movement desensitization and reprocessing (EMDR): A meta-analysis. *Journal of Consulting and Clinical Psychology, 69*, 305–316.

Department of Veterans Affairs & Department of Defense. (2004). *VA/DoD clinical practice guideline for the management of posttraumatic stress.* Washington, DC. Veterans Health Administration, Department of Veterans Affairs and Health Affairs, Department of Defense. Office of Quality and Performance publication 10Q-CPG/PTSD-04.

Dell, P. F., & O'Neil, J. A. (2009). *Dissociation and the dissociative disorders.* New York, NY: Routledge.

Devilly, G. J., & Spence, S. H. (1999).The relative efficacy and treatment distress of EMDR and a cognitive behavioral trauma treatment protocol in the amelioration of posttraumatic stress disorder. *Journal of Anxiety Disorders, 13*, 131–157.

Devilly, G. J., Spence, S. H., & Rapee, R. M. (1998). Statistical and reliable change with eye movement desensitization and reprocessing: Treating trauma with a veteran population. *Behavior Therapy, 29*, 435–455.

Edmond, T., Rubin, A., & Wambach, K. G. (1999). The effectiveness of EMDR with adult female survivors of childhood sexual abuse. *Social Work Research, 23*, 103–116.

Edmond, T., Sloan, L., & McCarty, D. (2004). Sexual abuse survivors' perceptions of the effectiveness of EMDR and eclectic therapy: A mixed-methods study. *Research on Social Work Practice, 14*, 259–272.

EMDR Database. Francine Shapiro Library (by Barbara J. Hensley). http://library.nku.edu/emdr/emdr.php.

EMDR Institute, Inc. (2009). Frequent questions: What is EMDR? Retrieved from website emdr.com April 24, 2009.

EMDR International Association. (2009). Appendix – Definition of EMDR. Retrieved from website www.emdria.org April 24, 2009.

Fernandez, I., Gallinari, E., & Lorenzetti, A. (2004). A school-based EMDR intervention for children who witnessed the Pirelli Building airplane crash in Milan, Italy. *Journal of Brief Therapy, 2,* 129–136.

Flannery, R., Jr. (1995). Posttraumatic stress disorder: The victim's guide to healing & recovery. New York: Crossroad.

Foa, E. B., Keane, T. M., & Friedman, M. J. (2000). *Effective treatments for PTSD: Practice guidelines of the International Society for Traumatic Stress Studies.* New York: Guilford Press.

Grainger, R. D., Levin, C., Allen–Byrd, L., Doctor, R. M., & Lee, H. (1997). An empirical evaluation of eye movement desensitization and reprocessing (EMDR) with survivors of a natural catastrophe. *Journal of Traumatic Stress, 10,* 665–671.

Ironson, G. I., Freund, B., Strauss, J. L., & Williams, J. (2002). A comparison of two treatments for traumatic stress: A community based study of EMDR and prolonged exposure. *Journal of Clinical Psychology, 58,* 113–128.

Jaberghaderi, N., Greenwald, R., Rubin, A., Dolatabadim, S., & Zand, S. O. (2004). A comparison of CBT and EMDR for sexually abused Iranian girls. *Clinical Psychology and Psychotherapy, 11,* 358–368.

Jackson, S. (1999). *Care of the psyche: A history of psychological healing.* New Haven: Yale University Press.

Jarero, I. (2002). The butterfly hug: An update. *EMDRIA Newsletter, 7*(3), 6.

Kavanaugh, D. J., Freese, S., Andrade, J., & May, J. (2001). Effects of visuospatial tasks on desensitization to emotive memories. *British Journal of Clinical Psychology, 40,* 267–280.

Kluft, R. P. (1987). First-rank symptoms as a diagnostic clue to multiple personality disorder. *American Journal of Psychiatry, 144,* 293–298.

Kluft, R. P. (1985). The natural history of multiple personality disorder. In Kluft, R. P. (Ed.), *The childhood antecedents of multiple personality.* Washington, D C: American Psychiatric Press.

Korn, D., & Leeds, A. (2002). Preliminary evidence of efficacy for EMDR resource development and installation in the stabilization phase of treatment of complex post-traumatic stress disorder. *Journal of Clinical Psychology, 58*(12), 1465–1487.

Kuiken, D., Bears, M., Miall, D., & Smith, L. (2001–2002). Eye movement desensitization reprocessing facilitates attentional orienting. *Imagination, Cognition and Personality, 21*(1), 3–20.

Laliotis, D. (2000). *Advanced applications of cognitive interweave and resource development in EMDR.* Paper presented at the annual meeting of the EMDR International Association, Austin, TX.

Lee, C., Gavriel, H., Drummond, P., Richards, J., & Greenwald, R. (2002). Treatment of posttraumatic stress disorder: A comparison of stress inoculation training with prolonged exposure and eye movement desensitisation and reprocessing. *Journal of Clinical Psychology, 58,* 1071–1089.

Leeds, A. M. (1998). Lifting the burden of shame: Using EMDR resource installation to resolve a therapeutic impasse. In P. Manfield (Ed.), *Extending EMDR: A casebook of innovative applications* (1st ed., pp. 256–281). New York: W. W. Norton.

Leeds, A. M. (2001). Principals and procedures for enhancing current functioning in complex posttraumatic stress disorder with EMDR resource development and installation. *EMDRIA Newsletter, Special Edition,* 4–11.

Leeds, A. M., & Shapiro, F. (2000). EMDR and resource installation: Principles and procedures for enhancing current functioning and resolving traumatic experiences. In J. Carlson, & L. Sperry (Eds.), *Brief therapy with individuals and couples* (pp. 469–534). Phoenix, Arizona: Zeig, Tucker & Theisen, Inc.

Lendl, J., & Foster, S. (2003). Brief intervention focusing protocol for performance enhancement. In J. Lendl and S. Foster (2003), EMDR performance enhancement for the workplace: A practitioners' manual (2nd ed., p. 97). EMDR Humanitarian Assistance Program.

Loewenstein, R. J. (1991). An office mental status examination for complex, chronic dissociative symptoms and multiple personality disorder. *Psychiatric Clinics of North America, 14,* 567–604.

Lohr, J. M., Tolin, D., & Kleinknecht, R. A. (1995). An intensive investigation of eye movement desensitization of medical phobias. *Journal of Behavior Therapy and Experimental Psychiatry, 26,* 141–151.

Lohr, J. M., Tolin, D. F., & Kleinknecht, R. A. (1996). An intensive investigation of eye movement desensitization of claustrophobia. *Journal of Anxiety Disorders, 10,* 73–88.

Luber, M. (2009a) *Eye movement desensitization and reprocessing (EMDR) scripted protocols: Basics and special situations.* New York: Springer Publishing.

Luber, M. (2009b). *Eye movement desensitization and reprocessing (EMDR) scripted protocols: Special populations.* New York: Springer Publishing.

Marcus, S., Marquis, P., & Sakai, C. (1997). Controlled study of treatment of PTSD using EMDR in an HMO setting. *Psychotherapy, 34,* 307–315.

Marcus, S., Marquis, P., & Sakai, C. (2004). Three– and six–month follow-up of EMDR treatment of PTSD in an HMO setting. *International Journal of Stress Management, 11,* 195–208.

Maxfield, L., Melnyk, W. T., & Hayman, C. A. G. (2008). A working memory explanation for the effects of eye movements in EMDR. *Journal of EMDR Practice and Research, 2*(4), 247–261.

Maxfield, L., & Hyer, L. (2002). The relationship between efficacy and methodology in studies investigating EMDR treatment of PTSD. *Journal of Clinical Psychology, 58*(1), 23–41.

Miller, E., & Halpern, S. (1994). *Letting go of stress.* San Anselmo, CA: Inner Peace Music.

Montgomery, R. W., & Ayllon, T. (1994). Eye movement desensitization across subjects: Subjective and physiological measures of treatment efficacy. *Journal of Behavior Therapy and Experimental Psychiatry, 25,* 217–230.

National Institute for Clinical Excellence. (2005). *Post traumatic stress disorder (PTSD): The management of adults and children in primary and secondary care.* London: NICE Guidelines.

Pitman, R. K., Orr, S. P., Altman, B., Longpre, R. E., Poire, R. E., & Macklin, M. L. (1996). Emotional processing during eye movement desensitization and reprocessing therapy of Vietnam veterans with chronic posttraumatic stress disorder. *Comprehensive Psychiatry, 37,* 419–429.

Propper, R. E., & Christman, S. D. (2008). Interhemispheric interaction and saccadic horizontal eye movements: Implications for episodic memory, EMDR, and PTSD. *Journal of EMDR Practice and Research, 2*(4), 269–281.

Power, K., McGoldrick, T., Brown, K., Buchanan, R., Sharp, D., Swanson, V., & Karatzias, A. (2002). A controlled comparison of eye movement desensitisation and reprocessing versus exposure plus cognitive restructuring, versus waiting list in the treatment of posttraumatic stress disorder. *Journal of Clinical Psychology and Psychotherapy, 9,* 299–318.

Puffer, M. K., Greenwald, R., & Elrod, D. E. (1998). A single session EMDR study with twenty traumatized children and adolescents. *Traumatology, 3(2).*

Putnam, F. W. (1989). *Diagnosis and treatment of multiple personality disorder.* New York: Guilford Press.

Putnam, F. W., Guroff, J. J., Silberman, E. K., Barban, L., & Post, R. M. (1986). The clinical phenomenology of multiple personality disorder. *Journal of Clinical Psychiatry, 47,* 285–293.

Renfrey, G., & Spates, C. R. (1994). Eye movement desensitization: A partial dismantling study. *Journal of Behavior Therapy and Experimental Psychiatry, 25,* 231–239.

Ross, C. A., Heber, S., Norton, G. R., Anderson, D., Anderson, G., & Barchet, P. (1989). The dissociative disorders interview schedule: A structured interview. *Dissociation, 2*(3), 169–189.

Ross, C. A., Miller, S. D., Reagor, P., Bjornson, L., Fraser, G. A., & Anderson, G. (1990). Schneiderian symptoms in multiple personality disorder and schizophrenia. *Comprehensive Psychiatry, 31,* 111–118.

Rothbaum, B. O. (1997). A controlled study of eye movement desensitization and reprocessing for posttraumatic stress disordered sexual assault victims. *Bulletin of the Menninger Clinic, 61,* 317–334.

Rothbaum, B. O., Astin, M. C., & Marsteller, F. (2005). Prolonged exposure versus eye movement desensitization (EMDR) for PTSD rape victims. *Journal of Traumatic Stress, 18,* 607–616.

Sanderson, A., & Carpenter, R. (1992). Eye movement desensitization versus image confrontation: A single-session crossover study of 58 phobic subjects. *Journal of Behavior Therapy and Experimental Psychiatry, 23,* 269–275.

Scheck, M. M., Schaeffer, J. A., & Gillette, C. S. (1998). Brief psychological intervention with traumatized young women: The efficacy of eye movement desensitization and reprocessing. *Journal of Traumatic Stress, 11,* 25–44.

Schleyer, M. A. (2000). *The trauma client's experience of eye movement desensitization and reprocessing: A heuristic analysis.* Union Institute, Cincinnati, OH.

Shapiro, F. (1989a). Efficacy of the eye movement desensitization procedure in the treatment of traumatic memories. *Journal of Traumatic Stress, 2(2),* 199–223.

Shapiro, F. (1989b). Eye movement desensitization: A new treatment for posttraumatic stress disorder. *Journal of Behavior Therapy and Experimental Psychiatry, 20*(3), 211–217.

Shapiro, F. (1991). Eye movement desensitization & reprocessing procedure: From EMD to EMDR/R-a new treatment model for anxiety and related traumata. *the Behavior Therapist, 14,* 133–135.

Shapiro, F. (2002). *EMDR as an integrative psychotherapy approach: Experts of diverse orientations explore the paradigm prism.* Washington, D.C: American Psychological Association Press.

Shapiro, F. (2006). *EMDR: New notes on adaptive information processing with case formulations principles, forms, scripts and worksheets, version 1.1.* EMDR Institute: Watsonville, CA.

Shapiro, F. (2009). *EMDR: Part 1 training manual.* Watsonville, CA: EMDR Institute, Inc.

Shapiro, F. (2008). *EMDR: Part 2 training manual.* Watsonville, CA: EMDR Institute, Inc.

Shapiro, F. (1991–1995). *EMDR: The lightstream technique.* Hamden, CT: EMDR-HAP.

Shapiro, F. (2002). *EMDR as an integrative psychotherapy approach: Experts of diverse orientations explore the paradigm prism.* Washington, DC: American Psychological Association.

Shapiro, F. (2001). *Eye movement desensitization and reprocessing: Basic principles, protocols and procedures* (2nd ed.). New York: Guilford Press.

Shapiro, F., & Forrest, M.S. (1997). *EMDR: The breakthrough therapy for overcoming anxiety, stress, and trauma.* New York, NY: BasicBooks.

Shapiro, F., Kaslow, F. W., & Maxfield, M. (2007). *Handbook of EMDR and family therapy processes.* Hoboken, NJ: John Wiley & Sons, Inc.

Sharpley, C. F., Montgomery, I. M., & Scalzo, L. (1996). Comparative efficacy of EMDR and alternative procedures in reducing the vividness of mental images. *Scandinavian Journal of Behaviour Therapy, 25,* 37–42.

Silver, S. M., Brooks, A., & Obenchain, J. (1995). Eye movement desensitization and reprocessing treatment of Vietnam War veterans with PTSD: Comparative effects with biofeedback and relaxation training. *Journal of Traumatic Stress, 8,* 337–342.

Soberman, G. B., Greenwald, R., & Rule, D. L. (2002). A controlled study of eye movement desensitization and reprocessing (EMDR) for boys with conduct problems. *Journal of Aggression, Maltreatment, and Trauma, 6,* 217–236.

Solomon, S. D., Gerrity, E. T., & Muff, A. M. (1992). Efficacy of treatments for posttraumatic stress disorder: An empirical review. *Journal of the American Medical Association, 268,* 633–638.

Solomon, R. M., & Kaufman, T. E. (2002). A peer support workshop for the treatment of traumatic stress of railroad personnel: Contributions of eye movement desensitization and reprocessing (EMDR). *Journal of Brief Therapy, 2,* 27–33.

Spiegel, D. (1993). Multiple posttraumatic personality disorder. In R. P. Kluft & C. G. Fine (Eds.), *Clinical perspectives on multiple personality disorder.* Washington, DC: American Psychiatric Press.

Sprang, G. (2001). The use of eye movement desensitization and reprocessing (EMDR) in the treatment of traumatic stress and complicated mourning: Psychological and behavioral outcomes. *Research on Social Work Practice, 11,* 300–320.

Taylor, S., Thordarson, D., Maxfield, L., Fedoroff, I., Lovell, K., & Ogrodniczuk, J. (2003, April). Comparative efficacy, speed, and adverse effects of three PTSD treatments: Exposure therapy, EMDR, and relaxation training. *Journal of Consulting & Clinical Psychology, 71*(2), 330–338.

United Kingdom Department of Health. (2001). *Treatment choice in psychological therapies and counseling evidence based clinical practice guideline.* London, England.

van den Hout, M., Muris, P., Salemink, E., & Kindt, M. (2001). Autobiographical memories become less vivid and emotional after eye movements. *British Journal of Clinical Psychology, 40*, 121–130.

van Etten, M.L. & Taylor, S. (1998). Comparative efficacy of treatments for posttraumatic stress disorder: A meta-analysis. *Clinical Psychology & Psychotherapy, 5*, 126–144.

van der Kolk, B. A., Spinazzola, J., Blaustein, M. E., Hopper, J. W., Hopper, E. K., Korn, D. L., & Simpson, W. B. (2007). Randomized clinical trial of eye movement desensitization and reprocessing (EMDR), fluoxetine, and pill placebo in the treatment of posttraumatic stress disorder: Treatment effects and long-term maintenance. *Journal of Clinical Psychiatry, 68*(1), 37–46.

Vaughan, K., Armstrong, M. F., Gold, R., O'Connor, N., Jenneke, W., & Tarrier, N. (1994). A trial of eye movement desensitization compared to image habituation training and applied muscle relaxation in posttraumatic stress disorder. *Journal of Behavior Therapy & Experimental Psychiatry, 25*, 283–291.

Watkins, J. G. (1971). The affect bridge: A hypnotherapeutic technique. *International Journal of Clinical and Experimental Hypnosis, 19*, 21–27.

Wilson, S. A., Becker, L. A., & Tinker, R. H. (1995). Eye movement desensitization and reprocessing (EMDR) treatment for psychologically traumatized individuals. *Journal of Consulting and Clinical Psychology, 63*, 928–937

Wilson, S. A., Becker, L. A., & Tinker, R. H. (1997). Fifteen-month follow-up of eye movement desensitization and reprocessing (EMDR) treatment for PTSD and psychological trauma. *Journal of Consulting and Clinical Psychology, 65*, 1047–1056.

Wilson, D., Silver, S. M., Covi, W., & Foster, S. (1996). Eye movement desensitization and reprocessing: Effectiveness and autonomic correlates. *Journal of Behavior Therapy and Experimental Psychiatry, 27*, 219–229.

Young, J. E., Klosko, J. S., & Weishaar, M. E., (2003). *Schema therapy: A practitioner's guide.* New York: Guilford Press.

Young, J., Zangwill, W. M., & Behary, W. E. (2002). Combining EMDR and schema-focused therapy: The whole may be greater than the sum of the parts. In F. Shapiro (Ed.). *EMDR as an integrative psychotherapy approach: Experts of diverse orientations explore the paradigm prism* (1st ed., pp. 181–208). Washington: American Psychological Association.

Zangwill, W. M. (1997, June). *The dance of the cognitive interweave.* Presentation at the annual meeting of the EMDR International Association, San Francisco, CA.

Wolpe, J. (1990). *The practice of behavior therapy* (4th ed.). New York: Pergamon Press.

Index

A

Abreactions, 162–167
  cautionary note, 170
  defined, 162–163
  guidelines for, 165–167
  preparing client for, 163
  process of abreaction, 163–165
  and retraumatization, 164
  strategies for blocked processing,
    161, 171–174
  strategies for maintaining
    processing, 168–171
Abreactive state, 28
Activation components of EMDR, 9
Acute stress response ("fight or flight"),
  131
Adaptive can become maladaptive
  behaviors, 27
Adaptive Information Processing (AIP)
  model, 1, 5–11, 178, 262, 289
  adaptive vs. maladaptive
    resolution, 7
  before and after EMDR, 11
  and dysfunctionally stored
    material, 8, 9
  and earlier life experiences, 7
  earlier life experiences, 7
  graphical representation of, 8, 10
  information processing system
    at work, 8, 10
  memory networks, 6
  as psychological self–healing
    construct, 6–7
  and train metaphor, 32
Adaptive vs. maladaptive resolution, 7
Addictions, and EMDR, 47
Affect dysregulation, 58
After scan, 136–137, 140
Aim of EMDR, 263
Alienation, 61
Alternating bilateral hand taps, 25

Alternating bilateral instrumental
  music, 25
American Medical Association, 283
American Psychological Association, 283
Anchoring in the present exercise, 59,
  269–270
Ancillary targets, 172, 174, 175
Anticipatory anxiety, and future
  templates, 155, 156
Assessment phase, 87–125
  case examples, 89–90, 109–117
    Henry, 115–117
    Jennifer, 89–90
    Jerry, 113–115
    Julia, 109–113
    Patrick, 119–123
    Terry, 105–109
  client, extent of knowledge about, 88
  cognition assessment, 91–99
    cognitions defined, 92–93
    criteria for negative and positive
      cognitions, 98
    elements of negative and positive
      cognitions, 91–92
    purpose of cognitions, 92
    stepping stones to adaptive
      resolution, 99, 100
    teasing out negative and positive
      cognitions, 93–99
    Validity of Cognition (VoC) scale,
      99–100
  current level of disturbance
    assessment, 101–103
    stepping stones to adaptive
      resolution, 103
    Subjective Units of Disturbance
      (SUD) scale, 91, 99, 101–103
  emotional assessment, 100–101
    stepping stones to adaptive
      resolution, 101
  physical sensations assessment,
    103–105

stepping stones to adaptive
resolution, 104
recent traumatic events, 119–123, 132
caveats when using protocol, 122
conclude with body scan, 122
obtain a narrative history, 119–120
process present stimuli, 122
protocol for, 123
target the most disturbing aspect of
the memory, 120–121
target the remainder of the narrative in chronological order, 121
visualize entire sequence of events,
121–122
when it is appropriate, 123
single-incident traumas, 90, 124
target assessment, 88–91
appropriateness of target, 90–91
characteristics of effective targets,
89
memory encoding, 89–90
multiple-trauma victims, 91
stepping stones to adaptive
resolution, 90
top 10 most disturbing childhood
memories, 91
targeting sequence plans, 124–125
See also Phases of EMDR
Associative processing, 67–68, 69–71,
72

B
Before and after EMDR, 11
Bilateral stimulation (BLS), 2, 25–27
options regarding, 56–58
problems that might complicate use
of, 46, 56–57
and "stuck" information, 56
See also Dual attention stimulation in
EMDR
Blanking out, 28
Blech, Scott, 289
Block (dysfunctionally stored material),
8, 9
Blocked or stalled processing, 161–162,
171–174
ancillary targets for, 172, 174, 175
comparison between strategies for
cognitive interweave and, 184, 185
defined, 171
identifying, 171–172
primary targets for, 172, 173–174

SUD scale, 171
See also Processing
Blocking beliefs, 20–21, 23, 143
Body scan, 79–80, 212–213
in recent traumatic events protocol,
122
reprocessing completion, 118
See also Phases of EMDR
Body sensations, 63, 206–212
Brain
storing disturbing events, 57
See also Memory ("neuro") networks
Breathing shifts, 59, 277
Breathing techniques, 58
Building blocks of EMDR. See Three-
pronged approach (past/present/future)

C
Calm (or safe) place exercise, 59–60,
270–274
bilateral stimulation in, 26
defined, 164
Case examples
assessment phase, 89–90, 109–117
client history and treatment
planning, 52–54
cognitive interweave, 178–179,
181–184, 186–192
future, 156–160, 240–247
past (earlier memories/touchstone
events), 138–140, 202–220
present, 144–149, 220–240
Case examples for past, present, and
future, 199–247
future, Jimmy, 240–247
past, 202–220
Jessica, 202–213
Karen, 213–220
present, 220–240
Brenda, 235–240
Delores, 220–234
questions to ask about EMDR
sessions, 200–202
CAT scans. See Computed axial
tomography (CAT) scans
Cautionary note
for abreactions, 170
for cognitive interweaves, 192–193
for dissociative disorders, 62
for specialized populations, 47
Channels of association, assessment
of, 68, 72

Childhood memories, top 10 most disturbing, 91
Children, and EMDR, 47, 118
Choice interweaves, 185–192
Client-centered psychotherapy, EMDR as, 174
Client history and treatment planning (Phase 1), 41–54
Clients
adequate level of trust with, 45
age of, 47
challenging and highly disturbed, 161, 162
and cognitive interweaves, 176–177
definition of EMDR for, 262
depression screen of, 133
diagnosis of, 47
EMDR Brochure for Clients, 56
expectations and fears of, 55, 62–63
explanation of EMDR process and its effects, 55–58
extent of knowledge about, 34–35, 39, 88
fears of, 22
individual and family belief systems, 133
medical history of, 133
natural healing process, 176, 192
preparing for abreactions, 163
presenting problems, 48
previous therapy of, 47
selection criteria for, 45–46, 49–50
selection of, 38, 49–50
suitability and readiness for EMDR, 46–47
tracking the client, 35–36
willingness to do EMDR, 48
Clinician
and abreations, 170
adequate level of trust with client, 45
definition of EMDR for, 262–266
dissociative disorders cautionary note, 62
first solo run, 38–39
newly trained, 11, 199, 248
quiet neutrality position of, 35
solo run, 38–39
specialized populations cautionary note, 47
stay off the tracks, 35
staying out of client's way, 39
supervision and consultation for, 162

writing down what the client says, 35, 117
Closure (Phase 7), 80–82
Cluster memories, 19
Cognitions
assessment of, 91–99
defined, 92–93
purpose of, 92
Cognitive behavioral techniques, 8, 39
Cognitive interweave, 174–198
case examples
Renee, 178–179, 181–184
Susie, 186–192
caution in use of, 192–193
for challenging and highly disturbed clients, 161, 162, 175
choice interweaves, 185–192
choices of, 179–184
comparison between strategies for blocked processing and, 184, 185
defined, 174–176
examples of, 194–197
graphic example of, 176
overuse/underuse/misuse/ misunderstanding, 174
responsibility interweaves, 185–192
safety interweaves, 185–192
using effectively, 176–177
when to use, 177–179
Combat veterans, and EMDR, 118
Complete target sessions, 81
Comprehensive history, 39. *See also* Phases of EMDR
Computed axial tomography (CAT) scans, and dual attention stimulation in EMDR, 58
Concepts to consider in EMDR, 27–33
adaptive can become maladaptive behaviors, 27
dual awareness or mindfulness, 28
ecological validity (soundness), 28–30
holistic nature of the approach, 31
side benefits of EMDR, 30–31
state vs. trait change, 27–28
train metaphor, 31–33
tunnel metaphor, 33
Container and conference room techniques, 59
Couples, and EMDR, 118

D
Definitions of EMDR, 41, 261–266

Depersonalization, 47
Derealization, 47
DES. *See* Dissociative Experiences Scale
Desensitization (Phase 4), 65–76
Developmental trauma, 5
Diagnostic and Statistical Manual of Mental Disorders, text revision (DSM-IV-Tr), posttraumatic stress disorder (PTSD) diagnostic criteria, 2, 131
Diaphragmatic breathing and exercise, 59, 268–269
Direct questioning, 135–136, 138–139, 140
Disorders in EMDR treatment, 248
Dissociation, defined, 61
Dissociative disorders, 28, 47, 61
  cautionary note, 62
  clinical signs and symptoms of, 291
  and EMDR, 118
  screening for, 47
Dissociative Experiences Scale (DES), 47, 61, 291–292
Disturbance assessment, current level of, 101–103
Dream sleep, 118
Dreams, 7
DSM-IV-TR. See Diagnostic and Statistical Manual of Mental Disorders, text revision
Dual attention stimulation in EMDR, 2, 25–27
  defined, 25
  effects of, 58
  length, speed, and number of sets, 26–27
  as only one component of EMDR, 26
  preferred means of, 25–26
  See also Bilateral stimulation (BLS)
Dual awareness or mindfulness, 28, 164
Dysfunctionally stored material, 8, 9

E

Earlier life experiences, 7
Eating disorders, 47
Ecological validity (soundness), 28–30, 75–76, 142
Educational learning materials, 1
Efficacy of EMDR. *See* Research on EMDR
Ego-state therapy, 61–62

EMDR: New Notes on Adaptive Information Processing with Case Formulation Principles, Forms, Scripts, and Worksheets (Shapiro), 47
EMDR and associated organizations, 287–289
EMDR Brochure for Clients, 56
EMDR components, order of, 63
EMDR-HAP Store Web site, 34
EMDR Humanitarian Assistance Programs (EMDR-HAP), 47, 288–289
  trainings, 94
  Web site, 34
EMDR Institute, 261, 289
EMDR International Association (EMDRIA), 41, 56, 261, 262, 287
Eye Movement Desensitization and Reprocessing (EMDR), 1–37
  activation components of EMDR, 9
  Adaptive Information Processing (AIP) model, 1, 5–11
  as client-centered psychotherapy, 174
  concepts to consider in, 27–33
  definitions of EMDR, 41, 261–266
    for clients, 262
    for clinicians, 262–266
    description from EMDR Institute's Web site, 261–262
  disorders in EMDR treatment, 248
  dual attention stimulation in EMDR, 2, 25–27
  educational learning materials, 1
  formal training for, 1, 12, 248
  an integrative psychotherapeutic treatment approach, 2, 5, 6
  introduction in 1989, 248
  offshoots of EMDR, 2
  order of EMDR components, 63
  "past is present," 8, 134
  practical tips for EMDR, 33–39
  pretraining readings, 2
  standard EMDR procedure (11 step), 118, 156
  targeting possibilities, 15–24
  three-pronged approach, 1, 11–15
  trauma, 2–5
  See also EMDR theoretical foundation and methodology; Phases of EMDR; Research on EMDR; Shapiro, Francine
EMDR Progress Notepads, 34, 38

EMDR scripts, 277–281
  breathing shifts, 277
  future template script, 278–279
  spiral technique, 278
  TICES log, 280–281
EMDR sessions, questions to ask about, 200–202
EMDR theoretical foundation and methodology, 262–266
  aim of EMDR, 263
  fidelity in application through training and observation, 266
  foundational sources and principles for evolution, 263
  framework, 263–264
  hypotheses of the EMDR model, 264–265
  methods, 265–266
  purpose of definition, 263
EMDRIA. *See* EMDR International Association
EMDRIA Foundation, 288
Emotional assessment, 100–101
Emotions, 63, 206
End of channel, 68, 73–74
Exercises, 267–276
  anchoring in the present, 269–270
  calm (or safe) place, 270–274
  diaphragmatic breathing and exercise, 268–269
  grounding and grounding exercise, 267–268
  sacred space, 274–276
Experiential approaches, 39
External focus, 28
Eye Movement Desensitization and Reprocessing: Basic Principles, Protocols, and Procedures (Shapiro), 1, 2, 10, 86, 87, 193, 248
Eye movements, 25

F
Fears of clients, 22
Feeder memories, 20, 39, 143
Fidelity in application through training and observation, 266
"Fight or flight" (acute stress response), 131
Flashbacks, 7, 47
Floatback technique, 136, 139, 140
Flooding, 8
Fluid process, EMDR as, 1, 39

Foundational sources and principles for evolution of EMDR, 263
Four elements stabilization technique (Shapiro, Elan), 59
Fragmentation, 61
Framework for EMDR, 263–264
Francine Shapiro Library, 202, 289
Future templates, 12–13, 15, 128–129, 150–160
  alternative behaviors, 128
  anticipatory anxiety, 155, 156
  case examples, 199–247
  future desired state, 17–18
  goals of, 150
  imaginal future template development, 18
  misunderstood, disregarded, and forgotten, 154–156
  script for, 278–279
  skills building and imaginal rehearsal, 150–152
  steps in creating, 153–154

G
Giessl, Irene, 289
Grounding and grounding exercise, 59, 267–268
Guided imagery, 59
Guided visualization, 58

H
Hensley, Barbara J., and Francine Shapiro Library, 289
History-taking, 45, 51, 127, 143. *See also* Phases of EMDR
Holistic nature of EMDR, 31
Hypnosis, 58
Hypotheses of the EMDR model, 264–265

I
"I" statements, 91
Image (picture), 63, 90
Imagery techniques, 58
Imaginal exposure, 8
Imaginal future template development, 18
Imaginal rehearsal, 150–152
Incomplete target sessions, 80–81, 83
Information processing system
  and abreaction, 163
  process of, 8, 10

Informed consent and EMDR, 39,
    44–45, 283–285
Installation (Phase 5), 77–78
Intake Case Conceptualization Form, 47
Integrative psychotherapeutic treatment
    approach, EMDR as, 2, 5, 6
Intrusive thoughts, 47

L
Large "T" traumas and small "T"
    traumas, 3–5
Letting Go of Stress (Miller), 59
Lightstream technique, 59
Likert, Rensis, Likert scale, 101

M
Maladaptive behaviors, adaptive can
    become, 27
Maladaptive vs. adaptive resolution, 7
Memory encoding, 89–90
Memory lapses, 47
Memory ("neuro") networks, 6, 8
    dysfunctional, 88
    more adaptive in cognitive interweave,
        175
    state-dependent mode in, 3
    storing disturbing events, 57
Meta-analytic research, 266
Methods in EMDR, 265–266
Miller, Emmett, *Letting Go of Stress*
    (audiotape), 59
Multiple-trauma victims, 91
Muscle relaxation exercises, 58

N
Negative and positive cognitions
    criteria for, 98
    elements of, 91–92
    teasing out, 93–99
Negative cognitions (NC), 63, 204–205
Nodes or targets. *See* Targets or nodes

O
Obsessive-compulsive disorder (OCD),
    87
Offshoots of EMDR, 2
Optimal behavior, 3
Order of EMDR components, 63

P
Pain control, 87, 118

Past (earlier memories/touchstone
    events), 12–14, 38–39, 49, 134–142
case examples, 202–220
"past is present" (Shapiro), 8, 134
past targets, 16–17
strategies for assessing, 135–142
    after scan, 136–137, 140
    direct questioning, 135–136,
        138–139, 140
    floatback technique, 136, 139, 140
Peelback memories, 21–22, 143
Performance anxieties, 118
Phases of EMDR, 41–86
    Phase 1) client history and treatment
        planning, 41–54
    assessment, 48
    candidates for EMDR, 51–52
    case example 2a, Sally, 52–53
    case example 2b, Marie, 53–54
    client selection criteria, 45–46,
        49–50
    client willingness to do EMDR, 48
    client's suitability and readiness
        for EMDR, 46–47
    dissociative disorders screening,
        47
    elements pertinent to EMDR, 51
    history-taking, 45, 51, 127, 143
    informed consent and suitability
        for treatment, 44–45
    treatment planning in EMDR,
        45, 49, 127
Phase 2) preparation, 54–63
    calm (or safe) place and other
        coping stratetgies, 58–60
    client's expectations and fears, 55,
        62–63
    dissociation, 61
    ego-state therapy, 61–62
    explanation of EMDR process and
        its effects, 55–58
    Resource Development and
        Installation (RDI), 58, 60–61
    safe therapeutic environment,
        54–55
Phase 3) assessment
    63–65. *See also* Assessment phase
    assessing the NC and PC and emo-
        tional and physical sensations,
        63–64
    identifying the target, 63

measuring the VoC and SUD,
     64–65
Phase 4) desensitization, 65–76
  assessment of channels of
     association, 68, 72
  associative processing, 67–68,
     69–71, 72
  end of channel, 68, 73–74
  flow chart, 66
  graphic picture of, 76
  length of (spontaneously
     reprocessing), 74–75
  proceeding to installation phase,
     75–76
  purpose of, 67
  and reprocessing, 66–67
  returning to target, 74, 75
  SUD and VoC levels, 65, 75
  taking a break, 76
  when it begins, 65
Phase 5) installation phase, 77–78
  appropriateness of original
     cognition, 77
  completion of installation, 78
  discerning presence of a blocking
     belief, 78
  link to original target, 78
  validity of positive cognition, 77–78
  what occurs, 77
Phase 6) body scan, 79–80
Phase 7) closure, 80–82
  assessment of client's safety, 81–82
  complete target sessions, 81
  incomplete target sessions, 80–81
  levels of, 80
  what happens after a session, 82
Phase 8) reevaluation, 82–86
  final stage, 85–86
  pivotal points in, 86
  resuming reprocessing in an
     incomplete session, 83
  of targets, 84–85
  treatment effects, 84
  and treatment planning, 84
  what has changed and what is left
     to do, 82–83
  table listing goals and objectives of
     each phase, 42–44
Phobias, 87, 118
Physical sensations assessment, 103–105
Positive cognitions (PC), 63, 205. *See
  also* Negative and positive cognitions

Posttraumatic stress disorder (PTSD),
     2–3, 90, 131
  complex, 133
Practical tips for EMDR, 33–39
  follow the script verbatim, 33–34
  keep it simple, 36
  know the client, 34–35, 39
  one more time, 37–38
  practice, practice, practice, 33, 39, 199
  solo run, 38–39
  stay off the tracks, 35
  then or now?, 36
  tracking the client, 35–36
Practice, practice, practice, 33, 39, 199
Preparation (Phase 2), 54–63
Present (circumstances and triggers), 12,
     14–15, 17, 128–129, 142–150
  blocking beliefs, 143
  case examples, 220–240
  ecological validity, 142
  feeder memories, 143
  peelback memories, 143
  triggers remaining active, 143–144
  triggers subsumed by reprocessing
     of touchstone event, 149–150
Pretraining readings, 2
Primary targets, 172, 173–174
Procedure, standard EMDR procedure
     (11 step), 118, 156
Processing
  blocked or stalled, 161–162. *See also*
     Blocked processing
  overresponders and underresponders,
     168–170
  returning to target too soon, 170–171
  strategies for maintaining, 168–171
Progression, 19–20
Psychodynamic approaches, 39
Psychological self-healing construct,
     Adaptive Information Processing
     (AIP) model as, 6–7

R
Rapid eye movement (REM), 188
RDI. *See* Resource Development and
     Installation
Recent traumatic events, 119–123, 132.
     See also Assessment phase
Reevaluation (Phase 8), 82–86
REM. *See* Rapid eye movement
Reprocessing, 66–67
  completion of, 118

normal is 40 172, 202
order of, 13, 14
primary byproduct of, 9
spontaneous, 74–75, 192
Research on EMDR, 293–297
  international clinical guidelines, 294
  meta-analyses, 266, 295
  nonrandomized clinical trials, 297
  randomized clinical trials, 295–296
Resisting, 28
Resource Development and Installation
  (RDI), 58, 60–61, 290
Resource installation exercise, bilateral
  stimulation in, 26
Responsibility interweaves, 185–192
Retraumatization, and abreactions, 164

S
Sacred space defined, 59, 164
Sacred space exercises, 274–276
  bilateral stimulation in, 26
Safe therapeutic environment, 54–55
Safety interweaves, 185–192
Schleyer, Marilyn, 289
Schneiderian symptoms, 47
Second-order conditioning, 143–144
Secondary gain, 23–24
Self actualization hierarchy, three-
  pronged approach (past/present/
  future), 12
Self-confidence, 3
Self-control and relaxation exercises, 59
Self-definition, 3
Self-efficacy, 247
Self-esteem, 3
Self-regulation techniques, 58
Sexual abuse victims, and EMDR, 118
Shapiro, Elan, four elements stabilization
  technique, 59
Shapiro, Francine, 41
  on abreaction, blocks, and cognitive
    interweaves, 193
  abreaction guidelines, 165–167
  Adaptive information Processing (AIP)
    model, 5
  *EMDR: New Notes on Adaptive
    Information Processing with Case
    Formulation Principles, Forms,
    Scripts, and Worksheets,* 47
  *Eye Movement Desensitization
    and Reprocessing: Basic Principles,*

Protocols, and Procedures, 1, 2, 10,
    86, 87, 193, 248
  Francine Shapiro Library, 202
  on positive and negative cognitions, 95
  standard targeting sequence plan,
    124–125
  strategies for overresponders and
    underresponders, 169–170
Shock trauma, 5
Side benefits of EMDR, 30–31
Single-incident traumas, 90, 124
Single photon emission computed
  tomography (SPECT), and dual
  attention stimulation in EMDR, 58
Skills building and imaginal rehearsal,
  150–152
Small "T" traumas, 3–5
Socratic method, 133
Special populations, 87, 118
  cautionary note, 47
  special conditions or disorders, 118
SPECT. *See* Single photon emission
  computed tomography
Spiral technique, 59, 278
Spontaneous reprocessing, 74–75, 192
Stalled processing, 161–162
Standard EMDR procedure (11 step),
  118, 156
State-dependent mode in memory
  network, 3, 8
State vs. trait change, 27–28
Stepping stones to adaptive resolution.
  See Assessment phase
Subjective Units of Disturbance (SUD)
  scale, 20–21, 29–30, 63, 65, 75, 94
  in blocked or stalled processing, 171
  completion of reprocessing, 118
  current level of disturbance, 91, 99,
    101–103
  example, 206
Substance abuse, 118
SUD. *See* Subjective Units of
  Disturbance
SUD/VoC Scale Chart, 34, 94
Systematic desensitization, 8

T
Target assessment, 88–91. *See also*
  Assessment phase
Targeting possibilities, 15–24
  from the future, 17–18

from the past (touchstone memory), 16–17

from the present (circumstances and triggers), 17

types of targets, 16, 17, 18–24
  blocking belief, 20–21, 23
  cluster memories, 19
  fears, 22
  feeder memory, 20, 38
  node, 18–19
  peelback memory, 21–22
  progression, 19–20
  secondary gain, 23–24
  wellsprings of disturbance, 22–23

types of targets with examples, 24

Targeting sequence plans, 124–125, 129

Targets or nodes, 14, 18, 203–204
  ancillary, 172, 174, 175
  primary, 172, 173–174
  reevaluation of, 84–85
  returning to, 74, 75

Three-pronged approach (past/present/future), 1, 11–15, 127–160
  case examples
    Betty (past), 138–140
    Michael (future), 156–160
    Peter (present), 144–149
  clinical presentation possibilities, 129–134
    multiple issues/symptoms presentations, 132–133
    single-incident presentations, 131–132
    symptomology, 129
    vague or diffuse presentations, 133–134
  future templates, 12–13, 15, 128–129, 150–160. *See also* Future templates
  importance of, 14–15
  order of reprocessing, 13, 14
  past (earlier memories/touchstone events), 12–14, 38–39, 128–129, 134–142. *See also* Past
  present (triggers), 12, 14–15, 128–129, 142–150. *See also* Present
  self actualization hierarchy, 12
  targeting sequence plan, 12
  targets or nodes, 14

TICES (target=image, cognition, emotion, and sensation), 169, 280–281

Top 10 most disturbing childhood memories, 91

Touchstone events. *See* Past (earlier memories/touchstone events)

Traditional talk therapy, 162

Train metaphor, 31–33, 118, 163, 164

Training for EMDR, 1, 12, 248
  fidelity in application through training and observation, 266
  formal, 1, 12
  pretraining readings, 2

Trait vs. state change, 27–28

Trauma, 2–5
  defined, 2–3
  developmental trauma, 5
  large "T" traumas and small "T" traumas, 3–5
  posttraumatic stress disorder (PTSD), 2–3
  shock trauma, 5
  types of traumatic events, 4

Treatment planning in EMDR, 45, 49, 84, 127. *See also* Phases of EMDR

Triggers. *See* Present (circumstances and triggers)

Tunnel metaphor, 33, 164

V

Validity of Cognition (VoC) scale, 20–21, 30, 63, 65, 75, 94
  in cognition assessment, 99–100
  example, 205
  reprocessing completion, 118

Video metaphor, 118, 163

Visualization, 59

VoC. *See* Validity of Cognition scale

W

Wellsprings of disturbance, 22–23

Wolpe, Joseph, SUD scale, 29, 101

Y

Yannarella, Philip, 289

Z

Zangwill, William, floatback technique, 136